THE STATE OF THE WORLD'S CHILDREN 2007

© The United Nations Children's Fund (UNICEF), 2006

Permission to reproduce any part of this publication is required. Please contact the Editorial, Design and Publications Section, Division of Communication, UNICEF NY (3 UN Plaza, NY, NY 10017) USA, Tel: 212-326-7434 or 7286, Fax: 212-303-7985, Email: nyhqdoc.permit@unicef.org. Permission will be freely granted to educational or non-profit organizations. Others will be requested to pay a small fee.

Commentaries represent the personal views of the authors and do not necessarily reflect UNICEF positions.

ISBN-13: 978-92-806-3998-8
ISBN-10: 92-806-3998-6

UNICEF, UNICEF House, 3 UN Plaza,
New York, NY 10017, USA

Email: pubdoc@unicef.org
Website: www.unicef.org

Cover photo: © UNICEF/HQ95-0980/Shehzad Noorani

Acknowledgements

This report was made possible with the advice and contributions of many people, both in and outside of UNICEF. Important contributions were received from the following UNICEF field offices: Bangladesh, Bolivia, Brazil, China, the Gambia, India, Islamic Republic of Iran, Jamaica, Jordan, Madagascar, Montenegro, Mozambique, Nepal, Nicaragua, Papua New Guinea, Serbia, Sri Lanka, Tajikistan, Uganda, Uzbekistan and Zimbabwe. Input was also received from Programme Division, Division of Policy and Planning, Office of UN Affairs and External Relations, and Division of Communication at New York Headquarters, UNICEF regional offices and the Innocenti Research Centre.

Sincere thanks to Casimira Rodríguez Romero, Minister of Justice, Bolivia, for her special contribution.

EDITORIAL
Patricia Moccia, *Editor-in-Chief*; David Anthony, *Editor*;
Allyson Alert; Chris Brazier; Christine Dinsmore;
Hirut Gebre-Egziabher; Emily Goodman;
Paulina Gruszczynski; Tamar Hahn; Pamela Knight;
Amy Lai; Catherine Langevin-Falcon; Jodi Liss;
Najwa Mekki; Lorna O'Hanlon; Catherine Rutgers

STATISTICAL TABLES
Tessa Wardlaw, *Acting Chief*, Statistical Information
Section, Division of Policy and Planning; Priscilla Akwara;
Claudia Cappa; Friedrich Huebler; Rouslan Karimov;
Edilberto Loaiza; Nyein Nyein Lwin; Mary Mahy;
Maryanne Neill; Ngagne Diakhate; Khin Wityee Oo;
Emily White Johansson

DESIGN AND PRE-PRESS PRODUCTION
Prographics, Inc.

STEERING COMMITTEE
Rima Salah, *Chair*; Gordon Alexander; Maie Ayoub
von Kohl; Liza Barrie; Wivina Belmonte; Samuel Bickel;
Susan Bissell; Mark Hereward; Eva Jespersen; Afshan Khan;
Gabriele Koehler; Erma Manoncourt; Peter Mason;
Sidya Ould El-Hadj; David Parker; Mahesh Patel;
Marie-Pierre Poirier; Dorothy Rozga; Fabio Sabatini;
Christian Schneider; Susana Sottoli; Yves Willemot;
Alexandre Zouev

RESEARCH AND POLICY GUIDANCE
Elizabeth Gibbons, *Chief*, Global Policy Section, Division
of Policy and Planning; David Stewart, *Senior Policy
Advisor*, Global Policy Section; Raluca Eddon;
Ticiana Maloney; Annalisa Orlandi; Kate Rogers

PRODUCTION AND DISTRIBUTION
Jaclyn Tierney, *Production Officer*; Edward Ying, Jr.;
Germain Ake; Eki Kairupan; Farid Rashid; Elias Salem

TRANSLATION
French edition: Marc Chalamet
Spanish edition: Carlos Perellón

PHOTO RESEARCH
Allison Scott; Susan Markisz

PRINTING
Gist and Herlin Press

EXTERNAL ADVISORY PANEL
Anne Marie Goetz; Edmund Fitzgerald;
Geeta Rao Gupta; Kareen Jabre; Sir Richard Jolly;
Azza M. Karam; Elizabeth M. King; Laura Laski;
Joyce Malombe; Carolyn Miller; Agnes Quisumbing;
Gustav Ranis

BACKGROUND PAPERS
Lori Beaman, Esther Duflo, Rohini Pande and
Petia Topalova; Elizabeth Powley; Sylvia Chant;
Leslie A. Schwindt-Bayer

CONTENTS

1 A call for equality

2 Equality in the household

Women and Children
The Double Dividend of Gender Equality

Message from the Secretary-General of the United Nations

Eliminating gender discrimination and empowering women are among the paramount challenges facing the world today. When women are healthy, educated and free to take the opportunities life affords them, children thrive and countries flourish, reaping a double dividend for women and children.

© UN/DPI/Sergey Bormeniev

In the 27 years since the adoption of the Convention on the Elimination of All Forms of Discrimination against Women, much has been done to advance the progress of women. But we have fallen far short of what we need to achieve the Millennium Development Goals. Until there is gender equality, there can be no sustainable development. It is impossible to realize our goals while discriminating against half the human race.

As study after study has taught us, there is no tool for development more effective than the empowerment of women. No other policy is as likely to raise economic productivity or to reduce child and maternal mortality. No other policy is as sure to improve nutrition and promote health, including the prevention of HIV/AIDS. No other policy is as powerful in increasing the chances of education for the next generation. That is why discrimination against women of all ages deprives the world's children – all of them, not just the half who are girls – of the chance to reach their potential. This is an issue that goes to the heart of UNICEF's mission: protecting the rights of all children.

In my 10 years as Secretary-General, I have been proud to add my voice to UNICEF's in calling on the world to pay more attention to children's lives, needs and rights. Among the many issues UNICEF has addressed over the past decade, none is more central to its mandate than the rights of women.

Kofi A. Annan
Secretary-General of the United Nations

Foreword

The State of the World's Children 2007 reports on the lives of women around the world for a simple reason: Gender equality and the well-being of children go hand in hand. When women are empowered to live full and productive lives, children prosper. UNICEF's experience also shows the opposite: When women are denied equal opportunity within a society, children suffer.

Working within countries to achieve Millennium Development Goal 3 – promoting gender equality and empowering women – will reap the double dividend of bettering the lives of both women and children. It will also contribute to achieving all the other goals, from reducing poverty and hunger to saving children's lives, improving maternal health, ensuring universal education, combating HIV/AIDS, malaria and other diseases, ensuring environmental sustainability, and developing new and innovative partnerships for development.

© UNICEF/HQ05-2284/Christine Johnston

Despite the international community's commitment to gender equality, the lives of millions of women and girls throughout the world are plagued by discrimination, disempowerment and poverty. This report illustrates the many challenges that remain. Women and girls are disproportionately affected by the AIDS pandemic. Many girls are forced into child marriages, some before they are 15 years old. Maternal mortality figures remain indefensibly high in many countries. In most places, women earn less than men for equal work. Around the world, millions of women and girls suffer from physical and sexual violence, with little recourse to justice and protection.

Declarations, conventions and goals are not enough. It is imperative that we move resolutely from the realm of words to the realm of concrete action. As these pages will make clear, the day when women and girls have equal opportunities to be educated, to participate in government, to achieve economic self-sufficiency and to be secure from gender violence and discrimination will be the day when the promise of gender equality is fulfilled and UNICEF's mission of a world fit for children can be realized.

Ann M. Veneman
Executive Director
United Nations Children's Fund

SUMMARY Gender equality is central to realizing the Millennium agenda, which risks failure without the full participation of all members of society. Within the Millennium Declaration and the Millennium Development Goals, and at the heart of the United Nations itself, is the acknowledgement that the vulnerable, especially children, require special care and attention. Gender equality will not only empower women to overcome poverty, but also their children, families, communities and countries. When seen in this light, gender equality is not only morally right – it is pivotal to human progress and sustainable development.

Moreover, gender equality produces a double dividend: It benefits both women and children. Healthy, educated and empowered women have healthy, educated and confident daughters and sons. The amount of influence women have over the decisions in the household has been shown to positively impact the nutrition, health care and education of their children. But the benefits of gender equality go beyond their direct impact on children. Without it, it will be impossible to create a world of equity, tolerance and shared responsibility – a world that is fit for children.

Yet, despite substantial gains in women's empowerment since the Convention on the Elimination of All Forms of Discrimination against Women was adopted by the UN General Assembly in 1979, gender discrimination remains pervasive in every region of the world. It appears in the preference for sons over daughters, limited opportunities in education and work for girls and women, and outright gender-based violence in the forms of physical and sexual violence.

Other, less obvious, forms of gender discrimination can be equally destructive. Institutional discrimination is harder to identify and rectify. Cultural traditions can perpetuate social exclusion and discrimination from generation to generation, as gender stereotypes remain widely accepted and go unchallenged.

Eliminating gender discrimination and empowering women will require enhancing women's influence in the key decisions that shape their lives and those of children in three distinct arenas: the household, the workplace and the political sphere. A change for the better in any one of these realms influences women's equality in the others and has a profound and positive impact on children everywhere. This report intends to provide a road map to accelerate progess towards gender equality and empowering women through education, financing, legislation, legislative quotas, engaging men and boys, women empowering women and improved research and data.

A call for equality

Equality between men and women has been a goal of the United Nations since its inception. The 1945 Preamble to the UN Charter notes its objective "to reaffirm faith in fundamental human rights, in the dignity and worth of the human person, in the equal rights of men and women and of nations large and small."

These words link equality to human development, recognizing that both women and men are essential for the social and economic progress of nations. More than 60 years ago, global leaders envisioned a world where all people shared equally in rights, resources and opportunities, where abundance ruled and every man, woman and child was free from despair and inequity.

The call for equal rights evolved into a quest for gender equality when a distinction was made between gender and sex. Sex is biological: Females have two X chromosomes and males have one X and one Y chromosome. Gender, on the other hand, is a social construct that describes what is feminine and what is masculine. Recognizing that gender roles are not inborn but rather learned, proponents of gender equality challenged the stereotypes and pervasive discrimination that kept women and girls socially and economically disadvantaged.

Despite calls for gender equality in such documents as the Universal Declaration of Human Rights, adopted by the UN General Assembly in 1948, and other related proclamations, the cause of women's rights did not take its rightful place in the international agenda until 1974. Then, the UN Commission on the Status of Women, which had been established in 1946 and already succeeded in having sev-

eral legal instruments adopted, was tasked with preparing an internationally binding instrument that would protect human rights and fundamental freedoms for women. The result of its work, the Convention on the Elimination of All Forms of Discrimination against Women (CEDAW), was adopted by the UN General Assembly in 1979.[1] The Convention on the Rights of the Child (CRC), which focuses on the inalienable rights of children, was adopted a decade later.

World leaders know that human development is stunted by entrenched discrimination and injustice. Yet although 27 years have elapsed since CEDAW was adopted – and despite the fact that the convention has received 184 ratifications, accessions and successions by States parties – millions of women and girls throughout the world remain powerless, voiceless and without rights. The negative consequences of women's inequality reverberate throughout society.

The State of the World's Children 2007 examines the discrimination and disempowerment women face throughout their lives – and outlines what must be done to eliminate gender discrimination and empower women and girls. It begins by examining the status of women today, and then discusses how gender equality will move all the Millennium Development Goals (MDGs) forward, and how investment in women's rights will ultimately produce a double dividend: advancing the rights of both women and children.

The rights of women and children are mutually reinforcing

A logical question that arises from the topic of this report is, "Why does UNICEF, an

have equal access to food, health care, education and opportunities. Evidence has shown that women whose rights are fulfilled are more likely to ensure that girls have access to adequate nutrition, health care, education and protection from harm.

Second, gender equality is essential to creating the world envisioned in the Millennium Declaration, a world of peace, equity, tolerance, security, freedom, respect for the environment and shared responsibility, in which special care and attention is given to the most vulnerable people, especially children. This is the world that the international community has pledged to strive for – a world fit for both women and children.

Nothing less than the full participation of all members of society is needed to ensure sufficient human progress to meet the Millennium Agenda. World leaders at the UN Millennium Summit in 2000 understood this. They acknowledged that gender equality will empower women to overcome poverty, with multiple benefits for their families, communities and countries.

The Millennium agenda reflects this recognition of the centrality of gender equality to human development. The Millennium Declaration specifically calls for the full implementation of both the Convention on the Elimination of All Forms of Discrimination against Women and the Convention on the Rights of the Child; the conventions are identified as key human rights standards for meeting the Millennium Development Goals. These goals, the international community's guides to sustainable development, set time-sensitive benchmarks for promoting gender equality and empowering women. But gender equality, according to the Millennium agenda, is not simply a method for accelerating human development: It is also morally right.

Complementarities and tensions between the two conventions

Since the status of women and the well-being of children are deeply intertwined, advocates for children would be remiss if they failed to champion the cause of gender equality. The Convention on the Elimination of all Forms

organization that advocates for children, monitor women's rights?" The answer is twofold.

First, as this report demonstrates, gender equality furthers the cause of child survival and development. Because women are the primary caregivers for children, women's well-being contributes to the well-being of their offspring. Healthy, educated and empowered women are more likely to have healthy, educated and confident daughters and sons. Women's autonomy, defined as the ability to control their own lives and to participate in making decisions that affect them and their families, is associated with improved child nutrition (*see Chapter 2, pages 24*). Other aspects of gender equality, such as education levels among women, also correlate with improved outcomes for children's survival and development.[2]

By upholding women's rights, societies also protect girl children and female adolescents. Gender equality means that girls and boys of Discrimination against Women (CEDAW) and the Convention on the Rights of the Child (CRC) are sister treaties – inexorably linked in moving communities towards full human rights. Each delineates specific entitlements that cannot be abrogated due to age, gender, economic class or nationality. The two treaties are complementary, overlapping in their call for precise rights and responsibilities and filling in crucial gaps that may exist when either stands alone.

Several articles of CEDAW address rights pertinent to children, including equality (articles 2 and 15), protecting maternity (article 4), adequate health care (article 12) and shared parental responsibility (article 16). The CRC calls for equal access for girls and boys to education and health care. Both conventions demand freedom from violence and abuse and are based on principles of non-discrimination, participation and accountability.

The treaties are not perfectly harmonious: There are areas of tension. For instance, some supporters of gender equality believe that the CRC stereotypes women as mothers, limiting their life options. Some child rights advocates think that CEDAW focuses too much on a woman's right to self-actualization and may unintentionally subvert the importance of motherhood. Despite these differences, the two conventions hold more in common than in opposition – they set the standards for an equitable world in which the rights of every human being – female and male, old and young – are respected.

The rights of women are less widely accepted than those of children

Although both treaties have gained widespread endorsement, CEDAW has had the tougher road to acceptance and ratification. Some nations that readily accept the concept that children have rights are less willing to concede that women also have rights. And while 184 countries are parties to CEDAW, many of the signatures were submitted with reservations to specific articles. In fact, CEDAW contains among the highest number of reservations of any United Nations treaty, underscoring worldwide resistance to women's rights.[3]

Rhetorical support for CEDAW and the CRC has been strong. In practice, however, neither

Figure 1.1 In many developing regions, girls are more likely than boys to miss out on a secondary education

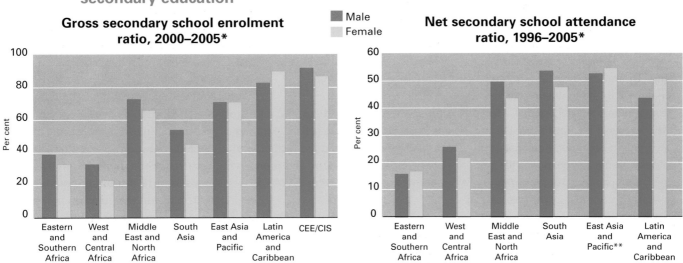

Notes: Gross secondary enrolment ratio refers to the number of children enrolled in secondary school, regardless of age, expressed as a percentage of the total number of children of official secondary school age. Net secondary school attendance ratio refers to the number of children attending secondary school who are of official secondary school age, expressed as a percentage of the total number of children of official secondary school age. These data come from national household surveys.
* Data refer to the most recent year available during the period specified.
** Excludes China.

Sources: *Gross secondary enrolment ratio:* UNESCO Institute of Statistics. *Net secondary school attendance ratio:* Demographic and Health Surveys and Multiple Indicator Cluster Surveys. The underlying data can be found in the Statistical Tables of this report, page 98.

Gender discrimination across the life cycle

Foeticide and infanticide

Gender discrimination begins early. Modern diagnostic tools for pregnancy have made it possible to determine a child's sex in the earliest phase. Where there is a clear economic or cultural preference for sons, the misuse of these techniques can facilitate female foeticide. Although there is no conclusive evidence to confirm such illegal misuse, birth histories and census data reveal an unusually high proportion of male births and male children under five in Asia, notably in China and India, suggesting sex-selective foeticide and infanticide in the world's two most populous countries – despite initiatives to eradicate these practices in both countries.

The middle years

A principal focus of the middle years of childhood and adolescence is ensuring access to, and completion of, quality primary and secondary education. With a few exceptions, it is mostly girls who suffer from educational disadvantage.

Primary education

For every 100 boys out of school, there are 115 girls in the same situation. Though the gender gap has been closing steadily over the past few decades, nearly 1 of every 5 girls who enrols in primary school in developing countries does not complete a primary education. Missing out on a primary education deprives a girl of the opportunity to develop to her full potential. Research has shown that educated women are less likely to die in childbirth and are more likely to send their children to school. Evidence indicates that the under-five mortality rate falls by about half for mothers with primary school education.

Secondary education

Recent UNICEF estimates indicate that an average of only 43 per cent of girls of the appropriate age in the developing world attend secondary school. There are multiple reasons for this: There may simply be no secondary school for girls to attend – many developing countries and donors have traditionally focused on offering universal primary education and neglected to allocate the resources to increase enrolment and attendance in secondary education. A girl's parents may conclude that they cannot afford secondary education or may take the traditional view that marriage should be the limit of her ambitions.

Secondary education has multiple benefits for women and children. It is singularly effective in delaying the age at which a young woman first gives birth and it can enhance freedom of movement and maternal health. It also strengthens women's bargaining power within households (*see Chapter 2*), and is a crucial factor in providing opportunities for women's economic and political participation (*see Chapters 3 and 4*).

Adolescence

Among the greatest threats to adolescent development are abuse, exploitation and violence, and the lack of vital knowledge about sexual and reproductive health, including HIV/AIDS.

Female genital mutilation/cutting

Female genital mutilation/cutting (FGM/C) involves partial or total removal of, or other injuries to, female genitalia for cultural, non-medical reasons. The practice of FGM/C mainly occurs in countries in sub-Saharan Africa, the Middle East and North Africa and some parts of South-East Asia. It is estimated that more than 130 million women and girls alive today have been subjected to FGM/C. FGM/C can have grave health consequences, including the failure to heal, increased susceptibility to HIV infection, childbirth complications, inflammatory diseases and urinary incontinence. Severe bleeding and infection can lead to death.

Child marriage and premature parenthood

Child or early marriage refers to marriages and unions where one or both partners are under the age of 18. Globally, 36 per cent of women aged 20–24 were married or in union before they reached their 18th birthday, most commonly in South Asia and sub-Saharan Africa. Child marriage is a long-standing tradition in areas where it is practised, making protest sometimes barely possible. Parents may consent to child marriages out of economic necessity, or because they believe marriage will protect girls from sexual assault and pregnancy outside marriage, extend girls' child-bearing years or ensure obedience to their husband's household.

Premature pregnancy and motherhood are an inevitable consequence of child marriage. An estimated 14 million adolescents between 15 and 19 give birth each year. Girls under 15 are five times more likely to die during pregnancy and childbirth than women in their twenties. If a mother is under 18, her baby's chance of dying in the first year of life is 60 per cent greater than that of a baby born to a mother older than 19. Even if the child survives, he or she is more likely to suffer from low birth-weight, undernutrition and late physical and cognitive development.

Sexual abuse, exploitation and trafficking

The younger girls are when they first have sex, the more likely it is that intercourse has been imposed on them. According to a World Health Organization study, 150 million girls and 73 million boys under the age of 18 experienced forced sexual intercourse or other forms of physical and sexual violence in 2002. The absence of a minimum age for sexual consent and marriage exposes children to partner violence in some countries.

An estimated 1.8 million children are involved in commercial sex work. Many are forced into it, whether they are sold into sexual slavery by desperately poor families or abducted and trafficked into brothels or other exploitative environments. Children exploited in the commercial sex industry are subjected to neglect, sexual violence and physical and psychological abuse.

Sexual and reproductive health

Because unprotected sex carries the risk of pregnancy and sexually transmitted infection, including HIV, knowledge of sexual and reproductive health is essential for the safety of young people. Information alone cannot provide protection, but it is certainly a first step. Nonetheless, adolescents around the world continue to have limited knowledge of reproductive health issues and the risks they face.

HIV/AIDS

By 2005, nearly half of the 39 million people living with HIV were women. In parts of Africa and the Caribbean, young women (aged 15–24) are up to six times more likely to be infected than young men their age. Women are at greater risk of contracting HIV than men. One important explanation is physiological – women are at least twice as likely as men to become infected with HIV during sex. The other crucial, and largely reversible, factor is social – gender discrimination denies women the negotiating power they need to reduce their risk of infection. High rates of illiteracy among women prevent them from knowing about the risks of HIV infection and possible protection strategies. A survey of 24 sub-Saharan African countries reveals that two thirds or more of young women lack comprehensive knowledge of HIV transmission.

The dramatic increase in infection among women heightens the risk of infection among children. Infants become infected through their mothers during pregnancy, childbirth or breastfeeding. In 2005, more than 2 million children aged 14 years or younger were living with HIV.

Motherhood and old age

Two key periods in many women's lives when the pernicious effects of both poverty and inequality can combine are motherhood and old age.

Maternal mortality

It is estimated that each year more than half a million women – roughly one woman every minute – die as a result of pregnancy complications and childbirth. Some 99 per cent of all maternal deaths occur in developing countries, with over 90 per cent of those in Africa and Asia. Two thirds of maternal deaths in 2000 occurred in 13 of the world's poorest countries. The same year, India alone accounted for one quarter of all maternal deaths. One out of every 16 sub-Saharan African women will die as a result of pregnancy or childbirth, compared to just 1 out of every 4,000 in industrialized countries. Moreover, motherless newborns are between 3 and 10 times more likely to die than newborns whose mothers survive.

Many of these women's lives could be saved if they had access to basic health care services, including skilled attendants at all births and emergency obstetric care for women who develop complications.

Women in old age

Elderly women may face double discrimination on the basis of both gender and age. Women tend to live longer than men, may lack control of family resources and can face discrimination from inheritance and property laws. Many older women are plunged into poverty at a time of life when they are very vulnerable. Only a few developing countries have safety nets for older people in the form of non-contributory or means-tested pensions.

Grandmothers in particular possess a great deal of knowledge and experience related to all aspects of maternal and child health and care. In many families, they are a mainstay of childcare for working parents. Experience has shown that children's rights are advanced when programmes that seek to benefit children and families also include elderly women.

See References, page 88.

convention has been fully implemented. While giving lip service to equality, governments often fail to invest often limited public resources in women and children or to challenge discriminatory customs, attitudes and beliefs.

Too often, legal watchdogs, civil society organizations and the media also shirk their responsibilities when they fail to monitor, publicly scrutinize or hold officials accountable for unfulfilled promises.

Enforcement of international conventions and national laws pertaining to women and children falls mainly to governments, and they must be ultimately held accountable for the slow pace of progress. But resistance by individuals, families and communities has also waylaid gender equality and children's rights. Male privilege, or the belief that girls and women must be submissive, can leave them last in line for food, health care, education and economic opportunity.

All obstacles to gender equality, regardless of origin, must be dismantled so that development can move forward. Although women and girls are most directly harmed by gender inequality, its pernicious effects reverberate across societies. Failure to secure equality for all has deleterious consequences for the moral, legal and economic fabric of nations.

The pernicious nature of gender inequality

Gender discrimination is pervasive. While the degrees and forms of inequality may vary, women and girls are deprived of equal access to resources, opportunities and political power in every region of the world. The oppression of girls and women can include the preference for sons over daughters, limited personal and professional choices for girls and women, the denial of basic human rights and outright gender-based violence.

Figure 1.2 Men's discriminatory attitudes towards women vary across regions but are significant everywhere

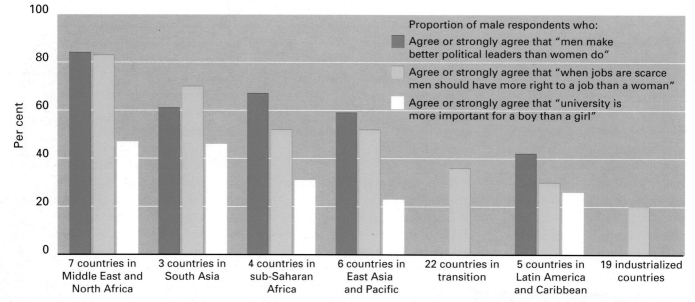

UNICEF calculations are based on data derived from the World Values Survey, Round 4 (1999–2004). Data for each country and territory in the regional aggregates are for the latest year available in the period specified. The following countries and territories are included in the regional aggregates cited: **Middle East and North Africa:** Algeria, Egypt, Islamic Republic of Iran, Iraq, Jordan, Morocco, Saudi Arabia. **Latin America and Caribbean:** Argentina, Bolivarian Republic of Venezuela, Chile, Mexico, Peru. **South Asia:** Bangladesh, India, Pakistan. **East Asia and Pacific:** China, Indonesia, Philippines, Republic of Korea, Singapore, Viet Nam. **Sub-Saharan Africa:** Nigeria, South Africa, Uganda, United Republic of Tanzania. **Countries in transition:** Albania, Belarus, Bosnia and Herzegovina, Bulgaria, Croatia, Czech Republic, Estonia, Hungary, Kyrgyzstan, Latvia, Lithuania, Montenegro, Poland, Romania, Republic of Moldova, Russian Federation, Serbia, Slovakia, Slovenia, Ukraine, The former Yugoslav Republic of Macedonia, Turkey. **Industrialized countries:** Austria, Belgium, Canada, Denmark, Finland, France, Greece, Iceland, Ireland, Italy, Japan, Luxembourg, Malta, Netherlands, Portugal, Spain, Sweden, United Kingdom, United States. Notes on the methodology employed can be found in the References section, page 88.

Source: World Values Survey, <www.worldvaluessurvey.org>, accessed June 2006.

Inequality is always tragic and sometimes fatal. Prenatal sex selection and infanticide, prevalent in parts of South and East Asia, show the low value placed on the lives of girls and women and have led to unbalanced populations where men outnumber women.[4]

Despite overall growth in educational enrolment, more than 115 million children of primary school age do not receive an elementary education. With few exceptions, girls are more likely than boys to be missing from classrooms across the developing world. Girls who do enrol in school often drop out when they reach puberty for many reasons – the demands of household responsibilities, a lack of school sanitation, a paucity of female role models, child marriage or sexual harassment and violence, among others.

Violence against women and girls

Girls and women are frequently victims of physical and sexual violence inside and outside the home. Although such assaults are under-reported because of the stigma of the crime, a recent multi-country study by the World Health Organization revealed that between 15 per cent and 71 per cent of women had experienced physical or sexual assault from an intimate partner.[5] Domestic violence is the most common form of violence perpetrated against women.[6]

During armed conflict, rape and sexual assault are often used as weapons of war. When complex emergencies force people to be displaced from their homes, women and girls are at increased risk of violence, exploitation and abuse – sometimes from the very security personnel or other persons charged with their protection and safety.

Insidious forms of gender inequality

As despicable as deliberate negligence or brutal violence can be, insidious gender inequality may be equally destructive.

Gender discrimination and inequalities across regions

Attitudes, beliefs and practices that serve to exclude women are often deeply entrenched, and in many instances closely associated with cultural, social and religious norms. Surveys, opinion polls and case studies provide a good indication of the prevalence of gender discrimination in many countries.

A Gallup Poll conducted in five Latin American countries (Argentina, Brazil, Colombia, El Salvador and Mexico) found that half of the respondents believed society favours men over women. In Brazil, only 20 per cent of respondents, both men and women, believe that society treats both sexes equally, while more than half of respondents in that country, and in neighbouring Argentina, consider that women and men do not enjoy equal job opportunities. Although these results are drawn from a small sample, they may well be indicative of a broader recognition of gender discrimination in society.

Examining social attitudes on specific issues, such as access to education and income-generating opportunities for women, reveals even more clearly the extent of gender discrimination and how it compares across countries. The World Values Survey reveals that an alarmingly large number of men – who, as this report will show, often hold power in the household allocation of resources for vital services such as education and health care – believe that university education is more important for a boy than for a girl (*see Figure 1.2, page 6*).

Around two thirds of male respondents in Bangladesh indicate that university education for boys should be prioritized over that of girls – an opinion echoed by around one third or more of male respondents from the Islamic Republic of Iran, Mexico and Uganda, among others. In some countries, men's opinions on this particular issue were less discriminatory, with only 1 out of every 10 male respondents in China and less than 1 out of every 13 male respondents in the United States holding the same view.

These views on education are largely mirrored in attitudes to women's work and participation in politics. More than 80 per cent of men in seven countries surveyed in the Middle East and North Africa believe that when jobs are scarce, men have more right to work than women, and that they make better political leaders than women. In other regions, the proportion of men holding these views is lower, but still significant.

The survey revealed that women's views can also be equally discriminatory towards their own sex, if not quite as extreme. A surprisingly large number of women respondents from the survey agreed or strongly agreed with the statement that men make better political leaders than women – including over half of women respondents from Bangladesh, China, Islamic Republic of Iran and Uganda, over one third from Albania and Mexico, and one out of every five from the United States. This underlines the fact that discriminatory attitudes towards women and girls are not simply held by men, but also reflect norms and perceptions that may be shared by the entire society. Research has shown that when women set aside these norms and the pressure to conform is relaxed, their choices and values are very different.

While such opinion polls and surveys offer a window into the views of societies, they cannot show the true extent of gender discrimination. Quantifiable indicators are needed in order to gain a clearer picture of the inequalities and inequities produced by gender discrimination against women and girls. But as many national and international surveys and censuses are often not disaggregated by sex, such indicators are relatively scarce. Nonetheless, the data available point to a clear conclusion: gender inequalities remain stubbornly entrenched in all regions of the world.

An attempt to capture gender discrimination in a single indicator is the United Nations Development Programme gender empowerment measure (GEM), which assesses gender equality in key areas of economic and political participation in decision-making. The measure includes estimated earned income (a crucial determinant of a family member's influence on household decisions), the percentage of women working in senior positions and the percentage of women in parliament. Gender empowerment as measured by GEM is lowest in countries in the Middle East and North Africa and South Asia, and highest in industrialized countries, although there is wide variation across regions.

While poorer countries tend to have lower levels of gender empowerment, there is no clear evidence that gender inequalities automatically diminish at higher levels of income. Accordingly, low income need not be a barrier to higher levels of gender empowerment.

See References, page 88.

Institutional discrimination is harder to identify and rectify. Cultural traditions can perpetuate inequality and discrimination from generation to generation, as gender stereotypes remain accepted and unchallenged.

The unequal division of household labour, such as requiring girls and women to trek many kilometres to fetch water and fire-wood, or the uneven allocation of household resources, such as giving women and girls less food or medical care, are examples of more subtle forms of inequality. These ingrained forms of discrimination often keep individuals, families and societies trapped in poverty and undermine economic, political and social development.

If poverty is to become history, then gender inequality must first be eliminated. Bold initiatives and unflinching determination

are required to end individual and institutional gender discrimination. Attitudes, customs and values that are detrimental to women and girls must be confronted. No history, legacy, religion or cultural tradition can justify inequality and disempowerment.

The double dividend of gender equality

Despite ingrained gender inequality, the status of women has improved in the past three decades. An increased awareness of discriminatory practices and outcomes – including physical and sexual violence, female genital mutilation/cutting (FGM/C), disproportionate numbers affected by HIV/AIDS and female illiteracy, among others – has fostered greater demand for change. By promoting legal and social reforms, proponents of gender equality have begun to reshape the social and political landscape. And while gender continues to influence people's choices and challenges, in many parts of the world a girl born in 2007 will probably have a brighter future than a girl born when CEDAW was adopted in 1979.

Today, women and girls have access to opportunities that were previously restricted. Primary school enrolment rates for girls have jumped and the educational gender gap is narrowing. Women are entering the labour force in greater numbers. And women's political representation is increasing in many parts of the world.

In 2006, for instance, Chile and Jamaica elected women for the first time as their heads of government. (Chile's president, Michelle Bachelet, is also head of state.) In addition, the Republic of Korea appointed its first woman prime minister in April 2006, bringing the total number of female heads of state or government in the world to 14.[7]

While that number is miniscule, considering that there are 192 UN Member States, female government leadership was unheard of less than 50 years ago.[8]

Gains in gender equality not withstanding, far too many women and girls have been left behind and remain voiceless and powerless. Women are disproportionately affected by poverty, inequality and violence. It is widely estimated that women make up the majority of the world's poor,[9] comprise nearly two thirds of the people who are illiterate,[10] and, along with children, account for 80 per cent of civilian casualties during armed conflict.[11]

All Member States of the United Nations, regardless of their political, religious or ethnic composition, spoke with one voice when the UN pledged to make the world fit for children at the General Assembly Special Session on Children in May 2002.

Figure 1.3 In sub-Saharan Africa, young women are more vulnerable to HIV infection but have less comprehensive knowledge about HIV than young men

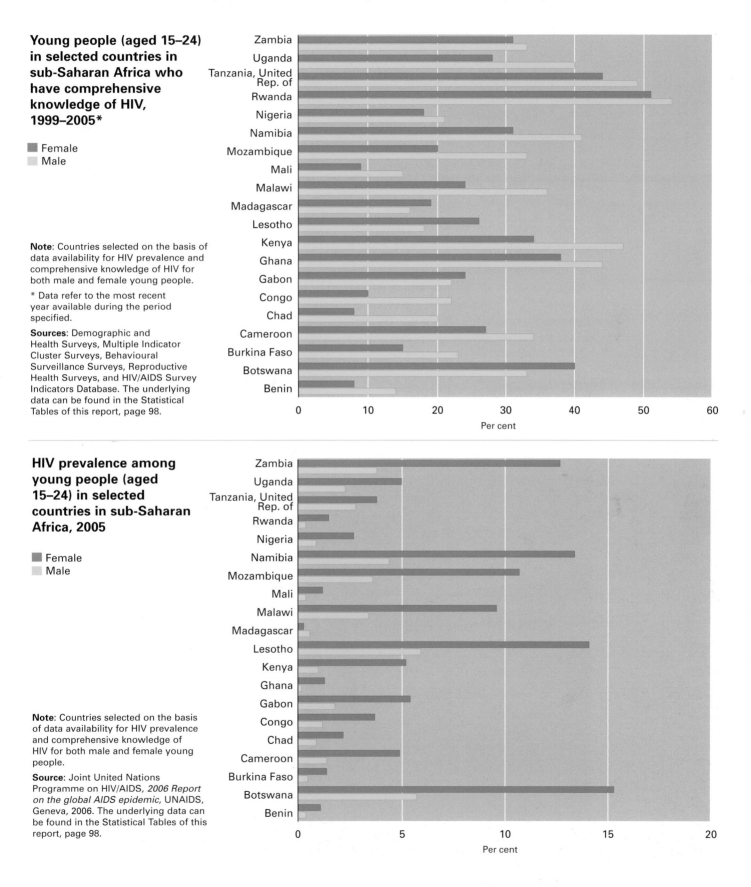

Young people (aged 15–24) in selected countries in sub-Saharan Africa who have comprehensive knowledge of HIV, 1999–2005*

■ Female
■ Male

Note: Countries selected on the basis of data availability for HIV prevalence and comprehensive knowledge of HIV for both male and female young people.

* Data refer to the most recent year available during the period specified.

Sources: Demographic and Health Surveys, Multiple Indicator Cluster Surveys, Behavioural Surveillance Surveys, Reproductive Health Surveys, and HIV/AIDS Survey Indicators Database. The underlying data can be found in the Statistical Tables of this report, page 98.

HIV prevalence among young people (aged 15–24) in selected countries in sub-Saharan Africa, 2005

■ Female
■ Male

Note: Countries selected on the basis of data availability for HIV prevalence and comprehensive knowledge of HIV for both male and female young people.

Source: Joint United Nations Programme on HIV/AIDS, *2006 Report on the global AIDS epidemic,* UNAIDS, Geneva, 2006. The underlying data can be found in the Statistical Tables of this report, page 98.

But rallying around the cause of children without championing gender equality is like stocking a sports team with players but failing to teach them how to play the game.

The intergenerational dividends of gender equality

Women are the primary caregivers for children and thus ultimately shape children's lives. This is especially true in the most traditional, patriarchal societies where roles and responsibilities are strictly delineated by gender. The well-being of women and children is inseparable. What is good for women is good for children with few, if any, exceptions.

Nations bear the consequences when women are disempowered and deprived of human rights. The cycle of poverty and despair is passed from generation to generation. Conversely, countries reap double dividends when gender equality is promoted and ultimately attained. Women become healthy, educated, productive and able to help their children survive and thrive. These benefits are bequeathed to current and future generations.

To maximize gender equality's impact on poverty reduction, education and sustainable development, women must have influence in decision-making in three distinct areas: the household, the workplace and the political sphere. A change for the better in any one of these realms influences women's equality in the others. But halfway measures towards human rights are unacceptable. Anything less than unqualified support for gender equality in all three areas will sabotage meaningful progress towards fulfilling the MDGs.

Equality in the household (Chapter 2)

Women's access to power at the household level has the most direct impact on families and children. Here is where decisions are

© Arege Douglas Mogeni/2006

Figure 1.4 More than 1 out of every 4 births to an adolescent mother (aged 15–19) occurs in the least developed countries

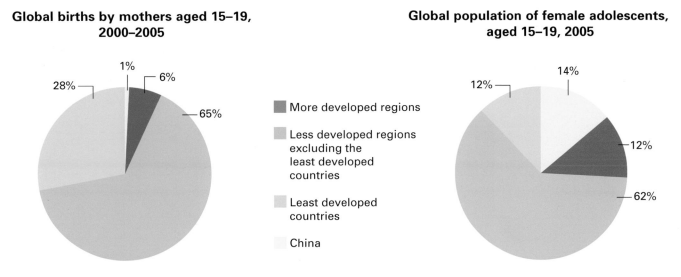

Global births by mothers aged 15–19, 2000–2005

Global population of female adolescents, aged 15–19, 2005

- More developed regions
- Less developed regions excluding the least developed countries
- Least developed countries
- China

Source: United Nations Population Division, 'World Population Prospects: The 2004 Revision Database', <www.esa.un.org/unpp/>, accessed September 2006. Note: The country composition of each regional group can be found in References, page 88.

made about the allocation of resources for food, health care, schooling and other family necessities.

When women are locked out of decisions regarding household income and other resources, they and their children are more likely to receive less food, and to be denied essential health services and education. Household chores, such as fetching water, gathering firewood or caring for the young or infirm, are delegated to mothers and daughters, which keeps them out of the paid labour force or school. When women share equally in household decisions, they tend to provide more adequately and fairly for their children.

Equality in the workplace (Chapter 3)

At work, women are often victimized by discrimination. They may be excluded from more highly remunerated occupations and are frequently paid less than men for the same work. Women and girls are often recruited into domestic work outside their own homes and may be forced to live away from their families, at times in oppressive, dangerous conditions. Destitute women and girls may find the sex trade their only option

for employment when all other economic doors have been shut.

Ending the wage gap, opening higher-paying fields to women and allowing female workers more decision-making power will greatly benefit children. As women become economically productive, their spheres of influence increase. They become able to make choices not only for themselves, but also for their children. When a woman brings income or assets into the household, she is more likely to be included in decisions on how the resources will be distributed. Historically, when women hold decision-making power, they see to it that their children eat well, receive adequate medical care, finish school and have time for recreation and play. Women who have access to meaningful, income-producing work are more likely to increase their families' standards of living, leading children out of poverty.

Equality in government and politics (Chapter 4)

Increasing women's political participation is an MDG objective in its own right (MDG 3, Target 4, Indicator 12). Empowering women in the political arena can help change societies.

Figure 1.5 High rates of maternal death are associated with limited access to health-care services for expectant mothers

Health-care services for expectant mothers, 1997–2005*

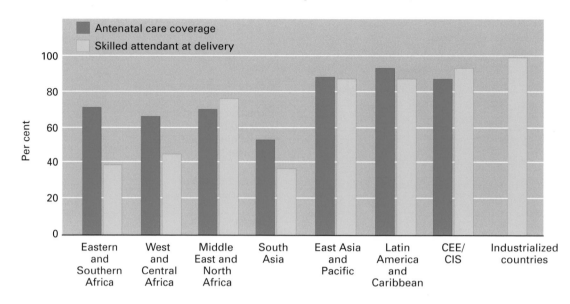

Note: Antenatal care coverage refers to the percentage of women aged 15–24 attended at least once during pregnancy by a skilled attendant (doctor, nurse or midwife). Data on antenatal care coverage are not available for industrialized countries. Skilled attendant at delivery refers to the percentage of births attended by skilled health personnel (doctors, nurses or midwives).

* Data refer to the most recent year available during the period specified.

Sources: Demographic and Health Surveys, Multiple Indicator Cluster Surveys, World Health Organization and UNICEF. The underlying data can be found in the Statistical Tables of this report, page 98.

Lifetime risk of maternal death, 2000

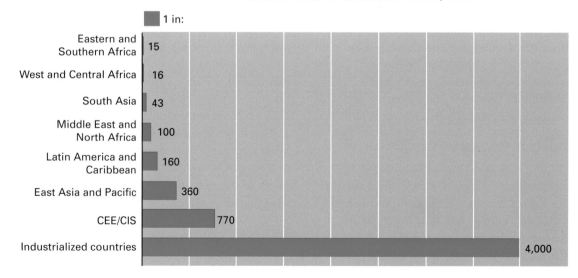

Note: The lifetime risk of maternal death takes into account both the probability of becoming pregnant and the probability of dying as a result of that pregnancy, accumulated across a women's reproductive years.

Source: World Health Organization and UNICEF. The underlying data can be found in the Statistical Tables of this report, page 98.

Their involvement in governing bodies, whether local or national, leads to policies and legislation that focus on women, children and families. In a survey of 187 women who hold public office in 65 countries, the Inter-Parliamentary Union found that about nine-tenths believe they have a responsibility to represent women's interests and advocate for other members of society.[12]

Women can play key roles in securing peace. Female representation in peace negotiations and post-conflict reconstruction is vital to ensuring the safety and protection of children and other vulnerable populations. Women's direct influence on politics and public policy bodes well for peace, security and prosperity.

Empowering women and girls

The status of women is a crucial element for accurately gauging the state of the world's children and assessing what the future holds for them. Disaggregated data on life expectancy, infant and under-five mortality, educational enrolment and completion, as well as other quantifiable statistics, are necessary to assess progress towards the MDGs. But attitudes, cultural beliefs and ingrained bigotry are difficult to quantify; consequently, qualitative evidence and women's reporting on their experiences are also needed to promote gender equality, poverty reduction and sustainable development.

The following chapters will analyse both quantitative indicators and qualitative evidence about the status of women and its relationship to child survival and development. The final chapter of the report intends to provide a road map for maximizing gender equality through seven key modes: education, financing, legislation, legislative quotas, engaging men and boys, women empowering

women, and improved research and data. For only when equality is achieved will women be empowered, and only then will they and their children thrive.

It has been nearly 30 years since CEDAW was adopted by the United Nations. One can only imagine what the lives of girls born in 1979 would have been like had the convention been fully supported and implemented. A generation of empowered women would have made a world of difference.

As a Chinese adage says, "Women hold up half the sky." The next generation cannot wait another three decades for its rights. Women and girls must have the means and support to fulfil their potential and fully enjoy their rights.

A world fit for women is a world fit for children

Two years after the Millennium Summit, the UN General Assembly Special Session on Children in May 2002 linked economic development to the creation of a world fit for children. A world fit for children is also a world fit for women. They are inseparable and indivisible – one cannot exist without the other.

Lofty ambitions, good intentions and catchy slogans will not produce human progress. The road to sustainable development cannot be paved with half measures. Sound investments and a resolute commitment to justice, gender equality and children are required.

If all citizens are allowed the opportunity to reach their potential, then nations will thrive. No argument against gender equality, whether based on traditions, customs or outright bigotry, can disprove the claim that women's rights are good for children and ultimately good for the world.

SUMMARY For children, the most important actors in the world are not political leaders and heads of development agencies, but the parents and care-givers who make crucial household decisions each day. Evidence suggests that men and women frequently have very different roles and priorities when it comes to household decision-making. Women generally place a higher premium on welfare-related goals and are more likely to use their influence and the resources they control to promote the needs of families, particularly children.

- A growing body of evidence indicates that household decisions are often made through a bargaining process that is more likely to favour men than women. Factors underlying women's influence in decision-making processes include control of income and assets, age at marriage and level of education.

- According to data from the Demographic and Health Surveys, in only 10 out of the 30 developing countries surveyed did half or more of women participate in all household decisions, including those regarding major household spending, their own health care and their visits with friends or relatives outside the home.

- The consequences of women's exclusion from household decisions can be as dire for children as they are for women themselves. According to a study conducted by the International Food Policy Research Institute, if men and women had equal influence in decision-making, the incidence of underweight children under three years old in South Asia would fall by up to 13 percentage points, resulting in 13.4 million fewer undernourished children in the region; in sub-Saharan Africa, an additional 1.7 million children would be adequately nourished.

- A woman's empowerment within the household increases the likelihood that her children, particularly girls, will attend school. A UNICEF survey of selected countries across the developing world found that, on average, children with uneducated mothers are at least twice as likely to be out of school than children whose mothers attended primary school.

- Men play a vital role in promoting egalitarian decision-making. Through simple and direct strategies, such as sharing responsibility for household chores and childcare, men can help combat gender discrimination in households and communities.

- Women themselves are the most important catalysts for change. By challenging and defying discriminatory attitudes in their communities, women's groups can advance the rights of girls and women for generations to come.

2

Equality in the household

Everyone interested in development and the progress of the world's children waits on the 'big' decisions: the conclusions of the G8 on aid and debt; the outcome of the Doha Round of trade negotiations; statements by international organizations and world leaders on major initiatives and positions. There is no doubting the importance of these negotiations in determining development outcomes. But there are other decisions, closer to home, that can have a larger and more direct impact on children's lives: How will scarce food be divided among parents and siblings? Who will go to school and who will work in the field? Is a child's temperature high enough to warrant a costly and distant trip to the doctor's office?

For children, the most important actors in the world are not political leaders and heads of development agencies, but the parents and caregivers who make these crucial household decisions on a daily basis. How members of the household use their collective resources determines the levels of nutrition, health care, education and protection that each family member receives.

Household decisions: More bargaining than cooperation

Every family is unique, and there is no simple set of rules that can explain the dynamic of decision-making processes. Studies that examine the dynamics of family decision-making often focus on the household. While this focus does not necessarily represent all interactions among family members, it does provide a practical means of understanding and analysing everyday family dynamics.

Much of the study of household dynamics is predicated on the assumption that households function as a unit in which family members pool their time and resources to achieve a common set of goals (the unitary model). While many households are characterized by such cooperation and act as a redistributive or sharing unit, individual household members do not always share the same priorities or preferences. Evidence suggests that men and women frequently have very different roles and priorities when it comes to household decision-making. Decisions are often made through a bargaining process in which household members each attempt to use the resources they control for their own priorities.

Inequalities in household decision-making

The factors that determine which family member will have the strongest say in household decisions vary among households and across cultures. The Demographic and Health Surveys provide one of the most direct sources of information on household decision-making dynamics. Questions from the surveys, which asked women in developing countries to specify their level of influence in household decisions, were aggregated by the research team to examine regional patterns of gender influence in household decision-making. Overall, the data paint a picture of extreme gender inequality. In only 10 of the 30 countries surveyed did 50 per cent or more of women participate in all household decisions, including those taken in regard to their own health care, major household purchases, daily household spending, and their visits with family or relatives outside of the household.[1]

© UNICEF/HQ98-0609/Alejandro Balaguer

Figure 2.1 Many husbands are making the decisions alone on their wife's health

Percentage of women who say their husbands alone make the decisions regarding their health, 2000-2004*

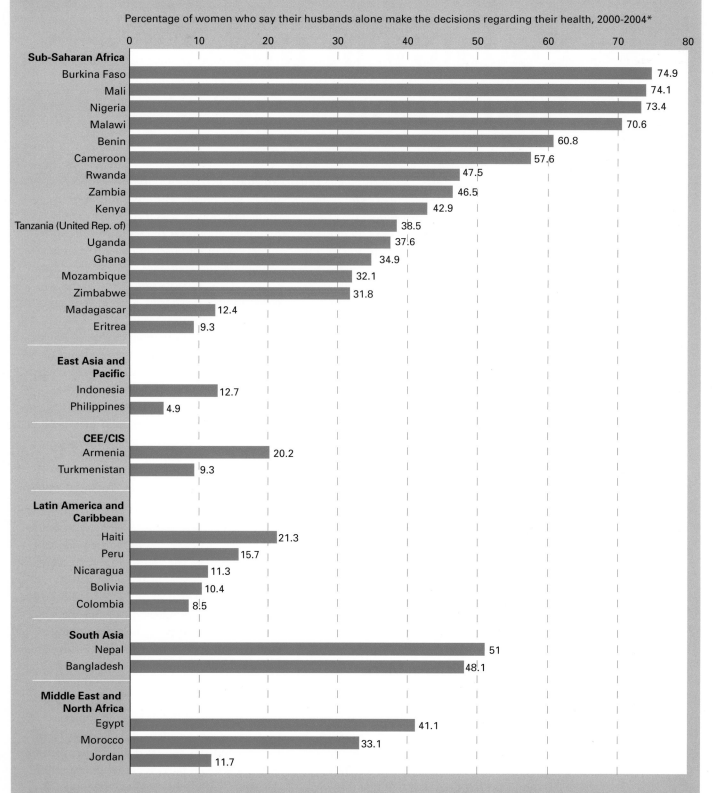

*Data refer to the most recent year available during the period specified. All countries with available data are presented in the chart.

Source: UNICEF calculations based on the data derived from Demographic and Health Surveys. The data were accessed from the DHS Statcompiler in June 2006. Notes on the methodology employed can be found in the References section, page 88.

Figure 2.2 Many husbands are making the decisions alone on daily household expenditure

Percentage of women who say their husbands alone make the decisions on daily household expenditure, 2000-2004*

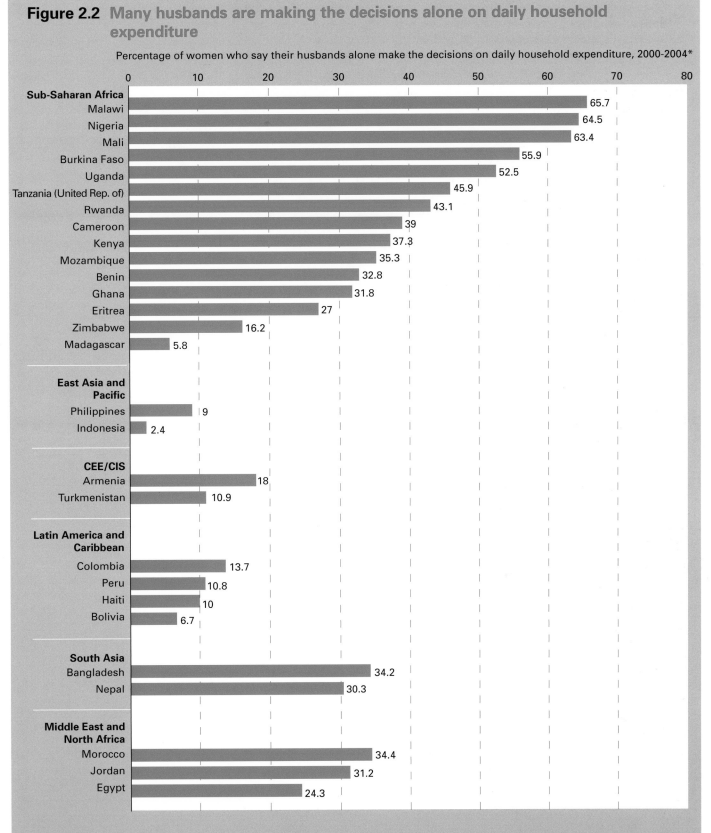

*Data refer to the most recent year available during the period specified. All countries with available data are presented in the chart.

Source: UNICEF calculations based on the data derived from Demographic and Health Surveys. The data were accessed from the DHS Statcompiler in June 2006. Notes on the methodology employed can be found in the References section, page 88.

Figure 2.3 Many husbands are making the decisions alone on visits to friends and relatives

Percentage of women who say their husbands alone make the decisions regarding visits to friends and relatives, 2000-2004*

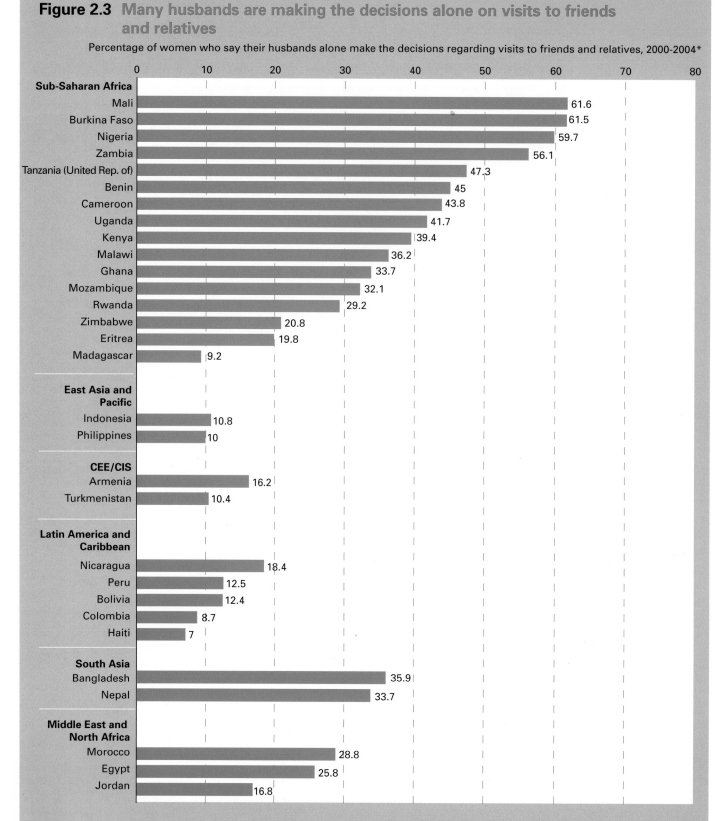

Sub-Saharan Africa
- Mali — 61.6
- Burkina Faso — 61.5
- Nigeria — 59.7
- Zambia — 56.1
- Tanzania (United Rep. of) — 47.3
- Benin — 45
- Cameroon — 43.8
- Uganda — 41.7
- Kenya — 39.4
- Malawi — 36.2
- Ghana — 33.7
- Mozambique — 32.1
- Rwanda — 29.2
- Zimbabwe — 20.8
- Eritrea — 19.8
- Madagascar — 9.2

East Asia and Pacific
- Indonesia — 10.8
- Philippines — 10

CEE/CIS
- Armenia — 16.2
- Turkmenistan — 10.4

Latin America and Caribbean
- Nicaragua — 18.4
- Peru — 12.5
- Bolivia — 12.4
- Colombia — 8.7
- Haiti — 7

South Asia
- Bangladesh — 35.9
- Nepal — 33.7

Middle East and North Africa
- Morocco — 28.8
- Egypt — 25.8
- Jordan — 16.8

*Data refer to the most recent year available during the period specified. All countries with available data are presented in the chart.

Source: UNICEF calculations based on the data derived from Demographic and Health Surveys. The data were accessed from the DHS Statcompiler in June 2006. Notes on the methodology employed can be found in the References section, page 88.

- **Lack of control over health-care needs:** Decisions on women's health care are vital to the health and well-being of both women and children. In many households, notably in those countries examined in South Asia and sub-Saharan Africa, women have little influence in health-related decisions. In Burkina Faso, Mali and Nigeria, for example, almost 75 per cent of women reported that husbands alone make decisions about women's health care; in the two countries surveyed in South Asia, Bangladesh and Nepal, this ratio was around 50 per cent. This exclusion compromises the health and well-being of all family members, particularly children.

- **Limited management of daily household expenditure:** Household decisions on daily expenditure have a decisive impact on children's well-being, education and, particularly, their health. Whether a family decides to spend its financial resources on the needs of children or the personal preferences of adults often depends on which family members are involved in the decision-making process. In many households across the developing world, men have a firm upper hand in decisions on household expenditures. In 7 of the 15 countries surveyed in sub-Saharan Africa, more than 40 per cent of women indicated that their husbands had exclusive control over daily household expenditures. In the countries examined in the Middle East and North Africa and South Asia, approximately 30 per cent of women felt excluded from decisions on household purchases, while in those countries surveyed CEE/CIS, East Asia and Pacific and Latin America and Caribbean, women reported having a greater degree of control over these decisions.

- **Exclusion from decisions on major household purchases:** Household decisions on large expenditures such as land, cars and livestock can be crucial for families. Money spent on large purchases may be regarded as a wise long-term investment. However, the short-term cost of acquiring these assets can consume a large share of household income that might otherwise be used for more immediate household needs, such as medicine, school supplies and food.

Data from the Demographic and Health Surveys suggest that men generally decide how much the household will allocate towards major expenditures. In Nigeria, for example, 78 per cent of women indicated that their husbands have exclusive control over large purchases. Approximately 60 per cent of women in Egypt and over a third of women in Bangladesh and Nepal felt excluded from such decisions. This contrasts with attitudes in the two countries surveyed in East Asia and Pacific, Indonesia and the Philippines, where fewer than 18 per cent of women in both countries felt that they had no say in such matters.

- **Restricted mobility and freedom:** Household decisions regarding women's mobility directly affect their ability to provide for their own needs as well as the needs of their children. Survey data suggest a high degree of male control over women's mobility in each of the regions surveyed. In Burkina Faso and Mali, approximately 60 per cent of women reported that husbands alone decide when wives can visit with family or relatives. One third of Bangladeshi husbands control their wives' mobility outside of the home. In Latin America and the Caribbean, data from Nicaragua show that 18 per cent of women require a man's permission before leaving home to visit friends and family; in CEE/CIS, 16 per cent of Armenian women need to first secure their husbands' permission.[2]

Factors underlying household decision-making processes

Household assessments such as Demographic and Health Surveys can provide a good indication of which family members are likely to participate in household decisions, but they cannot explain why certain individuals in each household are able to dominate decision-making processes. To understand the dynamics that influence household decision-making processes, it is useful to consider the factors that determine the structure of the family unit, as well as each family member's role within the household.

Gender discrimination in household decision-making is often rooted in patriarchal attitudes

that value the social status of men over women. But the extent to which individual households conform to 'traditional' ideas about the roles of men and women varies. The ability of family members to impose their own preferences in household decisions (bargaining power) is influenced by social attitudes and other, more tangible, factors.[3]

According to a study based on household decisions and gender, major determinants of influence in household decision-making include control of income and assets, age, and access to and level of education. Examining these factors across a wide range of countries offers insights into the distribution of bargaining power in individual households.[4]

Control of income and assets: The family member who controls the greatest share of household income and assets often has the strongest say in deciding whether those resources will be used to meet household needs.[5] As the next chapter will illustrate, in both industrialized and developing countries, women continue to lag behind men in terms of income-earning opportunities and ownership and management of assets.

Age gaps: The distribution of household bargaining power is also influenced by a woman's age at marriage and the age difference between a woman and her husband. Evidence from around the world shows that the age gap between husbands and wives can vary enormously among households. The average age at first marriage in Western Europe is estimated to be 27 for women and 30 for men. In developing countries, age differences are far greater. In South Asia, for example, husbands are approximately five years older than their wives; the gap rises to six years in sub-Saharan Africa (excluding southern Africa).[6] In cases of child marriage (defined as customary or statutory union where one or both of the partners is under the age of 18 years old), when the age gap between spouses is most extreme, the burden of domestic work and childcare severely constrains the life choices available to married girls and child mothers.[7] This, in turn, affects the power that women have over household decisions.

Levels of education: In addition to increased levels of knowledge, self-confidence and assertiveness, education confers social status and increases income-earning potential. As with age gaps between married couples, the levels of education of spouses vary among households. The findings of a study undertaken in 40 developing countries indicate that, on average, men tend to spend more time in education than women.

The education gap is widest in South Asia, where men on average spend 2.5 years more in school than women, declining to 1.3 years in sub-Saharan Africa, and 1 year in Latin America and the Caribbean.[8] Disparate levels of education between men and women may reinforce household gender inequalities, ensuring that women remain disadvantaged.

Domestic violence

Levels of education, earnings and asset ownership and age gaps are key in determining bargaining power between men and women within the household. Arguably of equal importance is the threat of domestic violence. While physical and sexual violence and other forms of abuse occur in different domestic environments and in different guises, there is substantial evidence to suggest that such acts are mainly perpetrated by adult men against women and girls.[9] Domestic violence threatens the physical health and emotional well-being of its victims and often forces them to endure subordinate positions and economic insecurity within their households.[10]

Household gender inequalities foster a permissive context for abusive relationships. A UNICEF study indicates that women who marry at a young age are more likely to believe that it is sometimes acceptable for a husband to beat his wife, and are more likely to experience domestic violence than women who marry at an older age. In Kenya, for example, 36 per cent of women who were married before the age of 18 believe that a man is sometimes justified in beating his wife, compared to 20 per cent of those who were married as adults.[11]

Violence against women and girls crosses the boundaries of race, culture, wealth and religion. Every year, thousands of women are maimed or killed by rejected suitors in many countries.[12] A landmark World Health Organization multi-country study on women's health and domestic violence against women reveals that of those interviewed, 37 per cent of women in a Brazilian province, 56 per cent of women in a province in the United Republic of Tanzania, and 62 per cent of women in a province in Bangladesh reported having experienced physical or sexual violence by an intimate partner.[13]

The pattern is broadly similar for industrialized countries. According to another key report from the same organization, the *World report on violence and health*, studies show that 40 per cent to 70 per cent of female murder victims in Australia, Canada, Israel, South Africa and the United States were killed by their husbands or boyfriends – often within the context of an ongoing abusive relationship.[14] In the United Kingdom, 40 per cent of female homicide victims are killed by their intimate partners.[15]

Where women have a fair say, children benefit

The consequences of women's exclusion from household decisions can be as dire for children as they are for women themselves. In families in which women are key decision-makers, the proportion of resources devoted to children is far greater than in those in which women have a less decisive role. This is because women generally place a higher premium than men on

Figure 2.4 Underweight prevalence among children under five in the developing regions*

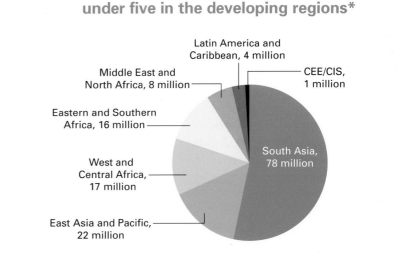

*UNICEF analysis is based on estimates of underweight prevalence in developing countries (1996-2005).

Source: United Nations Children's Fund, *Progress for Children: A report card on nutrition, Number 4*, UNICEF, New York, May 2006, page 2.

welfare-related goals and are more likely to use their influence and the resources they control to promote the needs of children in particular and of the family in general.[16] Case studies conducted in the developing world indicate that women who have greater influence in household decisions can significantly improve their children's nutritional status. Educating women also results in multiple benefits for children, improving their survival rates, nutritional status and school attendance.[17]

Women prioritize nutrition

Throughout the developing world, one out of every four children – roughly 146 million children – under the age of five is underweight.[18] Among developing regions, child undernutrition is most severe in South Asia and, to a lesser extent, sub-Saharan Africa.[19] For children whose nutritional status is deficient, common childhood ailments such as diarrhoea and respiratory infections can be fatal. Undernourished children who survive the early years of childhood often have low levels of iodine, iron, protein and energy, which can contribute to chronic sickness, stunting or reduced height for age, and impaired social and cognitive development.[20]

According to a study of three regions – Latin America and the Caribbean, South Asia and

Domestic violence against children

Every year, as many as 275 million children worldwide become caught in the crossfire of domestic violence and suffer the full consequences of a turbulent home life. Violence against children involves physical and psychological abuse and injury, neglect or negligent treatment, exploitation and sexual abuse. The perpetrators may include parents and other close family members.

Children who survive abuse often suffer long-term physical and psychological damage that impairs their ability to learn and socialize, and makes it difficult for them to perform well in school and develop close and positive friendships. Children who grow up in a violent home are more likely to suffer abuse compared to children who have a peaceful home life. Studies from some of the largest countries in the developing world, including China, Colombia, Egypt, India, Mexico, the Philippines and South Africa, indicate a strong correlation between violence against women and violence against children.

The behavioural and psychological consequences of growing up in a violent home can be just as devastating for children who are not directly abused themselves. Children who are exposed to violence often suffer symptoms of post-traumatic stress disorder, such as bed-wetting or nightmares, and are at greater risk than their peers of suffering from allergies, asthma, gastrointestinal problems, depression and anxiety. Primary-school-age children who are exposed to domestic violence may have more trouble with schoolwork and show poor concentration and focus. They are also more likely to attempt suicide and abuse drugs and alcohol.

The incidence of sexual violence in domestic settings is well known. Recent studies indicate high levels of sexual violence in childhood – up to 21 per cent according to a multi-country study conducted by the World Health Organization – with girls far more likely to be abused than boys. Sexual and gender-based violence is prevalent in schools and colleges, with much of the violence directed towards girls.

Working in someone's home can also entail the risk of violence. Child domestic workers – often girls under 16 – have indicated severe abuse at the hands of their employers, including physical punishment, sexual harassment and humiliation. Unlike other forms of domestic violence, much of the humiliation and physical punishment is perpetrated by women, although girls in particular are also vulnerable to sexual violence from men living in the household.

The consequences of domestic violence can span generations. The effects of violent behaviour tend to stay with children long after they leave the childhood home. Boys who are exposed to their parents' domestic violence are twice as likely to become abusive men as are the sons of non-violent parents. Furthermore, girls who witness their mothers being abused are more likely to accept violence in a marriage than girls who come from non-violent homes.

Although they often lack the means to protect themselves, abused women

sub-Saharan Africa – conducted by the International Food Policy Research Institute, a leading global research organization on hunger and nutrition, there is a clear link between regional differences in children's nutritional status and women's decision-making power. Where women have low status and are denied a voice in household decisions, they are more likely to be undernourished themselves and less likely to have access to resources that they can direct towards children's nutrition.[21] In South Asia, where between 40 per cent and 60 per cent of women are underweight,[22] approximately 45 per cent of children were born with low birthweight in 2005 – the highest incidence of underweight births in the world.[23]

The same study concluded that if men and women had equal influence in decision-making,[24] the incidence of underweight children under three years old in South Asia could fall by up to 13 percentage points, resulting in 13.4 million fewer undernourished children.[25] In sub-Saharan Africa, where one in every six women and around one third of children under the age of five are underweight,[26] increasing gender equality would have smaller but still significant benefits for children's nutritional status. It would reduce

often provide protection for children who are exposed to domestic violence. But without the legal or economic resources to prosecute abusive spouses, countless women and children remain trapped in harmful situations. Government-led efforts to create protective policies for victims of domestic violence require a parallel effort to change social attitudes that condone such violence.

Shattering the silence that surrounds domestic violence is key to ending violent behaviour in the home. The Report of the Independent Expert for the United Nations Study on Violence against Children represents a crucial step towards unmasking the issue of violence against children, including abuses perpetrated in the household. The report's six guiding principles – quoted at right – are clear, none more so than the first: **No violence against children is justifiable**. Its recommendations are comprehensive, with overarching precepts complemented by specific measures to combat violence against children in the home and family, in schools and other educational settings, in care and justice systems,

in the workplace and community. These measures also include advising governments to establish an ombudsperson or commission for children's rights in accordance with the 'Paris Principles'. The report advocates for the establishment of a Special Representative to the Secretary-General on Violence against Children to advocate at the international level, in conjunction with UNICEF, the World Health Organization and the Office of the UN High Commissioner for Human Rights, and the creation of a UN inter-agency group on violence against children, with representation from NGOs and children themselves.

See References, page 88.

The guiding principles of the Report of the Independent Expert for the United Nations Study on Violence against Children

- No violence against children is justifiable. Children should never receive less protection than adults.

- All violence against children is preventable. States must invest in evidence-based policies and programmes to address factors that give rise to violence against children.

- States have the primary responsibility to uphold children's rights to protection and access to services, and to support families' capacity to provide children with care in a safe environment.

- States have the obligation to ensure accountability in every case of violence.

- The vulnerability of children to violence is linked to their age and evolving capacity. Some children, because of gender, race, ethnic origin, disability or social status, are particularly vulnerable.

- Children have the right to express their views, and to have these views taken into account in the implementation of polices and programmes.

the incidence of underweight children under three from 30 per cent to 27.2 per cent, and ensure that a further 1.7 million children are adequately nourished.[27]

A growing body of evidence, principally from West and Central Africa, suggests that when resources are scarce, women generally prioritize the nutrition of family members above other personal and household issues. Survey results from Cameroon show that income-earning women typically spend 74 per cent of their funds to supplement the family food supply, while men spend only an estimated 22 per cent of their income on food.[28] Research from Côte d'Ivoire and Ghana demonstrates that in the event of an external shock, such as surplus rainfall or drought, income received from the cultivation of crops tends to be spent differently by men and women. Whereas an increase in women's income led to additional household spending on food, an increase in men's income had no significant impact.[29]

Throughout much of the developing world, women play an important role in planting and harvesting crops, but rarely own the land on which crops are grown and lack control over the distribution of food and profits *(see Chapter 3, pages 41-42)*. Even on subsistence plots, where women generally retain a portion of what they produce, gender discrimination reduces the quantity of food available for children. Unequal access to education, labour and fertilizer results in women farmers having lower crop yields than their male counterparts. In Burkina Faso, for example, where members of the household simultaneously cultivate the same crop on different plots of similar size, evidence shows that, on average, yields are about 18 per cent lower on women's plots compared to men's plots. For vegetable crops, in which women tend to specialize, the decline in yields is about 20 per cent.[30]

Increasing women's access to the means of agricultural production, such as farming land or fertilizers, farm labour, credit and education is therefore crucial to guaranteeing food security and improving the nutritional status of children. Evidence from sub-Saharan Africa indicates that strengthening women's control over these inputs can increase agricultural output by an average rate of 10 per cent.[31]

Women prioritize family health care

As the primary caregivers for children, women tend to be the first to recognize and seek treatment for children's illnesses. Yet, as the findings of the Demographic and Health Surveys cited earlier confirm, many women around the world are denied a say in even the most basic decisions on family health, such as whether a child will be taken to the doctor, how much money will be spent on medication and the type of care they themselves will receive during pregnancy.

In households where women are routinely denied these rights, the husband – or his mother in some cases – determines when and how to seek health care for family members. For instance, a study from Gujarat, India, reports that approximately 50 per cent of women interviewed felt unable to take a sick child to the doctor without the approval of their husband or parent-in-law.[32]

Women who have greater influence in decision-making can promote better health-care practices for the family. As evidence from Nepal and India shows, even after accounting for differences in education and wealth among the households surveyed, women's participation in household decisions decreases stunting among children and reduces child mortality.[33]

Research from Ghana indicates that gender bias in household decisions can influence the quality of medical treatment that sick children receive. A study conducted in the Volta region found that men, typically the household decision-makers in rural villages, tend to treat malaria in children with local herbal remedies and generally regard formal medical treatment as a last resort. Women, in contrast, prefer to treat children immediately with antimalarial drugs from formal medical clinics, which are often located in neighbouring towns and therefore entail travel expenditures in addition to the costs of health care. Those women who lacked economic support from relatives or disagreed with their husbands or family elders about how the children should be treated struggled to obtain appropriate treatment for their ailing children. As a result, the local remedies preferred by men tended to prevail over formal medical treatment, often to the sick children's detriment.[34]

Even when women can influence household decisions on medical care, they may still need the help of family members, particularly husbands or mothers-in-laws, to carry out their decision. In Bangladesh, Egypt and India, for example, social norms often discourage or restrict women's mobility outside of the home. Restrictions on women's movement can compromise children's access to emergency health care by preventing women from travelling independently to shops, pharmacies or hospitals, and limiting women's direct contact with unrelated males, including doctors.[35]

Women prioritize education

Empirical research on the links between women's decision-making power in the household and children's education is in its infancy. Yet the evidence available indicates that women's empowerment within the household increases the likelihood that children, particularly girls, will attend school. Recent studies have found that where gender influences

outcomes for children, it tends to be related to the gender of the parent who controls the distribution of resources. A study of poor Brazilian households reveals that girls living with mothers who are educated and decision-makers are more likely to be enrolled in school and kept out of the informal labour market.[36]

Empowering women to prioritize girls' education generates positive outcomes that span generations. A UNICEF survey of selected countries across Latin America and the Caribbean, South Asia and sub-Saharan Africa – including Cameroon, Côte d'Ivoire, Eritrea, Guinea-Bissau, Guyana, India and Suriname – finds that on average, children with uneducated mothers are at least twice as likely to be out of primary school than children whose mothers attended primary school.[37] The importance of mothers' education is supported by a separate study of children aged 7 to 14 years in 18 sub-Saharan African countries; the study found that 73 per cent of children with educated mothers were in school, compared with only 51 per cent of children whose mothers lacked schooling.[38] Moreover, children with a formally educated primary caregiver are less likely to repeat a grade or leave school early.[39]

Figure 2.5 **Despite recent improvements, women's literacy rates are generally lower than men's**

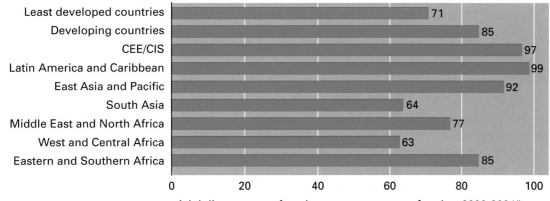

Adult literacy rate: females as a percentage of males, 2000-2004*

Notes: Adult literacy rate refers to the percentage of persons aged 15 and over who can read and write.

* Data refer to the most recent year available during the period specified.

Source: UNESCO Institute of Statistics. The underlying data can be found in the Statistical Tables of this report, page 98.

<figure style="position:relative">© UNICEF/HQ05-1159/Roger LeMoyne</figure>

Female-headed households: Proving that empowered women benefit children

The impact of women's decision-making on children's development is keenly evident in female-headed households. It was estimated in 1998 that roughly 20 per cent of households worldwide are headed by women.[40] Based on this estimate, female-headed households account for 24 per cent of all households in Latin America, 22 per cent in sub-Saharan Africa, 16 per cent in Asia, and 13 per cent in the Middle East and North Africa.

It is often assumed that households headed by women represent the poorest of the poor. This belief is grounded in the reality that in many countries and societies, men enjoy superior social status and earning power.[41] The evidence, however, is far less conclusive. Research on Latin America has shown that female-headed households may even generate higher earnings, or have more income earners than their male equivalents due to more effective use of household labour.[42]

Female-headed households do not fit neatly into any one social category or income bracket. The factors that motivate or force women to head households independently may determine a household's economic status.[43] A woman may have decided not to marry at all, or she may have chosen to leave her partner. She may head the household due to personal or economic circumstances that are beyond her control, as is the case for many widows, abandoned wives, or married women who become de facto household heads when their partners are migrant workers. Even among female heads of households who did not consciously choose to live without a partner, one should be wary of labelling them and children who live in these households as the 'poorest of the poor'. For instance, a 2005 study from rural Bangladesh shows that the proportion of female-headed households compared to male-headed households was highest among the poorest quintile (5.2 per cent) and the wealthiest quintile (7.4 per cent), while the intermediate quintiles had lower proportions ranging from 3.3 per cent to 4.5 per cent.[44]

Extended family members and community support systems can result in female-headed households being less disadvantaged in practice than they are often believed to be in principle. Among poor neighbourhoods in urban Mexico, for instance, more than half of female-headed households are extended families compared with just over one quarter of male-headed units.[45]

A study based on data from 17 developing countries in which at least 15 per cent of children lived in female-headed households reveals that single mothers manage to raise their children with outcomes similar to those of two-parent families, despite the numerous challenges they face.[46] Furthermore, levels of child work and labour are not significantly higher in female-headed households. In both male- and female-headed households, approximately 5 per cent of children reported helping with domestic work, 14 per cent worked on a family farm or business, and around 8 per cent worked outside the home.[47]

Children may benefit from the fact that a female household head has full control over the allocation of household income.[48] Evidence from rural Bangladesh indicates that the prevalence of undernutrition in children under five in female-headed households compared with male-headed households was significantly lower across income quintiles. Even though female household heads faced restricted access to employment opportunities, land holdings and social services, across all income quintiles they spent relatively more on food and health-care services, suggesting different priorities in household management that helped to achieve better nutritional outcomes. Children living in female-headed households consume a more diverse diet than those in male-headed households, especially micronutrient and protein-rich foods that provide the necessary nutrients for the growth and mental development of young children.[49] Furthermore, the proportion of mothers with at least one year of secondary education in female-headed households is greater across all quintiles than in male headed households, which may contribute to the better nutritional status of children observed in the former group.[50]

Men must play a crucial role in the lives of children

The interests of children are best served when the dynamic between men and women in the household is based on mutual respect and

shared responsibilities, and both mother and father are involved in the care, nurture and support of their children.[51]

Men play a pivotal role in promoting egalitarian decision-making. From the decisions they make about resource allocation to the care and support they give to women and children, they can help fight gender discrimination in their families and communities. The absence of fathers from the lives of their children can affect children's emotional, physical, and

Grandmothers and HIV/AIDS

One of the rarely told stories from sub-Saharan Africa is that of the grandparents who care for children orphaned by AIDS. Research in seven countries (Burkina Faso, Cameroon, Ghana, Kenya, Mozambique, Nigeria and the United Republic of Tanzania) with recent data reveals the enormous burden that orphaning is exerting on the extended family in general and grandparents – often grandmothers – in particular. By the end of 2005, 12 million children across sub-Saharan Africa had been orphaned by AIDS.

Children who have lost their fathers (paternal orphans) usually stay with their mothers; over 50 per cent of children in each of the seven countries assessed did so. However, fewer than half of the children who lost their mothers (maternal orphans) continued to live with their fathers. Women are therefore more likely to take care of orphaned children, irrespective of whether they have lost their mothers, fathers or both parents.

The strain of caring for orphans is telling on female-headed households, which have among the highest dependency ratios. Many of these households are headed by elderly women, often grandmothers, who step in to raise orphans and vulnerable children when their own children sicken and die. Grandparents – particularly grandmothers – care for around 40 per cent of all orphans in the United

Republic of Tanzania, 45 per cent in Uganda, more than 50 per cent in Kenya and around 60 per cent in Namibia and Zimbabwe.

In many poor countries, elderly women are among the most vulnerable and marginalized members of society. Unequal employment opportunities and discriminatory inheritance and property laws force many women to continue working well into old age. Following the deaths of husbands, many elderly women subsist on low wages earned in physically arduous jobs in the informal sector. For instance, in Uganda, a study by the UN Food and Agricultural Organization found that widows were working two to four hours more each day to make up for reduced income following their husbands' deaths.

HIV/AIDS is straining elderly people already struggling to make ends meet. Evidence shows that poverty rates in households with elderly people are up to 29 per cent higher than in households without. Elderly women who assume responsibility for family members affected by HIV/AIDS are often forced to work longer hours and sell personal possessions and household assets in order to pay for medicines, health care and funeral costs. Household studies conducted in Côte d'Ivoire found that families where one member was living with HIV/AIDS had roughly double the health spending

but only half the income of households in a control group where no one was living with HIV/AIDS. Funerals can absorb a large share of income; in four provinces in South Africa, a study showed that households with an AIDS-related death in the previous year spent an average of one third of their annual income on funerals.

The financial burden of caring for orphans can threaten household food security. A study in Dar es Salaam, United Republic of Tanzania, found that orphans are more likely to go to bed hungry than non-orphans. In Malawi, moderate to severe hunger is also more prevalent among households with more than one orphan. The latter study has suggested that although extended family members may be able to care for one orphan, the demands of caring for any additional orphans undermine their food security and, by extension, the nutritional well-being of all children in the household.

Against the odds, grandparents and single mothers make enormous efforts to send children to school. Research from 10 sub-Saharan African countries has found a strong positive correlation between school enrolment and biological ties between the child and the head of household. But the financial strain may prove too great if the household has to accommodate more than one orphan. While there is no conclusive evidence to suggest intellectual development.[52] Researchers estimate that one in three children living in the US – numbering roughly 24 million – live in homes without their biological fathers.[53] Evidence shows that children can suffer emotionally and psychologically if they feel that they are not part of a family that conforms to what is considered 'normal' in their community.[54]

A recent study examining the issue of family life from a male perspective revealed that most men aspire to be good fathers and to care for

that orphaning per se increases the risk of children missing school, research from Uganda suggests that double-orphans – children who have lost both parents – are most likely to miss out on an education.

A deepening crisis for orphans and caregivers

UNICEF predicts that the number of children who have lost one or both parents due to AIDS will rise to 15.7 million by 2010. At that point, around 12 per cent of all children in sub-Saharan African countries will be orphans due to all causes, with one quarter of these orphaned by AIDS. Disaggregated data provide an even bleaker panorama: Roughly one in every five children aged 12–17, and one in every six children aged 6–11 were orphans in 2005. At the same time, the number of widows is rising. HelpAge International estimates that the highest growth rate of any age group will be among those aged 80 and over, most of whom are women.

Programmes designed to provide cash and other forms of assistance to elderly household heads can help ease the burden of caring for young orphans. In Zambia, a pilot cash transfer scheme for older people caring for orphans has resulted in improved school attendance rates among children. In South Africa, girls living in households with older women in receipt of a pension have

been found to be 3–4 centimetres taller than girls in households with older women who do not receive a pension. Despite these successes, these programmes represent a short-term solution at best.

Addressing the crisis facing orphans and elderly women in sub-Saharan Africa, and elsewhere, requires a long-term strategy aimed at reversing the discriminatory social attitudes and customs that keep women and children mired in poverty. Many countries in sub-Saharan Africa, and in other regions, are developing national plans to address these challenges based on the five core principles of *The Framework for the Protection, Care and Support of Orphans and Vulnerable Children Living in a World with HIV and AIDS.* This framework, endorsed by international agencies and non-governmental organization partners in 2004, is based on five key principles:

• Strengthen the capacity of families to protect and care for orphans and vulnerable children by prolonging the lives of parents and providing economic, psychosocial and other support.

• Mobilize and support community-based responses.

• Ensure access for orphans and vulnerable children to essential

services, including health care and birth registration.

• Ensure that governments protect the most vulnerable children through improved policy and legislation and by channelling resources to families and communities.

• Raise awareness at all levels through advocacy and social mobilization to create a supportive environment for children and families affected by HIV and AIDS.

Across sub-Saharan Africa, initiatives are transforming the five principles into action. These include abolishing school fees in Kenya and Uganda; community-level interventions to support households in Malawi, Rwanda, Swaziland and the United Republic of Tanzania; and improved data collection through large population-based surveys. UNICEF is providing support and advocacy through the Global Campaign on Children and AIDS – *Unite for Children. Unite against AIDS.* Despite these efforts, however, coverage remains limited in all areas. With research revealing the disproportionate burden on female-headed households, there is an urgent need to provide them with assistance as part of broader actions to support orphans and vulnerable children and their families.

See References, page 88.

© UNICEF/2005/Warpinski

individual, who cares for children while women are at work.[60] In families throughout the Middle East and North Africa, studies indicate a significant change in household power dynamics. Whereas the 1980s saw university-educated Saudi men shy away from the prospect of marrying university-educated women, recent research shows a shift in attitudes: Saudi men now report that they value wives who can assist with the high costs of urban living. Moreover, Saudi wives who share the responsibility for family expenses have a greater say in household decisions.[61] These trends are not unique to Saudi Arabia. In the El Mashrek region of Morocco, women enter the workforce on account of personal preference rather than financial necessity,[62] and are less inclined to resign from their jobs after having children.[63]

their children.[55] But fathers often receive mixed messages regarding their rights and responsibilities as parents.[56] Existing social and cultural norms can have a strong influence on parents' levels of involvement with their children. The message that some men internalize is that it is not a father's place to become heavily involved in the lives of young children.[57]

Conventional notions about the roles of men and women in families are changing, albeit slowly. One reason is the high rate of divorce in many regions. Data from 2002 show the divorce rate in Western Europe at approximately 30 per cent, while in the Scandinavian countries, the United Kingdom and the United States, it was closer to 50 per cent.[58] In Latin America and the Caribbean, divorce rates among women aged 40 to 49 who have been married at least once range from 25 per cent to nearly 50 per cent, with the median having nearly doubled between the mid-1980s and late 1990s.[59]

In many parts of the world, rising living costs and the growing number of dual-income households are also transforming family dynamics. Evidence from the United Kingdom shows that in 36 per cent of two-income families, it is the father, more than any other

Women's participation in the community

Social attitudes towards gender can and do change. The most important catalysts for change are women themselves. Through social groups and networks, both formal and informal, women interact with each other, pool their economic and human resources, and collectively decide how those resources will be used or invested. Women who come together to challenge and defy discriminatory attitudes can have a dramatic impact on their communities.[64] By publicly denouncing discrimination and motivating other women to claim their social, economic and political rights, women's groups can set in motion a process of broad social change that promotes the rights of girls and women for generations to come.

Social networks increase women's influence at the community level

Social groups and networks encourage and support women's participation in decision-making at the community level. Evidence drawn from Demographic and Health Surveys suggests that in some developing countries much of the impact of women's overall decision-making power is concentrated at the community level.[65] Where women's access to community resources is severely restricted by physical impediments or gender discrimination, women collaborate to help provide each other and children with food, water, childcare, medicines and labour for farming – often beyond the purview of the men who control the formal decision-making processes.[66]

Community-based social networks can also provide women with an important source of moral support. If, for instance, a woman is denied a say in household decisions but is linked to a strong social network that promotes women's empowerment, peer support may persuade her to make independent decisions on issues such as children's health care.[67] But the impact of women's networks goes beyond merely helping their own members: By challenging the status quo, these networks and organizations are also proving to be powerful agents of social change.[68]

South Asia provides numerous examples of such efforts. One such initiative is BRAC, a non-governmental organization in Bangladesh that provides credit and employment opportunities for women. BRAC has strengthened women's bargaining power in their households and communities. For example, through collective action, women have successfully per-

suaded community elders to refrain from criticizing and ridiculing those women who work outside the home.[69] This social sanctioning of women's work empowers women who wish to pursue employment opportunities and increases the economic incentives for girls' education.

Women's groups throughout sub-Saharan Africa are mounting similar challenges to male dominance in community decision-making. In Mozambique, women's organizations are fighting discrimination by contesting the 1997 Land Law that denies them the right to own and sell land independently.[70] Another example can be found in Angola, where the Angolan Association for Women's Lawyers led a national campaign for legal reforms to protect women's rights.[71]

While some women's groups have been instrumental in lobbying policymakers through formal political channels, other groups have successfully mobilized constituency-level support for female legislators. These efforts are helping to turn the tide of gender discrimination in formal political processes (see Chapter 4).

Mother Centres in Central and Eastern Europe and the Gambia

Mothers in Central and Eastern Europe are leading the way in empowering women in their communities.

Mother Centres provide women with a vehicle for forging social networks and organizing community activities that support women in their roles as mothers and caregivers. Initiated in Germany in the 1980s, the Mother Centres movement has spread to Bosnia and Herzegovina, Bulgaria, the Czech Republic, Georgia and the Russian Federation.

Mother Centres arose in response to a perceived lack of support for mothers in their communities. In many Central and Eastern European countries, the tradition of community networks was dismantled under socialist rule. Since the transition of the early 1990s, high unemployment, poverty, political instability and a decrease in public childcare and support services have compounded the sense of social isolation experienced by many mothers and children. Mother Centres offer women and families an opportunity to access practical resources and social support. The centres help address the financial needs of families through services such as second-hand shops, meals, toy libraries, sewing and language classes, and job retraining programmes.

Neighbourhood Mother Centres reach between 50 and 500 families and have helped transform the lives of thousands of women in the region. Interviews with those involved testify to the positive impact that the centres are having on women and families: 58 per cent of women said they learned how to participate and speak up, while 55 per cent felt that their confidence had increased since joining the centres. A survey of men who participated in some of the events revealed that 67 per cent had a positive view towards family responsibilities.

By empowering women to enhance their quality of life, Mother Centres are helping to revitalize neighbourhoods and fostering a new sense of hope among women and families. In 46 per cent of cases, Mother Centres are represented in municipal councils. The success of the movement has inspired other women to replicate the model, and there are now 750 centres worldwide. This dramatic growth illustrates the powerful impact that women can have when they mobilize. It demonstrates women's tremendous capacity to lead the way in empowering themselves and those around them.

The Gambia

A similar initiative is operating in the Gambia, where women are banding together to promote girls' education at the community level.

In the Gambia, Mothers Clubs provide a unique platform for women to raise financial and moral support for girls' education. Through advocacy and fund-raising campaigns, women are expanding the educational opportunities available to girls and asserting the right to have their voices heard in their communities.

Mothers Clubs operate in some of the Gambia's most impoverished regions, where most families eke out a living from subsistence farming, and few can support the cost of educating all of their children. Although primary education is free in the Gambia, other hidden expenses, such as uniforms, writing materials and school lunches, can make education costs prohibitive. Owing to a range of economic, social and cultural factors, most parents prioritize boys' education; girls account for only 19 per cent of students in primary school in some poor communities.

Women are among the most vocal advocates of gender parity in schools. Advocacy campaigns organized by women promote access to education for girls, and focus attention on the retention and performance of girls in schools. UNICEF and the Forum for African Women Educationalists are supporting women in their roles as community advocates. UNICEF has provided the Mothers Clubs with seed money for income-generating activities, including gardening, making batik, tie-dye, soap and pomade manufacturing, poultry farming and crop cultivation, and has provided milling machines that give families an additional source of food and income and release women and girls from the burden of daily milling. Income generated from these entrepreneurial initiatives is used to pay for school fees, uniforms and shoes for girls in the community. Mothers Clubs have also invested their profits in providing interest-free loans to other disadvantaged women so that they can initiate their own income-generating activities.

Since the programme's inception, women have established 65 Mothers Clubs in three regions of the Gambia. The movement is having a visible impact on girls' education. Girls' enrolment rates increased on average by 34 per cent, and the incidence of girls withdrawing from school due to early marriage has diminished sharply.

Mothers Clubs are creating new opportunities for women, in addition to girls. By providing women with the skills and resources needed to generate their own sources of income, Mothers Clubs are helping to empower women in their communities. Moreover, by persuasively arguing the case for girls' education, women are challenging gender discrimination and highlighting the importance of women's involvement in community decision-making processes, an achievement that will benefit current and future generations of women and girls.

See References, page 88.

Including women in decision-making

Ensuring that women have a greater voice in household and community decisions is critical to fulfilling their rights as well as the rights of children. While international agencies, governments, civil society organizations and women themselves have made significant progress in promoting a more egalitarian dynamic, much remains to be done. Some key areas that urgently require attention include:

- **Increasing women's employment and income-earning opportunities:** Ownership or control of household assets and income is an important determinant of household bargaining power. Ensuring that women have opportunities to earn income, acquire land, a house and other property can help to strengthen women's bargaining power and influence in household decisions. Chapter 3 discusses in more detail initiatives that can increase women's employment and income-earning opportunities.

- **Involving men:** Persuading individuals to change their attitudes and behaviour is a slow and complex process. Through simple, direct and effective strategies, such as persuading other men to contribute to domestic chores, men are partnering with women to combat gender discrimination in households and communities. By creating specific roles for men in advocacy programmes, governments and development agencies can also promote men's involvement in child-friendly initiatives in parliament, schools and the workplace (*see Chapter 5*).

- **Supporting women's organizations:** One of the most important and effective avenues for women's empowerment is the dynamic of cooperation among women. Informal women's collectives that organize around issues such as nutrition, food distribution, education and shelter help improve the standard of living for women, their families and communities. Women's organizatioins can also be catalysts for change in the political arena (*see Chapter 4*).

SUMMARY While there has been great progress in recent decades in engaging women in the labour force, there has been considerably less advance on improving the conditions under which they work, recognizing their unpaid work, eliminating discriminatory practices and laws related to property and inheritance rights, and providing support for childcare. Ensuring that women and men have equal opportunities to generate and manage income is an important step towards realizing women's rights. Moreover, children's rights are more likely to be fulfilled when women fully enjoy their social and economic rights.

- For many women, unpaid work in and for the household takes up the majority of their working hours, with much less time spent in remunerative employment. Even when they participate in the labour market for paid employment, women still undertake the majority of the housework.

- When women work outside the household, they earn, on average, far less than men. They are also more likely to work in more precarious forms of employment with low earnings, little financial security and few or no social benefits.

- Women not only earn less than men but also tend to own fewer assets. Smaller salaries and less control over household income constrain their ability to accumulate capital. Gender biases in property and inheritance laws and in other channels of acquiring assets also leave women and children at greater risk of poverty.

- Paid employment for women does not automatically lead to better outcomes for children. Factors such as the amount of time women spend working outside the household, the conditions under which they are employed and who controls the income they generate determine how the work undertaken by women in the labour market affects their own well-being and that of children.

- In many countries, high-quality childcare remains prohibitively expensive for low-income families in the absence of state provision or subsidies. Parents often rely on extended family members or older children – most often girls – to provide childcare while they work, often at the expense of children's education.

- Challenging attitudes towards women at work requires a multifaceted approach. Governments should undertake legislative, financial and administrative measures to create a strong and enabling environment for women's entrepreneurship and participation in the labour market. Social policies should be promoted to tackle discrimination in the workplace and to enable women and men to reconcile their work and family responsibilities. For children, the most important strategies for ensuring that girls and boys will have equal income-earning opportunities as adults is to give them equal access to education.

3

Equality in employment

The story of women's economic empowerment is an account of great potential, all too often unfulfilled. It is not that women do not work – they often work longer hours than men – but they almost invariably earn less income as a result of their labours and own less property. While there has been progress in recent decades in engaging women in the global labour force, there has been considerably less advance on improving the conditions under which they work, recognizing their unpaid work, eliminating discriminatory practices and laws related to property and inheritance rights and providing childcare support.

Ensuring that women and men have equal opportunities to generate and manage income is an important step towards realizing women's rights under the Convention on the Elimination of All Forms of Discrimination against Women (CEDAW) and enhancing their development, self-esteem and influence both within the household and in society. Furthermore, children's rights are more likely to be realized when women fully enjoy their social and economic rights.

Policymakers are becoming attuned to the reality that women have an important economic role in addressing the poverty experienced by children; an increasing number of countries are channelling provisions to fulfil children's rights – such as cash transfers contingent on sending children to school – directly to mothers. Across the world, the livelihoods of households are already often sustained and enhanced by women who work outside the home – from those who cultivate subsistence crops or work on large farms where they oversee the output and marketing of produce, to those labouring in factories and offices. In both the Caribbean and sub-Saharan Africa, for example, women produce about 80 per cent of household food consumed.[1]

Women are working more but earning less than men

Whether they live in industrialized or developing countries, in rural or urban settings, in general, women work longer hours than men. While data on the way men and women use their time are sparse, surveys conducted in recent years confirm the validity of this assertion across developing countries. Oxfam estimates that women work around 60 to 90 hours per week,[2] and time-use surveys reveal that across a selection of developing countries in Asia, Latin America and sub-Saharan Africa, women's working hours exceed those of men, often by a wide margin[3] (see Figure 3.1, page 38).

For many women, unpaid chores in and for the household take up the majority of their working hours, with much less time spent in remunerative employment. Data from urban areas in 15 Latin American countries reveal that unpaid household work is the principal activity for 1 in every 4 women; the corresponding ratio for men is 1 in every 200.[4]

Even when they participate in the labour market for paid employment, women still undertake the majority of work in the home. Here again, this finding is substantiated by research in countries across developing regions. In Mexico, for example, women in paid employment also perform household tasks that absorb 33 hours of their time each week; in contrast, men's contribution to domestic chores amounts to just 6 hours per week.[5]

Time-use surveys in six states in India reveal that women typically spend 35 hours per week on household tasks and caring for children, the sick and elderly, against 4 hours per week for men.[6]

The division of household labour is not dissimilar in industrialized countries. Although

gender disparities in the overall work burden are less marked than in developing countries, women in the more affluent nations still spend a far greater proportion of working hours than men in unpaid work.[7]

Despite the limited time that many women spend in paid employment and their pivotal

Figure 3.1 Women are working longer hours than men across the developing world*

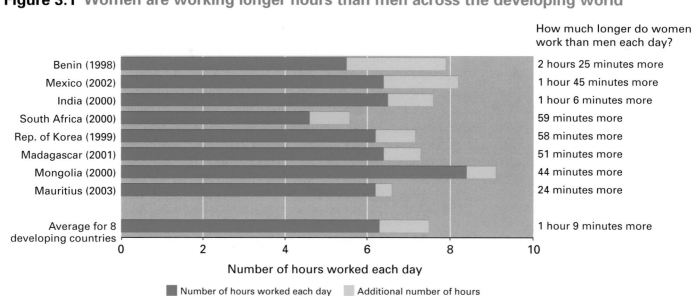

Number of hours worked each day

■ Number of hours worked each day by both women and men   ■ Additional number of hours a day women work

How much longer do women work than men each day?

Benin (1998) — 2 hours 25 minutes more
Mexico (2002) — 1 hour 45 minutes more
India (2000) — 1 hour 6 minutes more
South Africa (2000) — 59 minutes more
Rep. of Korea (1999) — 58 minutes more
Madagascar (2001) — 51 minutes more
Mongolia (2000) — 44 minutes more
Mauritius (2003) — 24 minutes more

Average for 8 developing countries — 1 hour 9 minutes more

*It is important to note that the data represent averages across each country that reflect high levels of underemployment. In some settings, women are working more than 12 hours a day.

Source: UNICEF calculations based on data derived from United Nations Development Programme, *Human Development Report 2006, Beyond Scarcity: Power, poverty and the global water crisis,* Oxford University Press for UNDP, New York, 2006, page 379.

contribution to the functioning of the household, there is a widespread view that women as well as men should contribute to household income. Findings from the World Values Survey reveal that when asked whether husbands and wives should both contribute to household income, a clear majority of respondents agreed – around 90 per cent on average in countries surveyed in East Asia and Pacific, Latin America, sub-Saharan Africa and transition economies, and more than two thirds in the Middle East and South Asia.[8]

These attitudes have, perhaps, contributed to the steady increase in women entering the labour force over the past two decades. By 2005, women accounted for roughly 40 per cent of the world's economically active population.[9] Trends in participation rates vary widely across regions, however, with much greater female economic activity rates in East Asia and Pacific (68.9 per cent), sub-Saharan Africa (62.3 per cent) and CEE/CIS (57.5 per cent) than elsewhere. Just over one third of women in the Arab States, and under one half in Latin America and South Asia are economically active.[10]

A more revealing statistic of the regional variation in women's relative economic activity outside the household is the gender parity activity index (defined here as the female economic activity rate as a percentage of the male rate). In the least developed countries, CEE/CIS, East Asia and Pacific, sub-Saharan Africa and the member states of the Organisation for Economic Co-operation and Development (OECD), the parity index exceeds 70 per cent. However, it drops to 52 per cent in Latin America and South Asia and below 50 per cent in the Arab States.[11]

The wage and earnings gap

Women not only spend significantly less time in paid employment than men; when they work outside the household their average income is also far lower. Although disaggregated data on nominal wages are scarce, the available evidence shows that, across regions, women's nominal wages are roughly 20 per cent lower than men's. While the data show that gender wage gaps exist across countries, these can vary significantly and can even be inverted. In Brazil, for example, women under the age of 25 earn a higher average hourly wage than their male counterparts.[12]

Because much of the work women do is underpaid and because they often perform low-status jobs and earn less than men,

women's per capita average earned income – measured by applying women's share of non-agricultural wages to gross domestic product – is far lower than men's (*see Figure 3.3, page 41*). Estimates based on wage differentials and participation in the labour force suggest that women's estimated earned income is around 30 per cent of men's in the countries surveyed in the Middle East and North Africa, around 40 per cent in Latin America and South Asia, 50 per cent in sub-Saharan Africa and around 60 per cent in CEE/CIS, East Asia and industrialized countries.[13] As Chapter 2 shows, income in the hands of women can reap benefits for children. Gender gaps in earnings, therefore, can decrease or limit the resources available to meet children's rights, such as health care, adequate nutrition and education.

With both parents working outside the home, and in the absence of adequate social support systems, children's rights to education, rest and leisure, care and protection are also at risk. One example of this negative externality is the mother-daughter substitute effect. As mothers take on paid work outside the home, children, especially girls, assume the domestic responsibilities, looking after the home and taking care of siblings – often at the expense of their education.[14] This highlights the importance of the role played by both parents in caring for children, whether or not they work outside the home (*see Panel, page 41*).

The asset gap

Women not only earn less than men, they also tend to own fewer assets. Smaller salaries and less control over household income constrain their ability to accumulate capital. But these are not the only reasons. Gender biases in property and inheritance laws and in other channels of acquiring assets – even state land distribution programmes – leave women and children at greater risk of poverty.[15]

The consequences of being excluded from owning property or assets can be even more direct, particularly when a marriage breaks down or a husband dies. Widows who upon their husband's death lose the right to their ownership of the family home or land, or divorced women who are driven from the husband's home, are easily pushed into the margins of society, further exacerbating the struggle to achieve health and well-being for themselves and their children.[16]

Figure 3.2 Nominal wages for women are significantly lower than for men*

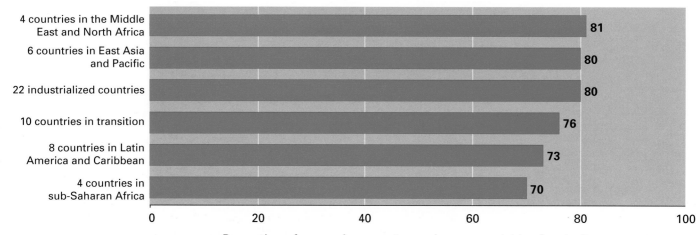

Proportion of women's wages to men's wages outside of agriculture

* UNICEF calculations for **Developing countries** include countries and territories in the following regional groups. *Middle East and North Africa:* Bahrain, Egypt, Jordan, Occupied Palestinian Territory. *East Asia and Pacific:* Malaysia, Myanmar, Philippines, Republic of Korea, Singapore, Thailand. *Countries in transition:* Bulgaria, Croatia, Czech Republic, Georgia, Kazakhstan, Latvia, Lithuania, Romania, Turkey, Ukraine. *Latin America and Caribbean:* Brazil, Colombia, Costa Rica, El Salvador, Mexico, Panama, Paraguay, Peru. *Sub-Saharan Africa:* Botswana, Eritrea, Kenya, Swaziland.

Industrialized countries: Australia, Austria, Belgium, Cyprus, Denmark, Finland, France, Germany, Greece, Hungary, Iceland, Ireland, Japan, Luxembourg, Malta, Netherlands, New Zealand, Norway, Portugal, Sweden, Switzerland, United Kingdom.

Source: International Labour Organization, LABORSTA database, <http://laborsta.ilo.org>, accessed March 2006.

Do girls risk missing out on school when women work?

Although increasing numbers of women are entering the workforce, their expanded participation is not always matched by an improvement in children's welfare. The need for substitute caregivers while mothers are at work places many children – most often girls – at risk of being kept out of or dropping out of school in order to care for younger siblings or perform household work, or both. The universally recognized rights of children to play, to receive an education and to be cared for by both parents are at risk, with negative implications for their well-being and future economic status. Evidence of these trends is consistent across many developing countries.

A recent survey in Nepal shows that eldest daughters tend to be at greatest risk of being withdrawn from school to help their working mothers take care of younger siblings and to assume household responsibilities. Evidence from the United Republic of Tanzania indicates that a lack of childcare facilities forces parents to take their children to work or pass on childcare responsibilities to their elder siblings. Increasing female employment in Peru has resulted in children, particularly girls, dedicating more time to household activities. Similarly, in countries in South-East Asia, as more mothers work outside the home, the

increased need for childcare is met by older children, aunts and grandmothers, who often become the primary caregivers of young children in rural areas.

See References, page 88.

Although there are even fewer statistics on gender asset gaps than on wage disparities, the evidence available suggests that the pattern of discrimination is broadly similar across the developing world. A study covering five Latin American countries indicates that women own only a fraction of the land compared with men (*see Figure 3.4, page 42*).[17] In other regions where data are available, women face similar inequalities. For example, in Cameroon, while

Figure 3.3 Estimated earnings* for women are substantially lower than for men

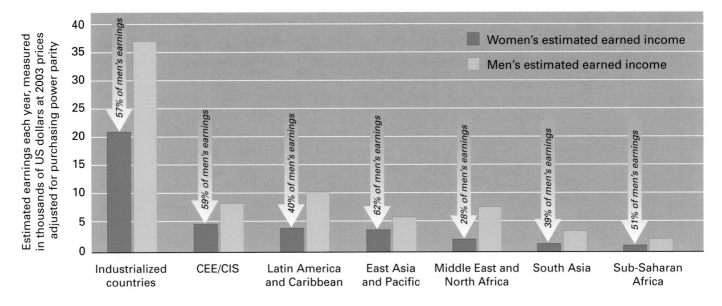

*Estimated earnings are defined as gross domestic product per capita (measured in US dollars at 2003 prices adjusted for purchasing power parity) adjusted for wage disparities between men and women.

Source: United Nations Development Programme, *Human Development Report 2005: International cooperation at a cross roads: Aid, trade and security in an unequal world,* Oxford University Press for UNDP, New York, 2005, Table 25, pages 299-302.

women undertake more than 75 per cent of agricultural work they own less than 10 per cent of the land. Comparable disparities have been identified in Kenya, Nigeria, the United Republic of Tanzania and other countries in sub-Saharan Africa.[18] In Pakistan, research reveals that women owned less than 3 per cent of plots in sampled villages, despite having the right to inherit land in most villages.[19]

Where women own assets they have more control over household decision-making. For example, in rural Bangladeshi households, when women's shares of pre-wedding assets are higher than their husbands', their influence in household decisions is greater and levels of sickness among their daughters decrease.[20]

The benefits of ownership can also extend beyond household bargaining dynamics, with positive implications for productivity and growth, particularly in agriculture. Giving women greater control over land and farm planning and management can enhance agricultural productivity. A study by the International Food Policy Research Institute suggests that if gender inequalities were reduced in Burkina Faso, and men and women farmers given equal access to quality agricultural inputs and education, agricultural pro-

ductivity could rise by as much as 20 per cent.[21] An earlier study on women farmers in Kenya revealed that crop yields could be increased by 24 per cent if all women farmers were to receive a primary education.[22] Another study in Bangladesh reached a similar conclusion, showing that providing women with specific resources such as high-yielding vegetable seeds and polyculture fish technology in fish ponds leased to groups of low-income women has a greater impact on poverty reduction than untargeted technology dissemination, which is more likely to benefit men and more affluent households.[23]

Empowering women through other types of investment can also have positive effects on economic growth and poverty reduction. Research indicates that providing women with skills training and access to new technologies gives them greater mobility and increases their control over resources, enhances their political awareness and reduces instances of domestic violence.[24]

Where women work matters for children

Female participation in the workforce can be beneficial to children, because it often results

Figure 3.4 Significant male-female gaps in land ownership in Latin America

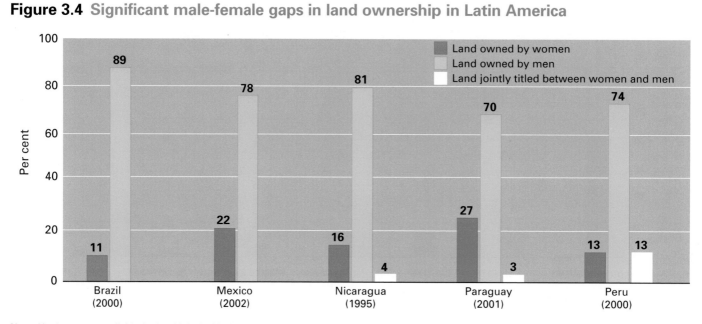

Note: No data were available for land jointly titled between women and men in Brazil and Mexico. Totals may not add up to 100 per cent due to rounding.
Source: Grown, Caren, Geeta Rao Gupta and Aslihan Kes, *Taking Action: Achieving gender equality and empowering women,* UN Millennium Project Taskforce on Education and Gender Equality, Earthscan, London/Virginia, 2005, page 78.

in women gaining greater access to, and control of, economic resources. But paid employment for women does not automatically lead to better outcomes for children. Factors such as the amount of time women spend working outside the household, the conditions under which they are employed and who controls the income they generate determine how their employment affects their own well-being and that of their children.

Women's informal employment and its impact on children

The increased participation of women in the labour force has not always been matched by an equivalent improvement in their working conditions or job security. Women are less likely than men to enjoy job security, working in positions with low earnings, little financial security and few or no social benefits. As growing numbers of women join the labour force, there has been a parallel increase in informal and non-standard forms of employment. In developing countries, the majority of women workers outside agriculture are concentrated in the informal sector. They are more likely than men to be own-account workers, domestic workers, industrial outworkers or unpaid workers in family enterprises.[25]

By its very nature, informal work is less visible in national statistics due to the lack of systematic reporting. Collecting accurate and comprehensive information on the informal sector remains problematic because of the wide-ranging nature of activities, non-formal organizational structures and diverse modes of operation involved.[26]

In nearly all developing regions, 60 per cent or more of women engaged in non-agricultural work activities are in informal employment. The exception is North Africa, where women's participation in the informal sector is 43 per cent. Of the developing regions, sub-Saharan Africa has the highest rate of informally employed women (84 per cent).[27] Individual developing countries show wide variation across regions (*see Figure 3.5, page 44*).

Women working in the informal sector often face difficult working conditions, long hours and unscheduled overtime. The lack of job security and benefits such as paid sick leave and childcare provisions can leave women and their children at a higher risk of poverty.[28] When mothers are poor, engaged in time-intensive, underpaid and inflexible informal work, and have little control over their earnings and few alternative caregivers, children are significantly more at risk of poor health and growth.[29]

Such conditions are prevalent in many areas of both informal employment and low-income work in the formal sector. One particular area that has received increasing scrutiny in recent years is domestic service. Women make up the majority of domestic workers, most of them informally employed. When mothers who work in domestic service take on childcare responsibilities for the employer's family, this often results in a conundrum: The day-to-day security of the employer's children is dependent on an employee who has to be away from her own children in order to work.[30]

A childcare crisis in the formal sector

The increasing participation of women in the labour force is challenging the traditional breadwinner-homemaker model of paid work by men and unpaid work by women. In its place, a new model is prevalent in many countries, such as the high-income OECD countries, transition economies and the rapidly growing nations of East Asia, where both men and women engage in paid employment.[31] In the United Kingdom and the United States, for example, two out of every three families are currently double-income families.[32] In the Russian Federation, in 52 per cent of households in which there are young children, all adults between the ages of 25 and 55 are working. The corresponding figure for Viet Nam is 88 per cent.[33]

But even as this new model of household income generation steadily takes root, in general women are still expected to take on the majority of the housework and childcare. As a result, and in the absence of greater participation by men in both domestic chores and childcare, it is becoming increasingly difficult for working mothers to reconcile work and family responsibilities.[34]

Women working in the formal sector are more likely to have shorter careers than men of equivalent age because there may be periods during their careers when they are unable to engage in full-time employment. Many women in high- and middle-income countries tend either to leave their jobs or work part-time to raise children – typically between the ages of 25 and 35 – and return to full-time employment at a later stage.[35] In the European Union, around half of working mothers with a child aged six or younger work part-time.[36] These temporary absences from full-time employment can result in lower pay or fewer promotions. In addition, positions that require long working hours, travel or even relocation may be less of an option for mothers in paid employment because of their family commitments.[37]

Figure 3.5 Many women across the developing world work in the informal sector

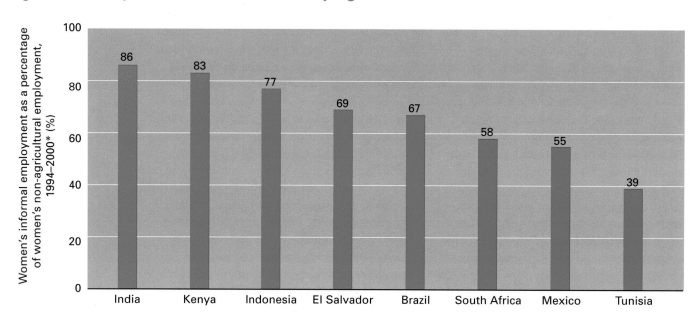

* Data refer to the most recent year available during the period specified.

Source: Employment Sector, International Labour Office, *Women and Men in the Informal Economy: A statistical picture,* International Labour Organization, Geneva, 2002, page 19.

THE STATE OF THE WORLD'S CHILDREN 2007

In the absence of policies to support working mothers, childbearing and childcare can interrupt women's careers and permanently constrain their earning power. Research indicates that mothers in paid employment tend to earn even less than other women. According to recent research in several industrialized countries, one child could lead to a 'penalty' of 6 per cent to 7 per cent of earnings for women; the penalty for two children can be as high as 13 per cent.[38]

Although research shows that quality parental care is an essential component of child development and that the early experiences of children have a significant impact on their future welfare,[39] working families are often struggling to balance the demands of work and childcare.

The demands of work also often leave parents with less time to spend with their children. A study from the United Kingdom shows that parents there are working longer hours or are increasingly focused on work activities.[40] Working long hours can be problematic for lower-income families, yet many employers do not regard work-schedule flexibility to be an option for low-wage workers.[41] More than two thirds of the low-income parents interviewed in a recent study in the United States reported having at least one child with either a chronic health issue or a special learning need, and that they were often unable to devote quality time to their children without jeopardizing their ability to support their families.[42]

These difficulties are exacerbated by a lack of affordable, quality, childcare facilities. Children who receive high-quality childcare that provides a safe, stable and stimulating environment and fosters their learning skills demonstrate stronger mathematical ability, cognitive skills and alertness and exhibit fewer behavioural problems than children who receive low-quality care.[43]

In many countries, the absence of state provisions or subsidies results in high-quality childcare remaining prohibitively expensive for low-income families. In others, quality childcare is expensive even for middle-income families.[44] Parents often rely on extended family members to care for their children while they work. Studies conducted in China and in West

Java, Indonesia, for example, show that grandmothers, in particular, play an active role in childcare when mothers are away at work.[45]

The availability of affordable, quality childcare outside the home increases the probability that mothers will enter the labour force. In poor areas in Rio de Janeiro, Brazil, access to public childcare facilities enables mothers to work outside the home, in full- or part-time employment. This also holds true for the Russian Federation, where subsidized out-of-home childcare raises maternal and household incomes and brings mothers into the labour market. In Kenya, the reduction of childcare costs has been shown to have a positive correlation with higher wages for working mothers.[46]

Some countries – notably those Scandinavian nations with high levels of gender equality as measured by the GEM (*see Chapter 1, page 8*) – have managed to attain and sustain elevated levels of high-quality, affordable childcare. One example is Sweden, where municipalities provide public childcare nurseries and centres, as well as publicly paid and regulated care for children in private homes and subsidized private childcare centres with fees based on income.[47] In the Netherlands, the Childcare Act (which entered into force in January 2005) places responsibility for the cost of childcare jointly on parents, employers and the government. The government provides subsidies directly to parents, who choose the day-care centre for their children. Employers are required to contribute one sixth of the cost of childcare per employee, while the local government monitors quality and regulates operators.[48]

In many industrialized countries, large companies have introduced family-friendly initiatives including parental leave, maternity benefits, career breaks, flexible hours, childcare arrangements and work-share schemes (*see Panel, page 46*).[49] Such initiatives can have substantial benefits for employers as well as employees. Working parents and employers agree that work-schedule flexibility reduces the conflict between work and family life, giving parents the opportunity to attend to their children's health and educational needs.[50]

The impact on children of women migrating for work

Around the world there are between 185 million and 192 million migrants living outside their country of birth, of whom roughly half are women.[51] While women's migration could potentially be beneficial, it also engenders new vulnerabilities for individuals and families.[52] One such risk is separation, as migration sometimes forces parents to leave their chil-

The impact of family-friendly workplaces in industrialized countries

Following the 1994 International Conference on Population and Development in Cairo, and the Fourth World Conference on Women in Beijing the following year, the ensuing decade saw the launch of many family-related initiatives focusing on gender equality and work-family reconciliation. The rationale for this increasing interest was the recognition that dual-working parents require special support and that, in the absence of such support, gender equality in the workplace cannot be achieved. In several industrialized countries, state and private support for working families, in particular for working women with young children, are composed of a broad range of initiatives. These include flexible working hours, telecommuting or working at home, parental leave, medical care for sick children and childcare provisions. In the absence of childcare provisions, part-time work may also help reconcile work and family life.

Some companies have begun implementing family-friendly initiatives. In Australia, in addition to flexible working hours, 35 per cent of labour agreements in large firms and 8 per cent in small firms include at least one family-friendly policy. BMW, the German automobile manufacturer, allocates funds for the family-related needs of its employees, such as purchase of baby carriages, children's clothing or hearing aids for elderly relatives. The company also provides facilities and financial support for childcare.

Family-friendly initiatives can be beneficial to both businesses and employees. Research conducted in Canada, Finland, Sweden and the United Kingdom shows that companies that have introduced family-friendly measures experience significant reductions in staff turnover, recruitment and training costs and absenteeism, and have increased the likelihood that mothers return to work after maternity leave. It is estimated that companies can generate a return of around 8 per cent by adopting family-friendly policies. AMP, a leading Australian wealth-management corporation, estimates that making its workplace more family-friendly has achieved as much as a 400 per cent return on investment, mainly through increasing staff return after maternity leave. However, further research shows that family-friendly policies are more likely to offer parental leave or childcare subsidies, or both, to highly paid employees rather than those with lower salaries. Such policies are particularly needed by low-wage working mothers who struggle with poor working conditions, low compensation and a lack of childcare facilities.

Family-friendly provisions are by no means uniform across industrialized countries. While in some countries parents may take up to three years of leave with some financial compensation, in others paid leave is restricted to the periods immediately before and after childbirth. In Scandinavian countries, employ-

ment-protected leave with relatively high compensation rates is an integral part of a family-friendly policy model. In Sweden, for example, working families are allowed 12 months of paid parental leave, to be divided between parents as they desire, provided that only one parent is on leave at any given time. Aided by the right to reduce their working hours until children go to school, almost half the mothers in dual-earner families in Sweden work less than 35 hours per week. Yet, while some countries encourage fathers to take temporary leave to care for their newborns, most countries continue to accept a traditional gender division of labour in which women stay at home, out of the labour force.

The lack of systematic reporting hampers measurement of the effectiveness of family-friendly policies (i.e., how well they achieve a balance between work and family life). While seemingly positive, two challenges remain even in the presence of family-friendly workplaces. First, working mothers continue to be the primary caregivers for their children, experience career interruptions and suffer from the double burden of working within and outside the household throughout their lives. Second, the family-friendly policy model frequently excludes low-skilled and low-wage workers, working mothers in particular, and typically benefits higher-paid workers.

See References, page 88.

dren behind. In the Philippines, for example, an estimated 3 million to 6 million children (10 per cent to 20 per cent of all under-18s) have been left by parents working overseas.[53]

Evidence from the Philippines, along with research on Indonesia and Thailand, suggests that, compared with non-migrants, the children of migrants might not be a particularly disadvantaged group in terms of income or access to basic services such as health care and education. This is because migration is generally an effective way for households to alleviate poverty, and because extended families help fill the gap left by absent parents.[54] Remittances sent by parents who have migrated are often an important source of income for the families left behind.[55]

Migration may improve women's self-esteem and status as they are able to assume a key role as providers by sending remittances home to their families and communities.[56] Several academic studies have found an increase in school attendance and an improvement in children's access to health-care services in households with parents working abroad.[57]

Although remittances sent by migrant workers can bolster household income, the migration of one or both parents can have negative effects on children, jeopardizing their development and well-being.[58] Research from Ecuador, Mexico and the Philippines suggests that children whose parents have migrated can suffer negative psychological effects.[59] In the Philippines, the children of migrant mothers reported feeling angry, lonely and afraid.[60] In other countries, the risks of abuse and trafficking increase when relatives and friends gain custody of children left behind – risks particularly emphasized in studies conducted in Albania and the Republic of Moldova.[61]

'Involuntary migration' also poses especially high risks to children. Refugee and internally displaced children face particular threats.[62] They may be separated from their families, lose their homes and find themselves living in poor conditions with grave risks to their health and education.[63]

Migrant women and girls are uniquely vulnerable to abuse and exploitation. With a greater likelihood of entering into low-status jobs, such as domestic service, migrant women often face human rights violations.[64] An International Labour Organization study reports that half of foreign female domestic workers interviewed said they were or had been victims of verbal, physical or sexual abuse.[65] When migrants have children in foreign countries they may also face discrimination in passing their nationality on to their children, or, if they are undocumented, may be reluctant to register their children for fear of deportation.[66]

A number of countries have made positive efforts to address migration and its effects on women and their families. In 2003, the Jordanian Government endorsed the Special Unified Working Contract for non-Jordanian domestic workers. The Philippines and Sri Lanka require that departing workers register with the government. Italy's immigration law provides a number of protections for migrants and their families.[67] However, while migration is moving up the development agenda, the significant implications for children still receive little focus and research.

Challenging attitudes towards women and work

The Convention on the Elimination of All Forms of Discrimination against Women guarantees women's equality before the law and establishes specific measures to eradicate discrimination against women in all areas of their lives, including those related to education, health, employment, marriage and the family.[68] While all but a handful of countries have endorsed CEDAW – albeit some with reservations – much more can be done to ensure discrimination does not exclude women from opportunities to work productively.

The workplace must be transformed to recognize the role that both parents play in child rearing, as required by article 18 of the Convention on the Rights of the Child. Social policies and programmes should be promoted to enable women and men to reconcile their work and family responsibilities and encourage men to take on an equal share of domestic chores and childcare.[69] It is also important to implement policies aimed at altering stereotypical attitudes towards women at work, addressing underlying factors including sectoral and occupational segregation, and lack of education and training.[70] Chapter 5 addresses the concrete actions and initiatives required to help eradicate gender discrimination in employment. A brief synopsis of some of these measures is presented below.

The vital role of education: One of the most important strategies for ensuring that boys and girls will have equal income-earning opportunities as adults is to give them equal access to education. Several strategies have proved to be effective in increasing girls' school enrolment in primary and secondary school, including the elimination of school fees. However, eliminating school fees is only one of several measures required to ensure gender parity in education. Governments, parents and inter-

Child labour: Are girls affected differently from boys?

Gender is a crucial determinant of whether a child engages in labour. While child labour is an infringement of the rights of all children – boys and girls alike – girls often start working at an earlier age than boys, especially in the rural areas where most working children are found. Girls also tend to do more work in the home than boys. As a result of adherence to traditional gender roles, many girls are denied their right to an education or may suffer the triple burden of housework, schoolwork and work outside the home, paid or unpaid.

In the Dominican Republic, for example, girls are expected to care for their siblings as well as complete household tasks. As a result, almost twice as many girls as boys perform domestic chores. In Egypt, girls are expected to do the majority of work in the home. Parents are often reluctant to send their girl children to school because educating them is not viewed as a good investment as they will soon marry and leave home.

Paid domestic service is often seen as a particularly suitable form of employment for girls. Research indicates that worldwide, domestic service is the main economic activity for

girls younger than 16, with more girls employed in this sector than in any other form of work. The majority of the children engaged in domestic service – over 90 per cent according to studies conducted in the 1990s – are girls. This is particularly true in Latin America. In Guatemala, for example, while twice as many boys as girls are engaged in child labour, more than 90 per cent of child domestic workers are girls. In some countries, the situation is reversed; in Nepal, for example, the majority of child domestic workers are boys.

In many countries in East and South-East Asia, parents send their daughters to work in domestic service because they see it as good preparation for marriage. In India, young girls will often accompany their mothers as they undertake domestic work and, at ages eight or nine, be hired as domestic workers themselves. In Ghana, where girls are traditionally seen as homemakers, many mothers encourage their daughters to start working as domestics.

Domestic work is among the least regulated of all occupations. Working in the privacy of individual homes,

child and adult domestic workers are often invisible to the outside world and thus particularly vulnerable to violence, exploitation and abuse. Domestic labour becomes even more hazardous when children are trafficked into another town or country to take up service, especially when they do not speak the local language. There is a close correlation between gender and the reasons for trafficking, with girls being trafficked mainly for domestic service and commercial sexual exploitation.

The different experiences of girls and boys make it important to integrate gender concerns into child labour research, advocacy, programmes and policies. Research that reflects gender disparities will provide a more solid basis for actions aimed at reducing child labour. Gender-sensitive programmes and policies that combat and prevent child labour are essential to fulfilling the rights of boys and girls, including the right to an education, a healthy childhood, protection from violence, abuse and exploitation, and rest and recreation.

See References, page 88.

national donors must work together to ensure that schools are 'girl-friendly' through several measures:

- Encouraging local school authorities and teachers to adopt flexible scheduling.

- Allowing married adolescents and unmarried parents to attend classes.

- Making school facilities safe from gender-based violence.

- Ensuring that schools have separate latrines for girls.

- Building schools close to girls' homes.

- Encouraging parents and community leaders to be actively involved in school management.[71]

In addition, it is important to emphasize that school curricula help students understand the importance of gender equality.

Eliminating gender disparities in legislation: Critical measures to eliminate gender discrimination in women's land and property rights must include, but should not be limited to:

- Bringing national legislation in line with international human rights standards.

- Reforming land and property rights to eliminate discrimination against women.

- Involving international agencies and non-governmental organizations in efforts to track and expose violations of women's property rights and in monitoring government compliance with international human rights treaties.[72]

The role of government in supporting working families: Governments should undertake legislative, administrative and financial measures to create a strong and enabling environment for women's entrepreneurship and participation in the labour market, including:

- Improved employment conditions.

- Creating career development opportunities.

- Eliminating pay gaps based solely on gender.

- Providing safe, affordable, high-quality childcare arrangements.[73]

A further step towards ensuring women's rights, greater public transparency and economic efficiency is the increasing use of gender-responsive budgets (*see Chapter 5, page 74*). This mechanism analyses the impact of government expenditure and revenue on women and girls compared to men and boys. It neither requires separate budgets for women, nor does it aim to solely increase spending on women-specific programmes. Instead, it helps governments decide how policies should be adjusted, and where resources need to be reallocated to address poverty and gender inequalities.

Budget initiatives aimed at eliminating gender disparities focus on national, provincial and municipal processes and may cover the overall budget or only selected parts of it. They can be carried out within government by the Ministry of Finance in conjunction with the Ministry of Women's Affairs or other branches of government related to social welfare, or by non-governmental organizations and independent researchers.[74]

The need for better data and analysis: Although there are sufficient data to show that women tend to work more and earn less than men, a lack of sex-disaggregated labour statistics precludes a more detailed analysis of the disparities. Better data on employment and income disaggregated by sex could significantly improve the analysis underlying policies and programmes – with benefits to women, children, families and entire economies.

SUMMARY Women's political participation is a Millennium objective in its own right. Empowering women in the political arena has the potential to change societies. Their involvement in governing bodies at the national and local levels leads to policies and legislation that are focused on women, children and families.

- A growing body of evidence suggests that women in politics have been especially effective advocates for children at all levels, sponsoring legislation and fostering tangible changes in policy outcomes that reflect the rights, priorities, experiences and contributions of women, children and families.

- Though women's parliamentary representation has steadily increased in the past decade, they remain underrepresented in almost all national legislatures – accounting for just under 17 per cent of parliamentarians worldwide. Many of the pernicious effects of gender discrimination, from lower levels of education to prevailing social attitudes that challenge women's competence as decision makers, as well as women's greater work burden, continue to hinder their participation in politics.

- The participation of women in local politics can have an immediate impact on outcomes for women and children, particularly in the distribution of community resources and in promoting provisions for childcare.

- Women's participation in peace negotiations and post-conflict reconstruction is vital to ensure the safety and protection of children and other vulnerable populations. Yet women's role in most peace processes remains, at best, informal. While governments and other political actors appear content to encourage engagement between women's groups that often cut across conflict lines, women rarely make it to peace table.

- Despite limited participation in national and local politics and in post-conflict reconstruction, women in politics and government are helping change the political environment. Their influence is not just being felt in stronger legislation for children and women; they are also helping decision-making bodies become more democratic and gender-sensitive.

- Increasing women's participation in politics is vital to promote gender equality, empower women and fulfil children's rights. The remaining formal entry barriers must be dismantled, and women encouraged and supported by political parties to stand for office. Legislative quotas are also gaining increasing recognition as a potentially effective vehicle for bolstering women's representation in local government, and in some countries, at the national level as well. Gender initiatives also need the involvement and support of men, especially male parliamentarians and political leaders. Better data and research are required to fully assess the impact of women legislators on policies related to children.

4

Equality in politics and government

Children have a powerful stake in political outcomes, but they have little power to shape them. Unable to vote or directly represent their own interests in governing bodies, their ability to influence policy is limited. The advocates who speak on their behalf – if there is anyone at all to do so – can make a vast difference to the fulfilment of children's rights to survival, development and protection.

A growing body of evidence suggests that women in politics have been especially effective advocates for children at the national and local levels. They are equally powerful advocates when represented in peace processes and post-conflict reconstruction. Women's participation in politics can significantly transform the governance of a country by making it more receptive to the concerns of all of its citizens. As this chapter will attest, their involvement in politics also fosters direct and tangible changes in policy outcomes that reflect the priorities, experiences and contributions of women, children and families. When women lack a voice in politics, powerful advocates for children remain unheard.

Women's participation in politics, however, remains limited. Although women's parliamentary representation has steadily increased over the past decade, gender parity in politics at all levels is still a long way off. At current annual rates of growth in the proportion of women members of national parliaments – about 0.5 per cent worldwide – gender parity in national legislatures will not be achieved until 2068.[1]

Advocating for women, children and families

For several reasons, assessing the impact of women's participation in politics in general,

and on child-related outcomes in particular, is a complex and challenging task. First, in many countries there are still far too few women in politics, and they have been in public life for too short a time, for their impact to be meaningfully assessed. Second, the behaviour of all parliamentarians is still an emerging area of investigation in political science. Third, there is the challenge of indicators: What is an adequate measure to gauge a legislator's impact? While bill sponsorship, voting patterns and political seniority are all significant, they represent relative rather than absolute measures of influence.

Despite these constraints, those cases where there is both a significant level of female political representation and a sufficient amount of data to assess its impact point to an unequivocal conclusion: Women in politics are making a difference in at least three important arenas – national legislatures, local government and post-conflict reconstruction.

- **National politics.** A better representation of women in parliament can make legislatures more gender- and child-sensitive and can influence legislation and policies that address the rights of both groups.

- **Local politics.** The presence of women leaders in local politics often serves to focus greater attention on issues related to women and children. Evidence from India shows that women's participation in local politics can significantly tilt the distribution of community resources in favour of women and children.[2]

- **Peace processes and post-conflict reconstruction.** There is an increasing recognition that the contribution of women is critical both to the long-term success of peace processes and to post-conflict stability.

Women in national politics

Promoting the interests of children and women

Research on the priorities of women parliamentarians comes mostly from industrialized countries, where there has been greater scrutiny of legislative behaviour than in developing countries.[3] Case studies examining lawmakers' patterns of bill sponsorship and legislative outcomes across a range of industrialized countries confirm a strong commitment by women legislators to issues related to children, women and families. This commitment translates into both active sponsorship of legislation in these areas and to ensuring that the bills become law. A number of studies have expanded this area of enquiry to developing countries, with similar findings.[4]

It would be a mistake to assume on the basis of these results that every woman legislator actively advocates on behalf of women and children; some certainly do not. What the following studies indicate, however, is that many of the issues of particular relevance and importance to women and children might not reach parliamentary agendas without the strong backing of women legislators.

A pioneering study of women legislators in Latin America found that in the 1993–1994 parliament, women deputies in Argentina were 9.5 per cent more likely to sponsor children and family bills than their male counterparts.[5] Furthermore, despite representing only 14 per cent of deputies, Argentina's women parliamentarians introduced no fewer than 78 per cent of the bills related to women's rights.[6]

Recent evidence suggests that this pattern of behaviour held true over the subsequent decade. In 1999, women legislators in Argentina played a critical role in ensuring the passage of a law that modified the country's penal code to explicitly define sexual crimes against women and children and toughened the penalties for such egregious acts. Several

years later, in the 2004–2005 parliament, women legislators helped pass the Law on the Integral Protection of the Rights of Children and Adolescents.[7]

Other Latin American countries display similar tendencies. In 1999, women deputies in Costa Rica initiated and helped pass the Law against Sexual Exploitation of Minors, together with reforms of the national penal code that toughened penalties for those convicted of sexual assault against children and the disabled. In 2003, women senators in Colombia helped promote groundbreaking equal opportunity legislation. The laws carry wide-ranging provisions to promote and guarantee the rights of girls and women, remove obstacles to the exercise of their rights, and incorporate gender-equitable policies at all levels of the State.[8]

This pattern of advocacy by women legislators on behalf of women and children is also found in industrialized countries. A recent examination of New Zealand's parliamentary debates on childcare and parental leave over a 25-year period (1975–1999) revealed similar tendencies on the part of women legislators (*see Figure 4.1, page 53*).[9] In the United Kingdom, a forthcoming analysis of more than 3 million words of text from the plenary debates of the National Assembly of Wales also finds important differences between the willingness of female and male legislators to engage in debate about childcare.[10]

Parliamentary advocacy on behalf of children and families can also bridge party and ideological lines. Countries where cross-party alliances of women parliamentarians have successfully advanced the cause of women and children include Egypt, France, the Netherlands, South Africa, Sweden, the Russian Federation and Rwanda.[11]

In the case of the Russian Federation, an examination of the role of women legislators in the 1995–1999 Duma (parliament) shows that they were able to set aside ideological and party differences to promote legislation benefiting children and families. The proposed measures favoured childcare and child support; benefits to citizens with children;

pregnancy benefits and leave; reduced taxes for families with many children; penalties for domestic violence; and equal rights for men and women with families.[12]

Initiatives to promote children's rights often accompany efforts to advance the rights of women. One such example occurred in Rwanda, where in 1999 women parliamentarians played a critical role in the passage of a law strengthening women's rights. The new legislation established women's right to inherit land for the first time. In the wake of the Rwandan genocide, which destroyed and scattered families, the exclusion of women from land ownership became a critical issue. In addition to being a violation of their rights, not allowing women to own land had a negative impact on such issues as food production and security, the environment, settlement patterns and the livelihood of families and children left behind.

Women legislators in Rwanda also actively advocated for increased spending on health and education, and for special support for children with disabilities. In 2006, the Forum of Women Parliamentarians, a cross-party cau-

cus formed in 2003, worked on and supported a bill to combat gender-based violence. The proposed legislation will define gender-based violence and address crimes committed during the genocide as well as ongoing violations.[13]

This activism on the part of women legislators in Rwanda is not an isolated phenomenon, but part of a trend that has been apparent in other countries in the region for several years. In South Africa, women parliamentarians provided significant support for the 1998 Domestic Violence Act. The act makes specific references to children, defines the different forms of domestic violence and explains how children can get a protection order against their abusers.[14] In neighbouring Namibia, women lawmakers supported groundbreaking legislation dealing with domestic and sexual violence, such as the Combating of Rape Act of 2000, which provides protection against rape to young girls and boys, and the Domestic Violence Act of 2003.[15]

Changing the face of politics

Women in parliament are not only having an impact on legislation. Their influence extends beyond their immediate actions and is encour-

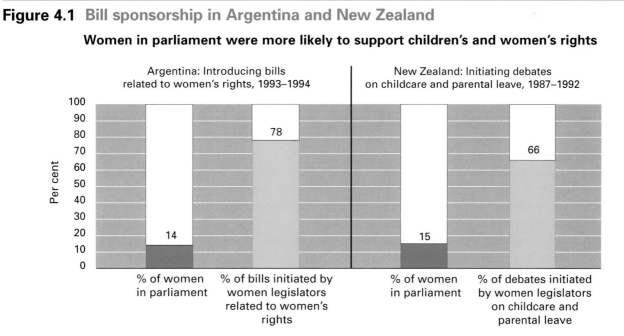

Figure 4.1 Bill sponsorship in Argentina and New Zealand

Women in parliament were more likely to support children's and women's rights

Argentina: Introducing bills related to women's rights, 1993–1994

New Zealand: Initiating debates on childcare and parental leave, 1987–1992

Per cent

- % of women in parliament: 14
- % of bills initiated by women legislators related to women's rights: 78
- % of women in parliament: 15
- % of debates initiated by women legislators on childcare and parental leave: 66

Source: UNICEF calculations for womens parliame ntary representation and patterns of bill sponsorship in Argentina are based on Jones, Mark P., 'Legislator Gender and Legislator Policy Priorities in the Argentine Chamber of Deputies and the United States House of Representatives', *Policy Studies Journal*, vol. 25, no. 4, 1997, pages 613-629. UNICEF calculations for women's parliamentary representation and patterns of bill sponsorship in New Zealand are based on Grey, Sandra, 'Does Size Matter? Critical mass and New Zealand's women MPs', *Parliamentary Affairs*, vol. 55, no. 1, January 2002, p. 6. Although the study covered the period 1975-1999, the data were for the period 1987-1992.

Women and politics: Realities and myths

Should one expect the involvement of women parliamentarians to lead to different policy outcomes? The reasons one can assume women might act from a different perspective than their male counterparts are practical rather than theoretical.

An alternative perspective

In an extensive survey of 187 women parliamentarians from 65 countries conducted by the Inter-Parliamentary Union (IPU) in 1999, the respondents consistently portrayed women as having different priorities from men. Four out of every five respondents believed that women held conceptually different ideas about society and politics. More than 90 per cent agreed that women's greater participation would bring about change, and almost 9 out of every 10 considered that women's participation in the political process significantly changed political outcomes.

Three reasons women politicians are likely to approach politics differently

Women's motivation for entering politics is often different from that of men. In the IPU survey, 40 per cent of the respondents stated that they had entered politics as a result of their interests in social work and 34 per cent through non-governmental organizations, as opposed to the more 'conventional' path of party politics often embraced by men. This finding accurately reflects a well-established tendency among women to engage in civil society as a way of promoting projects that support household survival, and to focus their energies at the local level.

Women are often exposed to different patterns of socialization and have different life experiences than men and are likely to bring their experience and expertise to bear on their political decisions. While important changes have been taking place over the past few decades, in most countries, women still bear the main caregiving responsibilities for their families, including children and the elderly.

Women are more likely to see themselves as representatives of women. A study of legislators in the United States, for example, found that women feel a special responsibility to represent other women and consider themselves more capable of representing their interests. In Northern Ireland, for example, almost one third of women who vote thought a woman would better represent their interests.

Why are there still so few women in politics?

Given their potential contribution to the political process, an obvious question arises: Why then are there still so few women participating in politics? The answer is multifaceted and differs across countries, societies and communities. But several common threads are outlined below.

Women are unlikely to run for political office. While exact numbers are difficult to come by, existing studies indicate that women are less likely than men to run for office. In the United States, for example, men are at least 50 per cent more likely to have investigated how to place their name on the ballot, or to have discussed running with potential donors, party or community leaders, family members or friends.

- *Double burden of public and private responsibilities:* As the preceding chapters have shown, women's work burdens are generally much heavier than men's, leaving less time and energy for involvement in political life. In the United States, evidence shows that as women's responsibilities for household tasks and caregiving decrease, their interest in running for office increases.

- *A culture of exclusion:* In many countries, both political and financial networks are controlled by men. Cultural practices that serve to nurture and consolidate bonds of male solidarity within these networks, such as drinking, smoking or golfing, are key stepping stones on the path to political office. A study in Thailand found that men typically dominate recruitment committees and tend to bypass women candidates, both in order to retain a structure they are familiar with and because they are more likely to know the male candidates personally.

- *Higher participation in education:* Those women who run for office successfully, especially in developing countries, tend to be educated to tertiary level at least. Out of the 187 women from 65 countries surveyed by the IPU in 1999, 73 per cent held an undergraduate degree and 14 per cent also held graduate degrees. The lack of women educated to tertiary levels in many countries can therefore act as a barrier to their participation in politics and government.

Women face an uphill struggle to win over public opinion. There are very few statistics about how many women run but fail to get elected.

Figure 4.2 In most of the countries surveyed, a majority of the public agrees or strongly agrees that men make better political leaders than women

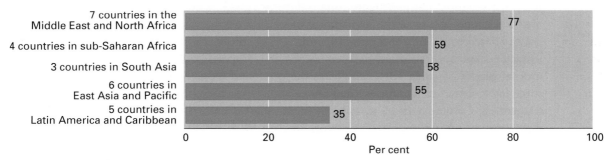

UNICEF calculations are based on data derived from the World Values Survey, Round 4 (1991-2004). Data for each country and territory in the regional aggregates are for the latest year available in the period specified. The following countries and territories are included in the regional aggregates cited: **Middle East and North Africa:** Algeria, Egypt, Iraq, Islamic Republic of Iran, Jordan, Morocco, Saudi Arabia. **Latin America and Caribbean:** Argentina, Bolivarian Republic of Venezuela, Chile, Mexico, Peru. **South Asia:** Bangladesh, India, Pakistan. **East Asia and Pacific:** China, Indonesia, Philippines, Republic of Korea, Singapore, Viet Nam. **Sub-Saharan Africa:** Nigeria, South Africa, Uganda, United Republic of Tanzania. Notes on the methodology employed can be found in the References section, page 88.

Source: World Values Survey, <www.worldvaluessurvey.org>, accessed June 2006.

Voter perceptions, however, can offer an instructive indication. On average, more than half the people surveyed in East Asia and the Pacific, South Asia and sub-Saharan Africa agreed or strongly agreed that men make better political leaders than women, with three quarters sharing that view in the Middle East and North Africa. However, in other parts of the world, the evidence is more positive. Far fewer respondents share this view in Latin America and the Caribbean, and over 80 per cent in Thailand think that a woman could be a good prime minister.

Women leave politics. There is little data available on whether women leave office more than men due to voter hostility or outright violence sometimes directed against women who are in office (or try to run for office). Women *pradhans* (leaders) in West Bengal, India, for example, revealed that even though women delivered an amount of public goods to their villages that was equal to or higher than that of their male counterparts, villagers were not only less satisfied with their leadership but

also blamed them for the inadequate quality of services outside of their jurisdiction. Perhaps unsurprisingly, about half of the *pradhans* said they would not run again. In Afghanistan, women candidates in the 2005 election were subject to violence and, in some instances, death threats.

Myths about women in politics

Myths about women in politics, both positive and negative, abound. Because such myths rely on unrealistic assumptions about women and politics, they can easily perpetuate stereotypes and discrimination. Two such myths are discussed below.

Myth 1: Every woman will make a difference for women and for children. Just because a legislator is a woman does not mean she will automatically promote legislation that advances the interests of women and children. Women in politics are individuals who can fall anywhere on a wide spectrum of personality and ideology. Women legislators are accountable to constituencies that represent a wide variety of backgrounds and interests, and may

often find themselves divided by ideological, regional, class or other differences. Furthermore, they are members of political parties and sometimes have to follow party discipline at the expense of their own policy preferences. Nonetheless, evidence strongly suggests that, on the whole, women parliamentarians are more likely than their male counterparts to use their political leverage to effect change in support of children, women and families.

Myth 2: Women are unsuited to the 'hard' jobs. A 2005 IPU tally of ministerial portfolios held by women counted 858 women ministers in 183 countries. The distribution of portfolios, however, is striking. While almost a third of all ministerial jobs held by women fell in the area of family, children, youth and social affairs or women's affairs and education, women accounted for only 13 ministers of defence and 9 ministers of the economy worldwide (or 1.5 per cent and 1 per cent, respectively).

See References, page 88.

aging changes in the priorities and policies of national legislators, including their male colleagues.

Research suggests that male legislators today are increasingly aware of the importance of issues related to women and families, and, in many cases, are important partners in promoting gender equality. For example, in the three Latin American countries cited above (Argentina, Colombia and Costa Rica), there is strong support among male legislators for both women's issues (68 per cent) and family and children's issues (66 per cent). Although these figures are below the corresponding indicators among women legislators (94 per cent for women's issues and 79 per cent for family and children issues), qualitative research, based on interviews with parliamentarians, suggests that men's interests in these issues are on the rise.[16]

Changes in legislative priorities have been accompanied by subtle but significant transformations of the parliamentary environment. Two examples of such changes relate to parliamentary schedules and the availability of childcare facilities in national legislatures. As a direct result of women entering legislatures in greater numbers, parliaments in several countries – including South Africa and the United Kingdom – have amended their sitting

hours to accommodate the schedules of women with family responsibilities.[17] In northern Europe, Sweden's parliament has established a day-care centre for legislators,[18] while in Scotland's National Assembly, a crèche was put in place for visiting constituents to "ensure that those with childcare responsibilities (usually women) can seek out and meet their representatives."[19]

Few women in parliament, but signs of progress

Despite the fact that women are often among the most active political advocates for children, women and families, and that increasing their participation in parliament is a key objective of the Millennium Development Goals (specifically MDG 3), the number of women in national parliaments remains low.

Women are under-represented in all national parliaments and in July 2006 accounted for just under 17 per cent of parliamentarians worldwide. Ten countries have no women parliamentarians, and in more than 40 others women account for less than 10 per cent of legislators. Nordic countries have the highest rates of participation, with women representing around 40 per cent of parliamentarians in the combined upper and lower chambers. Arab States rank lowest, with a regional average of less than 8 per cent.[20]

Figure 4.3 Women's participation in national parliaments across regions

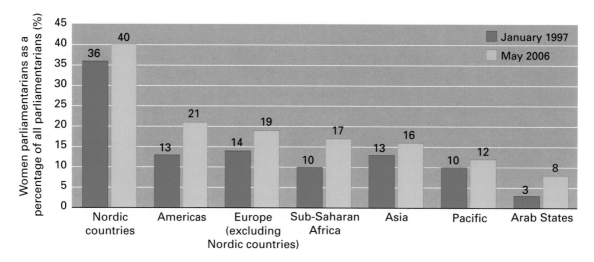

Source: Data are drawn from the Inter-Parliamentary Union database on 'Women in National Parliaments', <http://www.ipu.org/wmn-e/classif.htm> accessed June 2006.

There are, however, encouraging trends, to a large extent due to the introduction of quotas in an increasing number of countries. The number of parliaments where women account for 30 per cent or more of the legislature – the critical yardstick of women's parliamentary participation recognized by the 1995 Beijing Platform for Action – has increased fourfold in the past 10 years. Some of the most dramatic changes in women's political representation have occurred in countries formerly ravaged by conflict, such as Afghanistan where women were once excluded from politics but now account for 27.3 per cent of legislators. Burundi and Timor-Leste are also examples of post-conflict countries where women now account for a sizeable number of parliamentarians (30.5 per cent and 25.3 per cent, respectively). The levels of women's representation in all three countries are examples of the successful introduction of quotas during their political transitions.[21]

The election of Ellen Johnson-Sirleaf as president of Liberia in 2005 and of Michelle Bachelet to the presidency of Chile in early 2006 marked important moments in the history of women's political leadership in sub-Saharan Africa and Latin America, respectively. In Eastern Europe, Latvia became the first former Soviet Republic to choose a female president as chief of state in 1999. Finland, Ireland and the Philippines also currently have women presidents (in the first two countries the president is the chief of state, while in the latter the president is both chief of state and head of government). Women are heads of government in Bangladesh, Germany, Jamaica, New Zealand, Mozambique, Netherlands Antilles and the Republic of Korea.[22]

At the ministerial level, women are less well represented than they are in parliament. As of January 2005, women held 858 portfolios in 183 countries, accounting for only 14.3 per cent of government ministers worldwide.[23] Nineteen governments had no women ministers at all, and among those governments that did include women, most had a token presence of around one to three women ministers.

© UNICEF/HQ05-2038/Robert Grossman

As of March 2006, only three countries – Chile, Spain and Sweden – had achieved gender parity in ministerial portfolios.

Beyond the numbers

Women's representation in national parliaments is certainly a critical measure of their political empowerment and of a country's commitment to ensuring that powerful advocates for children can be heard. But numbers are merely a necessary benchmark and not a sufficient condition of women's empowerment. An extensive analysis of gender budgets in developing countries, undertaken by the Commonwealth Secretariat, has shown that changed gender attitudes, even where successful, must be accompanied by adequate resources as well as the requisite skills.[24]

Governments, in conjunction with women's organizations and political parties, have a vital role in ensuring women's empowerment. They do so by promoting gender-sensitivity among officials or establishing comprehensive women's policy forums, such as women's ministries and equal opportunity bureaus.

A comprehensive study of governments' responsiveness to violence against women between 1974 and 1994, for example, found no linear relationship between the number of women in parliament and policy initiatives aimed at reducing violence against women. Drawing on examples from 36 countries, the study revealed that governments with a high representation of women in parliament – such as Sweden, Finland and Denmark – sometimes lagged in their anti-violence policies behind such countries as Australia and Israel where the presence of women in the legislature was far weaker. The study concluded that what matters most in terms of a government's response to the needs and interests of women is not simply the number of women in parliament. Of equal importance are institutional mechanisms, such as support from political parties for women's rights, and the strength and coherence of women's organizations.[25]

Political parties and women's groups are central to the advancement of women's participation in politics. Parties have a critical function in recruiting and endorsing candidates for elections and putting their weight behind specific items in parliamentary agendas.[26] Women's groups often provide the civil society impetus and expertise that are required to promote, develop and sustain the legislative initiatives and accountability mechanisms that can advance the rights of women and children (see Panel, page 59).

Women in local politics

Prioritizing investments that benefit women and girls

The participation of women in local politics can have an even more immediate and direct impact on outcomes for women and children than national legislation or policies. Although evidence about the behaviour of local politicians is limited, a number of studies from both industrialized and developing countries indicate that women in local government tend to prioritize social issues. Moreover, in one important documented case in the developing world (India), women's increasing participation in local politics has led to a more equitable distribution of community resources, with direct benefits for women and children, especially girls.

In Norway, children's issues, and particularly the lack of childcare spaces, are one of the most frequently cited reasons for women entering local politics. A recent study, tracking data as far back as 1975, shows that during the first year when women were around some 30 per cent of local council members, the number of children receiving benefits increased. The most significant finding of the Norway study is that women in local government have the greatest policy impact early on in their careers because they bring a new set of concerns to the political agenda.[27]

In the United States, a 1994 analysis of more than 9,800 bills introduced in three states over a two-year period found that women legislators were twice as likely as their male counterparts to sponsor child health bills.[28] Another

Figure 4.4 Women in governance

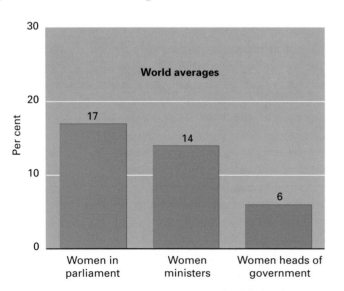

Source: Data on women in parliament and women ministers are drawn from the Inter-Parliamentary Union database on 'Women in National Parliaments', <http://www.ipu.org/wmn-e/classif.htm>, accessed June 2006. Data on women heads of government are derived from official websites of national governments.

Women's groups: A force for political change

There are at least two ways in which women's groups can be an important force for political change. First, these groups often provide support to women who have been elected to political office. Second, they conduct their own advocacy efforts on behalf of women, children and families. Across the world, women's groups and networks are providing examples of how grass-roots mobilization can advance human rights, especially for the most vulnerable.

Afghanistan: Women's groups have provided significant support in mobilizing women to participate in the presidential and parliamentary elections and in monitoring the electoral process. They have also organized workshops for women refugees in order to expand their awareness of their rights.

Australia: Women's groups, along with other groups in civil society, played an important role as advocates for the rights of children in immigration detention. They have lobbied for changes in domestic law and social policy and for improved services to enhance the ability of refugee families to rebuild their lives.

Morocco: In 2004, the advocacy and awareness-raising efforts of women's rights activists associated with the organization Printemps de l'Egalité (Spring of Equality) helped persuade government leaders to support a landmark family law that is meant to address women's inequality, protect children's rights and safeguard men's dignity.

Mozambique: A campaign against child marriage by several local women's groups contributed to the passage of a new family law in 2004 that raised the legal age of marriage without parental consent from 16 years to 18 years, and with parental consent from 14 years to 16 years.

Rwanda: In 2002, women parliamentarians and community leaders collaborated during the drafting of a national convention to support women's educational opportunities, small business loans provided by rural banks and the creation of a commission to lobby on behalf of vulnerable young people.

Tajikistan: The Tajikistan League of Women Lawyers drafted a national law on violence, which is currently pending approval by the president. The drafting of the law was a difficult task, but the League organized 32 workshops across the country for more than 1,100 participants, and eventually succeeded in obtaining the cooperation of local authorities, law enforcement and judicial bodies, ministries and other national institutions.

See References, page 88.

study, which examined women's political representation, showed that US states with a high percentage of women in the legislature are likely to be more supportive of efforts to address violence against women, increase child support, provide women with more extensive employment and unemployment benefits, and promote reproductive health care.[29]

In developing countries, research on the impact of women in local government is an emerging area of enquiry. The most comprehensive findings currently available come from India, where in 1998 one third of all leadership positions in village councils were reserved for women.[30] An extensive research project examining the impact of the reservation policy initially surveyed 165 village councils in the state of West Bengal. The study examined the level of public goods provision in councils that had reservation policies compared to those without such quotas.

The study found that in villages with reservation policies, investment in drinking-water facilities was double that of villages without quotas and that the roads were almost twice as likely to be in good condition. Furthermore, major roadways were 20 per cent more likely to have been recently repaired; new biogas (a substitute for cooking fuel and electricity) projects were introduced in 26 per cent of the villages with reservation policies (compared to 6 per cent in the villages without quotas); and, due to active monitoring, the number of visits by health workers in the six months covered by the study was significantly higher. These improvements were highly beneficial to women and girls, who bear the primary responsibility for collecting fuel and water and looking after family health-care needs, particularly those of children.

Building on these initial results, the research project was expanded to examine the impact of the reservation policies on child immunization and schooling. In a survey covering 100 villages in Rajasthan, immunization surveys were administered to 30 households in each village. The surveys collected information on the immunization record of every child under the age of five. The findings indicated that a child between the age of one and five years old residing in a village reserved for a woman *pradhan* (leader) has a slightly higher probability of having completed all vaccinations. The impact of the women leaders on the school attendance of girls is even more significant: The study revealed that the presence of a woman *pradhan* reduces the gender gap in school attendance by 13 percentage points.[31]

Simply having a greater number of women in local government, however, will not guarantee their effectiveness as advocates for the interests and rights of children, women and fami-lies. In South Africa, for example, an analysis of the problems and opportunities faced by women in local government revealed that, as with their colleagues in parliament, their effectiveness was largely determined by factors other than their numerical presence. These included cultural norms and expectations of women's roles; local hierarchies; the abilities and attributes of individual councillors; and the extent of political parties' commitment to gender equality.[32]

Catalysts of change

According to a comparative analysis of women in local government in 13 countries in East Asia and the Pacific, women have enjoyed more success at gaining access to decision-making positions in local government than at the national level. Local government tends to be easier for women to fit into their lives along with family and work responsibilities. It also tends to be more accessible to them, with more positions available and less competition than for parliamentary seats. Moreover, women's decision-making roles in city and community government may be more easily accepted because they are seen as an extension of women's involvement in their communities.[33]

Yet in many countries, women's participation in local politics is often undermined by gender inequality within families, by an inequitable division of labour within households, and by deeply entrenched cultural attitudes about gender roles and the suitability of women for decision-making positions[34] (*also see Chapter 1, page 8*). According to United Cities and Local Governments, an organization that has been collecting data on women in local decision-making since 1998, women account for just over 9 per cent of mayors worldwide and almost 21 per cent of local councillors.[35]

In spite of these obstacles, as more women are elected to local government, they are increasingly becoming important agents of change. In the previously cited example of villages with a reservation policy in West Bengal, India, the presence of women leaders at village meetings encouraged additional political interest and activism by other women. The attendance of women at village council meetings grew by a considerable margin – from 6.9 per cent to 9.9 per cent – when the chair was a woman *pradhan*.[36]

Women, war and peace

Women's ability to actively shape political processes at the national and local levels, as illustrated by the case studies above, is predicated on the existence of democratic institutions and a stable political environment. However, over the past few years there has been an increasing recognition that in conflict situations characterized by instability and weak application of the rule of law, women's participation in peace processes is essential to ensure their long-term success.[37] Preliminary research and case studies suggest that peace agreements, post-conflict reconstruction and governance have a better chance of success when women are involved, in part because women adopt a more inclusive approach towards security and address key social and economic issues that might otherwise be ignored.[38]

Recognizing the unique contribution that women can make to peace processes, in October 2000 the UN Security Council unanimously passed resolution 1325, which specifically addresses the impact of war on women, and women's contributions to conflict resolution and sustainable peace. Yet women's role in peace processes remains, at best, informal. While governments and other political actors appear content to encourage engagement with women's groups that often cut across the lines of conflict, women rarely make it to the peace table. On the few occasions that they do, their voices are rarely heard.

Women's exclusion from peace negotiations means that their rights and views – as citizens, as former combatants and as victims – are not fully represented in post-conflict reconstruction processes. A recent report examining 13 peace agreements reached between 1991 and 2001 that put an end to conflicts in Afghanistan, Bosnia and Herzegovina, Bougainville (Pacific Islands), Cambodia, El Salvador, Eritrea, Ethiopia, Guatemala, Kosovo, Liberia, Rwanda and Sierra Leone and Timor-Leste, among others, concluded that "there is no peace agreement that provides an overall model for appropriate provisions for ensuring that the needs of women are served alongside those of men."[39] These agreements included, in fact, few if any provisions that related specifically or even indirectly to women – an omission reflective of the overwhelming gender imbalance among the negotiators. While resolution 1325 has brought attention to the critical importance of including women in peace negotiations, half of the agreements signed since its adoption have omitted references to the needs of women and a gender perspective.[40]

Would women at the peace table make a difference?

The success of women's participation in other political arenas (as discussed earlier in this chapter) suggests that there is every reason to believe that the presence of women at the peace table would make an important difference for women and children. In the words of a former international mediator, when women are present, "the talks tend to adopt a more inclusive view of security and address issues related to the reintegration of children and women, preventing domestic violence when ex-combatants return to their homes, getting landmines out of the ground to allow women and girls to gather firewood and water more safely, and ensuring post-conflict accountability for human rights abuses against children and women."[41] In other words, the involvement of women increases the likelihood of issues critical to the rights and well-being of children, women and families being included in negotiations.

This notion is borne out by experiences in several countries across the world. Most famously, representatives of over 200 women's organizations met in 1996 to create the Northern Ireland Women's Coalition, the first female-dominated political party. The movement, which included members from both Protestant and Catholic communities, worked as a cross-community party to promote civil, human and workers' rights.[42] The coalition was eventually credited by George Mitchell, the US senator who mediated the Northern Ireland peace talks, with helping to achieve an agreement in those negotiations.[43]

Women's participation in conflict resolution processes

Across the world, women have become increasingly involved in conflict resolution processes. The Bonn talks on Afghanistan in late 2001 included 5 women out of approximately 60 delegates and advisers. During the negotiations, the women representatives fought hard for women's rights, and their achievements included the creation of a Ministry of Women's Affairs.[44] In Guatemala, the participation of women in the formal peace process of 1996 led to a national health programme for women and girls and a programme to reunite families and locate missing or separated children and orphans.[45] In the Philippines, women have held influential positions in formal peace processes and have pushed for cooperation across party and religious lines in the interests of peace.[46] In Sierra Leone, two women were involved in the Lome peace process. Although they were not chief negotiators, a key article of the final agreement calls for special attention to be paid to victimized women and girls in formulating and implementing rehabilitation, reconstruction and development programmes.[47] More recently, women have made a critical contribution to the Darfur peace talks (*see Panel at left*).

These experiences notwithstanding, in most conflicts women are either entirely excluded from peace negotiations or relegated to a 'parallel' track. Even establishing this type of track

Women and the Darfur Peace Agreement

In 2005, a Gender Experts Support Team, composed of 20 women members and backed by the governments of Canada, Norway and Sweden and by the UN Development Fund for Women was invited to participate in the seventh and decisive round of the Darfur Peace Agreement negotiations. The team gathered women from a variety of tribal and ethnic backgrounds in Darfur to create a unified platform of women's priorities and gender issues. The outcome document, 'Women's Priorities in the Peace Process and Reconstruction in Darfur', contains a number of key provisions related to women and children, including:

• Specific protections for women and children in conflict situations.

• Priority treatment for women and children in assessments related to compensation/reparations for damages and destruction caused by the war.

• An appeal to the government to pay particular attention to the education of women and children as a means of ensuring security.

• Provision of secondary education in the camps for refugees and internally displaced persons.

• A call to the international community to focus on the education needs of refugee girls.

• The creation of an institution to provide legal support, psychological counselling and other relevant services to women and children.

During the three short weeks that women were allowed to participate in the talks, they were able to negotiate for the inclusion of an impressive number of their priorities in the final agreement. The accord includes language that is gender-sensitive and, among other priorities, calls for the participation of women in decision-making bodies and in peace-building.

See References, page 88.

Women as mediators and peacekeepers

An increased presence of women among peace negotiators and peacekeeping forces, among other critical actors, would greatly enhance women's contributions to conflict resolution and post-conflict rehabilitation. As a District Officer from the Ituri Province in the Democratic Republic of the Congo explained in a report to the UN Department of Peacekeeping Operations (DPKO), "Local women [and girls] have difficulty in talking freely to uniformed men, such as male military observers, especially about sensitive issues such as sexual violence and abuse.... In many cases, especially where there is endemic violence, local women [and girls] prefer to speak to a woman peacekeeper because they fear further violence, including from male peacekeepers."

The UN is fully aware of this fact. While the number of women among the uniformed personnel (military and police forces) deployed by DPKO remains miniscule – at 4 per cent and 1 per cent, respectively – active steps taken by the department in recent years have increased the number of civilian positions held by women. These steps reflect a growing recognition that the presence of women among peacekeeping forces is critical to the success of their missions, and can reduce the possibility that peacekeepers engage in acts of sexual exploitation and abuse against the very populations they are mandated to protect, especially young girls. Among the key findings of an investigation initiated by the UN Secretary-General into such cases was the recognition that "the presence of more women in a mission, especially at senior levels, will help to promote an environment that discourages sexual exploitation and abuse, particularly of the local population."

At the behest of the UN General Assembly, as well as the Special Committee on Peacekeeping Operations, in June 2006 the UN Secretary-General issued a comprehensive strategy for assistance to victims of sexual abuse by UN personnel. This policy, which UNICEF helped formulate, proposes a comprehensive approach to victim support, including basic health, psychosocial, legal and administrative assistance for all victims and, in exceptional cases, financial assistance. Building on this policy, UNICEF, DPKO, the UN Office for the Coordination of Humanitarian Affairs and the United Nations Development Programme are organizing a high-level meeting to further address sexual exploitation and abuse in a comprehensive manner.

In addition to peacekeepers, mediators who represent the international community can act as 'tipping points' to help women secure representation in peace processes and post-conflict reconstruction. A recent assessment of women's participation in peace processes as 'track one' mediators – those involved in official negotiations through formal channels rather than unofficial contacts ('track two' mediators) – found that women remain largely excluded from conflict mediation and resolution processes. At the United Nations, women hold only 6.5 per cent of senior peace-related positions, while the European Union counts no women at all among its current and former high-level mediators. Similarly, despite Africa's deserved reputation of having strong female role models, women are entirely absent from the driving seat of the Peace and Security Council of the African Union. In conflicts where pre-agreement peace processes are ongoing, stalled or forthcoming, and where the United Nations or the European Union is not taking the lead role, only Uganda stands out for the presence of a lone female mediator.

See References, page 88.

is a challenge that requires women to fight hard to gain even limited representation, and often brings only modest success. Examples of such parallel tracks include:

- **Burundi:** In 2000, women overcame the resistance of the Burundian parties and were included as informal observers in peace talks held in Arusha, United Republic of Tanzania.[48]

- **Liberia:** Even though the Liberian Women's Initiative was unable to become an official participant in the regional peace talks of 1994, its leaders proved to be highly influential consultants during the process.[49]

- **Somalia:** In May 2000, 92 women delegates to the Somali National Peace Conference presented themselves as a 'sixth clan' for peace (Somalia has several major ethnic

© UNICEF/HQ04-1224/Giacomo Pirozzi

clans, all of which were represented by men). Despite resistance from some of their male colleagues, the group helped draft a national charter that guaranteed women 25 seats in the 245-member Transitional National Assembly.[50]

• **Sri Lanka:** In December 2002, a Subcommittee on Gender Issues was established, with a mandate to identify issues of concern to women and include them in the agenda of the peace process. The committee included 10 members, with each side appointing five women to focus on the gender dimension of post-conflict reconstruction. Among the top priorities of the committee were the equal representation of women in politics, educational structures and gender bias, and violence against women and girls.[51]

Conflict as an opportunity for change

The recognition that women are not merely victims of conflict, but critical actors whose contribution is essential to the success of peace processes and to long-term political stability is strikingly recent. As the renowned Indian economist Devaki Jain writes in *Women, Development and the United Nations,* "Until

1975, UN discussions on aspects of security and defence almost never referred to women; in the post-war conventions, male nouns and pronouns were used to represent both men and women."[52] It is therefore perhaps unsurprising that, as with other levels of political decision-making, the inclusion of women in peace processes requires far more than increasing their numbers and often depends on the active support of the international community.

As groundbreaking efforts by the UN Development Fund for Women to support the participation of women in peace processes in such countries as Burundi, Liberia and Somalia demonstrate, it takes many years of struggle and overcoming setbacks for these efforts to come to fruition. Sometimes simple things are needed to get women to peace negotiations. In the case of Burundi, the women's participation hinged on obtaining funding for two taxis, which enabled them to get to the peace talks in Arusha, United Republic of Tanzania. While the male participants travelled on officially sponsored planes for less than one hour, it took the women two days to get to Arusha – but they eventually arrived. Although their participation did not result in a formal mechanism for women's political participation, the group's influence did lead to the adoption of a number of gender-specific measures in the agreements in 2000.[53]

Inspiring the next generation

Women's participation in national legislatures, local government and peace processes are not only transforming the politics of the present – it is also altering its future, as women in politics are changing prevailing attitudes towards women and girls in decision-making roles. While patterns of causality are difficult to define across countries and societies, recent research suggests a strong relationship between the number of women in office and positive public attitudes towards women political leaders.[54] This correlation does not prove that the presence of women in politics is shifting public opinion towards greater gender equality. But it does show a strong link between the public's confidence in women's leadership abilities and its growing expectation of seeing women in office.

In Rwanda, for example, women's role in the transition to peace and democracy has paved the way for future generations of girls to assume public roles that would have been inconceivable only a generation ago.[55] In India, new associations are strengthened by elected women representatives, as well as women who were previously elected but who no longer formally participate in local councils.[56] These two countries represent just a sample of the growing involvement of women in politics across the world. Their influence is not just being felt in stronger legislation for children and women; they are also helping decision-making bodies become more democratic and gender sensitive. Despite discrimination and setbacks, young women and men who enter politics enter a world significantly transformed by the presence of women.[57]

Empowering women to participate in politics

Increasing women's participation in politics is vital to promoting gender equality and empowering women, the two tenets of Millennium Development Goal 3. As this chapter has shown, women in politics advocate more often and more strongly for the rights of women, children and families. Yet, at current rates of progress, we are still more than 60 years away from a world where women have an equal say in national parliaments. The situation is equally unbalanced at the local level where, today, women account for less than 1 in 10 of the world's mayors.[58]

While formal barriers to entering national and local parliaments have been eliminated in virtually every country, this has been insufficient to address gender imbalances in governance. Even when political spaces and processes have opened up, the number of women in decision-making positions has not automatically increased. Beginning in childhood women face discrimination, which ranges from lower levels of education to prevailing social attitudes doubting their competence as decision-makers. This discrimination, as well as women's significantly greater work burden, discourages and prevents women from entering politics and leaves them less time and energy for public life. Each of these issues needs to be addressed in its own right. Key measures – summarized below, but explored in greater detail in Chapter 5 – to ensure that women participate fully in politics include:

- **Education.** As previous chapters have underscored, a girl who is denied the right to go to school is denied much more than the knowledge she would have gained in the classroom. She is deprived of the opportunity to develop to her full potential in every area of life, including the right to political participation.

- **The involvement and support of men (in voting and in parliament).** While women's presence and active participation in politics is critical to advancing gender equality, gender initiatives require the involvement and support of men, especially male parliamentarians and political leaders.

- **Quotas.** The introduction of quotas has led to dramatic changes in women's political

The hope of justice for Bolivia's women and children

by Casimira Rodríguez Romero, Minister of Justice, Bolivia

Learning to survive

I remember that when I was six, my family was regularly hungry because of a drought. We didn't have enough to eat even twice a day, so my siblings and I were sent to another community where my grandparents grew some crops and had some goats and cows. All the same, my mom always wanted her kids, both boys and girls, to learn to read and write, so that's why she sent us to the mining town of Quioma in Mizque. There they rented a room for us.

When I got ready for school, I didn't have anyone to comb out my long braids. My brothers tried to brush them every day, but it was a disaster. The miners' kids at the school weren't used to being around indigenous girls like me. I'd never fought with anybody before, but they pulled my braids, treated me badly, and that's when I started to live with violence and discrimination. I could only speak Quechua, and it was really hard to study in Spanish. After school every day, my siblings and I went out and gathered firewood and swapped things with the local women. They gave us sugar, noodles and bread. We missed our folks terribly, but we learned to fight, earn money and survive.

From exploitation to discrimination

At age 13, I went to live in the city of Cochabamba. With promises of earning some money, I took a job working for a merchant family for two years. The exploitation was terrible: I worked 18 hours a day looking after 15 people. I was under a lot of psychological pressure, out of touch with my family and working without pay. Eventually, even my new clothes wore out. And since I was always helping the boss's kids with their homework, I started to really want to go to school again, but it was impossible.

Luckily, my mom turned up again and I went back to my hometown. From there, I went back to Cochabamba and worked for another family. I got paid there. They were always good about paying on time and giving me an extra month's pay at Christmas and other bonuses. But there was still a lot of discrimination: They gave me day-old bread to eat and food that had gone bad. My boss was a bit more humane, but when he died, I stayed on with his wife and she was like an evil stepmother: To her, I wasn't even a person. I worked for them as a housemaid for nine years, but it was so hard.

Consciousness and organization

A fighting spirit awoke in me when some other friends and I founded the Cochabamba Home Worker's Union in 1987. When we saw all the inequalities in the law, we realized that we only had half of our rights. We held meetings with domestic workers in La Paz, with women who were real fighters and with mining union leaders. We held national meetings and started to consolidate our group. For the next six years, we worked on the draft law, although lots of details were taken out. The first draft was pretty protectionist, but the process took on more of a

participation throughout the world. Though no such quotas exist for peace processes, their use is gaining increasing recognition as a potentially effective vehicle for ensuring women's representation at the peace table.

- **Party politics.** Political parties remain the gatekeepers to the advancement of women in politics. Within the context of party politics, however, the sanctions for non-compliance are particularly important. While it may seem impressive for a party to commit to a 40 per cent quota for women representatives, for example, that commitment can be rendered meaningless if the candidacies of women are not actively promoted.

- **Participation in peace negotiations.** Over the past five years, active steps have been taken, particularly by the UN Department of Peacekeeping Operations, to ensure that UN Member States, and other political actors adhere to resolution 1325. Nonetheless, efforts to include women in rights focus. We were able to turn our fears into courage and make the authorities listen to us. At first, our friends and even our own brothers and sisters didn't want to have anything to do with us, saying we were city folk now. But we took heart and started to hold demonstrations in order to open doors. Convinced that what we were doing was right, we started to break down the walls of discrimination – and, by insisting so much, we managed to gather support and seats on the councils of rural women's organizations. We made alliances with our peasant brothers, workers, miners, coca-leaf growers, indigenous groups and other sectors. It was a very interesting process that truly bore fruit.

The male world of politics

Along the way, we started to get support from Evo Morales's movement; as leaders, we started meeting here and there, coordinating national activities and international events. When they offered me the post of Minister of Justice, I didn't know what to do – I had to make a quick decision! You have your (personal) plans, your family...but I put it all aside. We're going through a historic process that I just couldn't say no to. There was no way to talk it over with my colleagues. If I said no, they would have never let me live it down. So I accepted, knowing it would be hard, but it was all about recognizing that this was the next step in everything we'd been doing so far.

At first I was very worried – soon I'd be entering a very different world. In our organizations, we always just worked around other women. The world of politics is a man's world and full of professionals with different types of education and experiences; I entered into this realm very carefully. When you are a leader, you have the freedom to say what you like, but now I have to be careful about what I say, and at the same time I have to leave something behind for other women and our *compañeros* (comrades).

There's still a long way to go. In this post, I want to meet the expectations of my brothers and sisters who have different kinds of problems. I want to fulfil the people's hopes for justice.

The boys and girls of Bolivia are living in difficult circumstances. There are huge inequalities. There are still lots of children who are going through what I did as a girl – not being able to go to school, not having safe food to eat. Our *wawas* (children) are the first ones to suffer from abuse, violence and rape. I would like to see a day when Bolivia's *wawas* can grow up enjoying the love of their parents without going hungry. It is a huge challenge. We have to make an effort to make everyone's dream of having a good life come true.

Casimira Rodríguez Romero, the current Minister of Justice in Bolivia, was born in a Quechua community in the valley of Mizque, Cochabamba. She is the fourth of 10 brothers and sisters. Her life was marked by poverty and discrimination, and her presence in Bolivia's cabinet represents the historically marginalized indigenous woman.

peace processes and post-conflict resolution remain confined to a handful of examples.

- **Better data and research.** Research on the impact of women on legislation and policy related to children remains limited, even in the industrialized countries. While UNICEF can and must play a critical role in child advocacy at all levels of government, this effort needs to be supported by better research on, and analysis of, the broader dynamic of decision-making and policy outcomes, with a particular focus on women and girls.

- **Creating an environment where women can make a difference.** The presence of women in politics is a necessary but not sufficient condition for their political empowerment. Women's ministries and other women's political forums, as well as the commitment of governments to greater participation of women in parliament, are equally important factors in advancing gender equality.

SUMMARY The final chapter of the report provides a road map for maximizing gender equality through seven key modes: education, financing, legislation, legislative quotas, women empowering women, engaging men and boys, and improved research and data.

- **Education:** Ensuring that girls and boys have equal educational opportunities is one of the most powerful steps towards combating gender discrimination. Key actions include abolishing school fees, encouraging parents and communities to invest in girls' education, and creating girl-friendly schools that are safe and without bias.

- **Focusing additional resources on achieving gender equality:** Far too little recognition has been given to the resources required to meet the goal of gender equality and women's empowerment.

- **Levelling the playing field in national legislation:** Legislative reform can be a powerful strategy of empowerment for women and girls and for the safeguarding of their rights.

- **Quotas can encourage women's participation in politics:** Quotas are a proven method of ensuring women break through the political glass ceiling. To be truly effective, however, quotas must to be supported by political parties and electoral systems that are committed to encouraging women's participation in politics and government.

- **Women empowering women:** Grass-roots women's movements have been the most vocal champions of women's equality and empowerment, but they are sometimes overlooked by national governments and international agencies. Involving women in the early stages of policy formulation helps ensure that programmes are designed with the needs of women and children in mind.

- **Engaging men and boys.** Men can be powerful allies in the struggle for women's equality. Advocacy initiatives designed to educate both women and men on the benefits of gender equality and joint decision-making can help nurture a more cooperative relationship between them.

- **Research and data on the situation of women and girls are sorely lacking:** An overwhelming lack of sex-disaggregated statistics often results in scant or weak quantitative evidence on the issues that affect women and, in turn, children. Better and more extensive data and analysis are urgently required.

Eliminating gender discrimination will produce a double dividend, fulfilling the rights of women and going a long way towards realizing those of children as well. Effective partnerships, involving governments, donors and international agencies, can support this process through the design and implementation of human rights-based development strategies. For women, men, and for children, the time to refocus our efforts is now.

5

Reaping the double dividend of gender equality

For children to achieve their fullest potential and to grow up in families and societies where they can thrive, gender discrimination must be banished once and for all. A world free of discrimination may seem like an impossible dream, but it is a dream within our reach. In recent decades, the goal of reducing gender discrimination has steadily grown in importance on the international agenda. Corresponding successes in empowering women and girls have become increasingly apparent. Since 1945, the proportion of women in parliament has increased more than fivefold.[1] Girls' education has increased dramatically in many regions, and more than 90 developing countries are on course to achieve the goal of gender parity in primary education, albeit only by 2015, which is already 10 years later than the original deadline set by the international community.[2] Discriminatory attitudes towards women and girls have been changing, not only over the course of generations, but also in some cases, through focused campaigns and discussion forums, in a matter of months.[3] Throughout the preceding chapters of this report, it has been clear that great change in favour of women and girls is possible and that for all children, such change is essential.

Progress is reflected in statistical outcomes and in the underlying social and political processes that have resulted in a strong international consensus in support of gender equality and the rights of girls and women. The ratification of the Convention on the Elimination of All Forms of Discrimination against Women by 184 countries by September 2006, and several world conferences on women, culminating in the Beijing Declaration and Platform for Action in 1995, have established in ever more concrete terms the challenges faced and actions required to empower women. But despite these gains and commitments, for many women, adolescent girls and girl children, the promises have not materialized. From children excluded from education because of their gender, to adolescent girls who may die from problems related to pregnancy and childbirth or face violence and sexual abuse, gender discrimination leads to rights violations that reverberate throughout the life cycle (see Chapter 1, page 4).

This final chapter brings together a number of concrete and achievable cross-cutting actions in several critical areas that can address this challenge. These actions will make an unprecedented difference to the lives of women and children and the achievement of the Millennium Development Goals. Measures include education, financing for development, legislation, legislative quotas, women empowering other women, engaging men and boys, and research and data. These recommendations are less about radical new ideas than they are about a firm commitment to and focus on what has proven to work and what needs to be done – as well as an equally firm commitment to working together in order to achieve gender equality and women's empowerment.

At its core, the goal of gender equality calls for a change in social attitudes and institutions

© UNICEF/HQ05-1566/Giacomo Pirozzi

Partnerships for girls' education

Gender parity in primary and secondary education is a central tenet of the Millennium agenda, and partnerships at all levels are increasingly recognized as the conduit to reaching this objective. The United Nations Girls' Education Initiative (UNGEI), launched in 2001, is a partnership between UN agencies and a broad spectrum of partners dedicated to achieving gender equality in education. UNGEI facilitates the coordination of girls' education strategies and interventions at the country level through partnerships with governments, donor countries, non-governmental organizations, civil society, the private sector, communities and families.

Other partnerships are also working towards the same objective. In 1999, four international civil society organizations – Oxfam International, ActionAid International, Education International, and the Global March against Child Labour – established the Global Campaign for Education (GCE) to work towards elimination of gender disparities in education

by 2015. Based on research in nine African and Asian countries, a report issued by the GCE entitled *A Fair Chance* identifies key actions to eliminate gender disparities in education.

The Forum for African Women Educationalists (FAWE), based in Kenya, is a non-governmental organization made up of cabinet ministers and other high-level educators from sub-Saharan African. Since 1993, FAWE has worked with governments, donors, non-governmental organizations, universities, communities and others to promote gender equity in education. Partners focus on influencing policy, increasing public awareness, practical interventions and mainstreaming best practices. The partnership's achievements include the publication of the *ABC of Gender Responsive Education Policies: Guidelines for analysis and planning*, which details the process for evaluating gender responsiveness in national education action plans and provides guidance on gender mainstreaming. So far, FAWE has

analysed and influenced action plans in 17 countries.

Reaching girls in rural areas of sub-Saharan African is the focus of the Campaign for Female Education (CAMFED), which currently operates programmes in Ghana, Zambia and Zimbabwe. CAMFED reports having enabled more than 56,000 girls to remain in primary school, with 98 per cent graduating to secondary schools, by working with a wide range of partners, including parents, local authorities and patriarchal chiefs. CAMFED's community approach includes establishing district committees to raise and distribute resources, building community confidence through dialogue and addressing threats to girls' health and safety. The 'virtuous cycle of girls' education' means that the young women who benefit from these interventions subsequently support them by contributing their insights and perspectives to local authorities and children in their communities.

See References, page 88.

that is based on the principles of equality and respect for human rights. Achieving social change at the local level, in communities and households, requires concerted and deliberate action by a broad array of actors, including men and boys, husbands and fathers, voters, teachers, religious and civic leaders, the media, the private sector and, indeed, women and girls themselves. Actions taken at the local level need to be encouraged and reinforced by governments and international donors, which have a pivotal role in the design and implementation of appropriate legislation and programmes that protect and advance the rights of women and girls.

Effective partnerships are essential to accelerating progress in all of the areas cited. While across the international community partnerships are being recognized as the most effective means to bring about real and lasting change, their role in tackling gender discrimination – an issue that cuts across all aspects of development – is of especially critical importance.

Establishing effective partnerships that bring together diverse actors with different agendas, perspectives and affiliations is an objective not without problems or costs. Each of the seven recommendations will focus on the role of partnerships in tackling gender discrimination.

Some of the following actions can reap quick rewards, others may take longer. But for women and children, for this and for future generations, the time to act is now.

Education: Attacking gender discrimination at its root

As this report has shown, ensuring that girls and boys have equal educational opportunities is one of the most important and powerful steps towards combating gender discrimination and advancing children's rights. Every girl and boy is entitled to education, regardless of their social or economic status. Enabling girls to access the intellectual and social benefits of basic education ensures that their rights are protected and fulfilled and greatly enhances the range of life choices available to them as women. Furthermore, girls' education has profound and long-lasting benefits for families and entire communities. Women with some formal education are more likely to delay marriage and childbirth, ensure their children are immunized, be better informed about their own and their children's nutritional requirements and adopt improved birth spacing practices. As a result, their children have higher survival rates and tend to be healthier and better nourished.[4] Moreover, in many countries, each additional year of formal education completed by a mother translates into her children remaining in school up to one half year longer than would otherwise be the case.[5]

Recent trends in girls' education provide grounds for some optimism. Over the past 30 years, for example, gross primary enrolment rates for girls in low-income countries have risen from 52 per cent to over 90 per cent.[6] But gender disparities remain, not only at the primary and secondary levels, but also in tertiary education, where a mere 5 per cent to 10 per cent of students in low-income countries are female.[7]

Abolishing school fees

In many developing countries, the direct and indirect costs of schooling represent one of the most significant barriers to education for both girls and boys, particularly those from poor families living in rural areas.[8] Abolishing school fees is one of the most effective policy measures for accelerating progress in this area. In 2005, UNICEF and the World Bank launched the School Fee Abolition Initiative (SFAI), which aims to increase access to basic education and scale up progress to meet the MDGs and the Education for All targets in the next decade. In Ethiopia, Ghana, Kenya, Malawi, Mozambique, the United Republic of Tanzania and other countries participating in the SFAI (Burundi and the Democratic Republic of the Congo are planning to abolish fees shortly), the elimination of school fees is making it possible for girls from disadvantaged backgrounds to enrol in primary education.[9]

Encouraging parents and communities to invest in girls' education

Even where schools fees are not an issue, the perceived and real opportunity costs asso-ciated with sending children to school can discourage parents from supporting girls' education.[10] Encouraging poor families to invest in their daughters' education may require such incentives as conditional cash transfers, meals, subsidies and other types of income support. Conditional cash transfers provide families with food and compensate parents for the opportunity costs associated with child labour on the condition that parents send their children to school and take them to health clinics for regular vaccinations and check-ups.

Girl-friendly schools: Safe and without bias

Children who are not in school tend to come from the poorest and most marginalized households and often live in remote rural areas.[11] Parents may object to sending their daughters to school because they feel the facility is unsafe, or that the long journey to school exposes girls to risk of sexual assault or other forms of violence.[12] Governments, parents and international donors must work together to promote flexible scheduling, increase the safety of school facilities, ensure that schools have separate hygiene and sanitation facilities for girls, and build schools close to their homes.

The school curriculum must impress upon teachers, as well as students, the importance of gender equality, and address male bias in the classroom. Studies show that teachers who perceive girls to be less intelligent than boys tend to treat boys and girls differently. Male students receive preferential treatment and are given time to learn and play at school. Girls, in contrast, are often encouraged to be subservient and to sit close to the back of the classroom. In some communities, girls are assigned janitorial work in schools while the boys play in the schoolyard.[13]

Girls outperform boys throughout much of the industrialized world. The picture is different in the developing world, however, where boys tend to achieve higher results on school exams than girls. A recent survey of francophone Africa and Eastern and Southern Africa shows that boys are outperforming girls in all of the low-income countries surveyed in the assessment.[14]

One way to help eliminate bias is to increase the number of female teachers in the classroom. In addition, textbooks and related school materials should avoid replicating gender stereotypes, such as those that portray women cleaning and cooking while men are shown as professional engineers and doctors.[15]

Focusing more resources on achieving gender equality

In addition to sound legislation, robust research and bold policies, achieving gender equality and fulfilling women's and children's rights also requires resources. Without financial resources to incorporate new laws and policies, strong legislation and better research will mean little. Equitable and efficient social investment to eliminate gender discrimination is a key strategy for the promotion of gender equality and the empowerment of women.

Perhaps because gender discrimination is so often viewed as the result of social attitudes alone, far too little consideration has been given to the financial resources required to achieve the goal of gender equality and women's empowerment. A great deal of knowledge exists about the policies and actions required to address gender inequality, but much more needs to be done to turn theory into practice.

The UN Millennium Project has taken the lead in assessing how much it will cost to achieve the Millennium Development Goals.[16] Detailed country assessments focus on the goods, services and infrastructure required, as well as capital and recurrent costs. As intensive and detailed as these projections are, they are unable to specify with precision the final cost of meeting the MDGs. Uncertainty arises from the inability to know how the Millennium Declaration is being implemented in specific communities and countries, as well as the variable costs associated with each of the eight MDGs.[17] Because gender equality cuts across all of the Goals, assessing the cost of achieving MDG 3 – promoting gender

Monitoring governments' commitments to women's empowerment through gender-responsive budgets

Budgets reflect the social and economic priorities of governments. A government budget that can be broken down according to its impact on women and men is considered 'gender-responsive'. The United Nations Development Fund for Women (UNIFEM) defines gender-responsive budgeting as "the analysis of actual government expenditures and revenue on women and girls as compared to men and boys."

According to a report by the Commonwealth Secretariat, the aim of gender budgets is fourfold:

• Improve the allocation of resources to women.

• Support gender mainstreaming in macroeconomics.

• Strengthen civil society's participation in economic policymaking, and

• Track public expenditure against gender and development commitments and contribute to the attainment of the Millennium Development Goals.

Gender-responsive budget analysis can provide a clear picture of the ways in which the distribution, use and generation of public resources affect women and men differently. It is an immensely useful tool not only to highlight the links between social investment and the realization of women's rights, but also to hold governments accountable for their commitments to gender equality and women's empowerment.

UNIFEM has strongly promoted gender-responsive budgets, which are currently being applied in over 50 countries. South Africa was among the first to implement gender-responsive budgeting in 1995. Rwanda's budget currently prioritizes gender equality, and all of the country's sectoral budgets are prepared with the participation of that country's Ministry of Gender.

In Latin America, UNIFEM has supported gender-responsive budget initiatives in Bolivia, Brazil, Chile, Colombia, Ecuador, Mexico and Peru. Such analyses have become codified in the formal budgeting process in Chile, where gender is one of six mandatory areas on which government ministries must report. Other interventions in the region have also included gender-based budget analyses at national, provincial and municipal levels, technical support to budget planning institutions, and advocacy initiatives with civil society and public sector organizations.

In India, female parliamentarians have taken a leading role in raising gender-based budgeting initiatives at the parliamentary level. Some states have gone even further by legislating for people's audits of local planning and spending, and enacting measures to ensure women's participation in these processes. For the 2005/6 fiscal year, 18 departments were directed to submit budgets showing resource allocations and expenditures benefiting women.

In Morocco, the 2006 budget contained an annex on gender equity priorities. This unprecedented development followed four years of collaboration between UNICEF and the Ministry of Finance in Morocco. The annex assesses the implications that the national budget has for gender equality and outlines specific gender targets. Key ministries, including education, finance, health, agriculture and rural development, participated in the preparation of the annex.

Gender-responsive budgets are proving to be effective in focusing attention on where financial resources are required to promote gender equality and empower women. Along with child budgets, which are also gaining increasing recognition as effective advocacy and policy instruments, they are practical tools to show whether sufficient resources are being dedicated to realize the rights of women and children.

See References, page 88.

equality and empowering women – has proved especially difficult. The UN Millennium Project has taken steps to modify its methodology in the hope of distilling more accurate estimates of the costs involved in meeting MDG 3.[18] The initial estimates come from a detailed analysis of Bangladesh, Cambodia, Ghana, the United Republic of Tanzania and Uganda that has subsequently been extended to cover all low-income countries.

In the initial group of five countries studied, it was estimated that between US$37 and US$57 per capita (measured in constant 2003 US dollars) was needed annually for supplies and services in girls' education, women's health and other areas. The MDG 3 specific interventions represent only 6-10 per cent of the total cost of interventions required to achieve the MDGs.[19]

Estimating costs requires outlining concrete areas where investments are needed. Many exercises estimating the cost of MDG 3 have focused solely on eliminating gender disparity in education,[20] which, however vital, is only part of the puzzle. A more complete cost estimation focuses on the seven strategic priorities identified in the Millennium Project task force report on gender equality and achieving the Millennium Development Goals:

- Strengthen opportunities for post-primary education for girls while meeting commitments to universal primary education.

- Guarantee sexual and reproductive health and rights.

- Invest in infrastructure to reduce women's and girls' time burdens.

- Guarantee women's and girls' property and inheritance rights.

- Eliminate gender inequality in employment by decreasing women's reliance on informal employment, closing gender gaps in earnings and reducing occupational segregation.

- Increase women's share of seats in national parliaments and local government bodies.

- Combat violence against girls and women.[21]

How much additional financing in total is required to meet MDG 3 depends on how government resources change between now and 2015, and how much of those resources are dedicated to gender equality and women's empowerment. According to a realistic scenario, low-income countries would need an additional US$28 billion (measured in constant 2003 US dollars) in 2006 from donor countries, rising to US$73 billion in 2015. Available estimates suggest, however, that governments currently target fewer resources to gender equality than other MDG areas.[22]

Getting the financing right is only the first step. Money must be put to the right use, and it must be integrated within existing government budgets and plans, as well as aligned with poverty reduction strategy papers and other planning processes in which all stakeholders participate. The road to gender equality can be long and complex, but without sufficient resources the destination will be impossible to reach.

Levelling the playing field in national legislation

Legislative reform can be a powerful strategy for empowering women and girls and safeguarding their rights. Over the past year alone, women obtained the right to vote and to stand for election in Kuwait,[23] pushed for legislation that would criminalize domestic violence in Tajikistan,[24] called for the greater inclusion of gender concerns in peace-agreement and post-conflict processes in Somalia,[25] and were a driving force behind the ratification of the Protocol on the Rights of Women in Africa, which entered into force in November 2005.[26] Nevertheless, in many countries, women still lack equal access to justice and legal protection, and in some countries, powerful legal obstacles continue to undermine their rights in key areas.

Domestic violence and gender-based violence in conflict

Violence against women and children has devastating consequences. It fills their lives with pain and terror, from which some may never recover.[27] It knows no boundaries of

Partnering to promote child rights and gender equality in political agendas

Partnerships between parliamentarians and advocates for women and children are also helping to focus greater attention on gender equality and protection against harm, exploitation, abuse and violence. One such partnership is the collaboration between Inter-Parliamentary Union (IPU) and UNICEF, which dates back over a decade and a half beginning with IPU's support for the Convention on the Rights of the Child. More recently, IPU jointly organized with UNICEF the Parliamentary Forum on Children during the UN Special Session on Children in May 2002. Since then, a strong partnership has developed between the two organizations, especially in the area of child protection and the promotion of gender equality. Some of the key joint actions have included:

- **Child protection handbook for parliamentarians:** *Child Protection: A Handbook for Parliamentarians*, launched in 2004, covers a wide range of themes related to child protection, including trafficking of children, violence against children, female genital mutilation/cutting, the sexual exploitation of children,

children and war, and juvenile justice. The handbook serves as a catalyst for action, providing concrete examples of ways to build a protective environment for children and parliamentarians' responses to the challenges of child protection.

- **Child trafficking handbook:** This jointly produced handbook by IPU and UNICEF was launched in 2005 at the IPU Assembly. *Combating Child Trafficking* served as a tool for a regional parliamentary seminar, 'Developing a Protective Framework for Children: The role of parliaments', in February 2006. The seminar, held in Hanoi at the invitation of the Vietnamese National Assembly, included parliamentarians from 13 countries.

- **High-level panels on gender equality and child protection:** In recent years, the two organizations have held a series of panels at the annual IPU assemblies to focus attention on gender equality and child protection. The first panel, which addressed the issue of commercial sexual exploitation, took place at the 2004 IPU Assembly in Mexico. The following year, the panel

addressed the issue of violence against women and children in situations of armed conflict. In 2006, the panel – which also featured the collaboration of the Joint United Nations Programme on HIV/AIDS (UNAIDS) – examined the impact of HIV/AIDS on children.

- **Regional forums:** On the recommendation of the IPU Task Force of Parliamentarians against female genital mutilation, the African Parliamentary Union, UNICEF and IPU organized a regional conference in Dakar, in December 2005 on parliamentary action to put an end to FGM/C. The conference brought together members of Parliament from 21 countries. It aimed at strengthening their action by familiarizing them with the experience of TOSTAN – a nongovernmental organization based in Senegal whose Community Empowerment Programme has been successful in discouraging the practice of FGM/C – and similar successful initiatives to combat protection abuses against children.

See References, page 88.

geography, culture or wealth. Anti-violence measures often require specific legislation, as well as a strong commitment by policymakers, the judiciary and law enforcement officials, and, in some cases, the international community, to ensure that perpetrators are prosecuted and that victims receive the full support they need to rebuild their lives.

The Report of the Independent Expert for the United Nations Study on Violence against Children, released in August 2006, confirms a widely held perception that domestic violence

has incalculable consequences for children.[28] Children suffer both directly, as targets of violence, and indirectly, as first-hand witnesses to the devastating impact that violence has on the family and household. Worldwide, at least 45 countries have specific legislation against domestic violence, 21 others are drafting more laws, and numerous countries have amended criminal laws to include domestic violence.[29] But the gap between the laws on the books and their implementation often remains as wide as it is deadly, and important regional differences prevail. While more than 80 per cent

of Latin American countries have specific legislation against domestic violence, this is true of less than 5 per cent of countries in Eastern Europe and the Commonwealth of Independent States, Africa and East Asia and the Pacific.[30]

Similarly, comprehensive mechanisms are needed to prevent and respond to gender-based violence in conflict. The increased law-lessness that accompanies the breakdown of social institutions and structures in times of conflict can contribute to a high incidence of sexual violence, exploitation and abuse. War exacerbates the violence that girls and women live with in times of peace. Many women and girls become victims of sexual slavery during conflict, forced to provide sexual services to armed forces or groups. In some cases, rape is employed as a strategic method of warfare in order to humiliate, degrade and displace com-munities, as well as to achieve wider military objectives, including ethnic cleansing and political terror.[31] Rape has also been perpe-trated by those with a mandate to protect, including United Nations staff and peace-keeping personnel.[32]

Since all such acts of sexual exploitation and abuse take place within a broader context of violence, long-standing gender inequality and a lack of empowerment of women and girls, strategies to address gender-based violence must address these underlying causes. Resolution 1325, adopted by the UN Security Council in 2000, took an important step forward by calling on "all parties to armed conflict to take special measures to protect women and girls from gender-based violence, particularly rape and other forms of sexual abuse, and all other forms of violence."[33] Much more remains to be done, however, including encouraging governments to codify rape and other forms of sexual violence as crimes in their national laws, holding states accountable for the actions of fighting forces, and increasing the numbers of women at all stages of peace-building.[34]

Property and inheritance rights

Equal land and property rights would repre-sent a significant step towards eliminating gender discrimination at the household level. For legal reform to change the lives of women and children, national laws based on human

Figure 5.1 The majority of countries with the most women in parliament use political quotas

| Rank | Country | Lower or single house of parliament | | | |
		Date of elections	% of women in parliament	Does the country have a quota?	Types of quota*
1	Rwanda	September 2003	48.8	Yes	1
2	Sweden	September 2002	45.3	Yes	3
3	Costa Rica	February 2006	38.6	Yes	2,3
4	Norway	September 2005	37.9	Yes	3
5	Finland	March 2003	37.5	No	-
6	Denmark	February 2005	36.9	Yes	3
7	Netherlands	January 2003	36.7	Yes	3
8	Cuba	January 2003	36.0	No	-
8	Spain	March 2004	36.0	Yes	3
10	Argentina	October 2005	35.0	Yes	1, 2, 3
11	Mozambique	December 2004	34.8	Yes	3
12	Belgium	May 2003	34.7	Yes	2,3
13	Austria	November 2003	33.9	Yes	3
14	Iceland	May 2003	33.3	Yes	3
15	South Africa	April 2004	32.8	Yes	3

* There are several types of quotas, including (1) constitutional quotas; (2) election law quotas; and (3) political party quotas for electoral candidates. For definitions, see Panel, page 79.

Sources: Data are drawn from the Inter-Parliamentary Union database on 'Women in National Parliaments', <http://www.ipu.org/wmn-e/classif.htm>, accessed May 2006. The figures for those legislatures using quotas are derived from the Global Database of Quotas for Women, <http://www.quotaproject.org/country.cfm>, also accessed May 2006.

rights laws and principles must necessarily be upheld over male-biased customary laws and traditional practices. National legal reforms in property law and inheritance rights represent one of the most direct strategies for increasing women's access to land and property. In the wake of land reform in Costa Rica, for example, women represented 45 per cent of land-titled beneficiaries between 1990 and 1992, compared with only 12 per cent before the reform. Similarly, in Colombia, after a ruling in 1996 on joint titling, land titled jointly to couples made up 60 per cent of land adjudications, compared to 18 per cent in 1995.[35]

No compromise on protecting women and girls

Legislative reform is likely to require different actions in different legal contexts. The fulfilment of the rights of women and girls in one country may be contingent upon the abolition or amendment of discriminatory legislation. In other countries, equal access to justice and legal protection may require the enactment of new laws or specific mechanisms that neutralize the power of other legal structures – such

as customary laws and religious codes – which often discriminate against women.[36] However, while understanding that customary law and religious codes are important, efforts at harmonizing these codes with statutory law cannot be conducted at the expense of the rights and well-being of women and girls.

Quotas can encourage women's participation in politics

Chapter 4 showed that, whether women are transforming political processes, directly representing the interests of women and children, or inspiring the next generation of girls, the political participation of women is vital for children. With Kuwait granting women the right to vote and stand for election in May 2005, there are now very few countries with elected parliaments where women do not have the right to vote and stand for public office.[37] But while the legal barriers to entry into politics and government for women have been removed, women still account for only one out of every six national parliamentarians in the world.[38]

Quotas: One size does not fit all

Quotas have proved effective in increasing the participation of women in politics in countries across the world. The mechanisms by which they apply vary widely and have differing effects in each country. As a means to understanding the concept of quotas, the following definitions and associated terms are presented, as classified by the International Institute for Democracy and Electoral Assistance, an inter-governmental organization whose mandate is to support sustainable democracy worldwide.

• **Gender quota systems** aim to ensure that women constitute at least a 'critical minority' of 20, 30 or 40 per cent of legislators, or a true gender balance of 50 per cent. In some countries quotas are applied as a temporary measure, that is to say, until the barriers to women's entry into politics are removed. Most countries with quotas, however, have not limited their use over time.

• **Legal quotas** regulate the proceedings of all political parties in a country and may also prescribe sanctions in case of non-compliance. Legal quotas can be mandated in a country's constitution (as in Burkina Faso, Nepal, the Philippines and Uganda) or by law, usually electoral (as in many parts of Latin America and, for example, in Belgium, Bosnia and Herzegovina, Serbia and Sudan).

• **Voluntary party quotas** are decided by one or more political parties in a country. In some countries, including Argentina, Bolivia, Ecuador, Germany, Italy, Norway and Sweden, several political parties have some type of quota. In many others, only one or two parties have opted to use quotas. If the leading party in a country uses a quota, such as the African National Congress in South Africa, this can have a significant impact on the overall rate of female representation. Most of the world's political parties, however, do not employ any kind of quota at all.

Quotas can target different parts of the selection and nomination process

• The first stage involves finding aspirants, or those willing to be considered for nomination, either by a primary or by the nominations committee and other parts of the party organization. Gender quotas at this stage are rules that demand that a certain number or percentage of women or either sex be represented in the pool of potential candidates. This has been used in countries with plurality-majority electoral systems, like the controversial 'women's short lists' in the United Kingdom.

• At the nomination stage, quotas are applied to the nomination of candidates to be placed on the party ballot. This implies that a rule (legal or voluntary) requires that, for instance 20, 30, 40 or even 50 per cent of the candidates must be women.

• At the electoral stage, quotas are applied as 'reserved seats', where a certain percentage or number among those elected must be women. Increasingly, gender quotas are being introduced using reserved seat systems.

See References, page 88.

Quotas can make an important difference. Whether legally mandated through constitutional or electoral law – often but not always the most effective approach – or based on voluntary actions by political leaders, quotas have led to dramatic changes in women's political participation throughout the world. According to the Inter-Parliamentary Union, as a result of the introduction of quotas, Rwanda, for example, jumped from 24th place in 1995 to 1st place in 2003 in terms of women's representation in parliament, while Costa Rica advanced from 25th in 1994 to 3rd place in 2006. Afghanistan, previously unranked as women were denied the right to vote under the Taliban regime, now stands in the 25th position.[39] Similar statistics hold true for countries as diverse as Argentina, Burundi, Iraq, Mozambique and South Africa.[40]

Overall, of the 20 countries in the world with the most women in parliament, 17 (or 85 per cent) are using some form of quota system (*see Figures 5.1 and 5.2, pages 78 and 80*). While quotas are most widely used to increase the political representation of women in national parliaments, to date there are 30 countries that have constitutional or statutory quotas at the subnational level. In India, for example, the results have been dramatic, as one third of seats in all local legislatures are reserved for women by a constitutional amendment. This stands in contrast to the national parliament, where women account for less than 10 per cent of all parliamentarians.[41]

Quotas are also gaining increasing recognition as a potentially effective vehicle for ensuring women's representation at the peace table. In 1999, for example, after women were key participants in helping settle hostilities in southern Sudan, the United Nations Development Fund for Women partnered with a local organization on the 'People to People' peace process, which reserved a third of the seats in local and regional peace reconciliation meetings for women.[42] Similarly, in South Africa, 41 per cent of the commissioners of the Truth and Reconciliation Commission were women.[43] Neither of these examples, however, involves formal peace processes. At present, no examples of such quotas exist.

While they can be effective, however, quotas are no panacea. To be effective, quotas have to match the electoral system of a country; unless

they do, and unless commitments are reinforced by a political system in which rules matter and failure to comply carries consequences, the role of quotas is merely symbolic.[44]

Women empowering women

One of the most important and effective avenues for women's empowerment is the dynamic of cooperation among women. Informal women's collectives organize around such issues as nutrition, food distribution, education and shelter, contributing to an improved standard of living for women, their families and communities.[45] But even though women's social networks tend to be wider than those of men, they tend to command fewer economic resources.[46]

Women's groups need to be recognized as important agents of empowerment and development. Governments and development agencies must include them in poverty reduction strategies and nurture long-term partnerships. By working with women's organizations at the community level and channelling development resources through them, international development agencies can help increase the likelihood that resources will reach the most vulnerable members of poor communities –

Figure 5.2 Countries with the most women in parliament are also the most likely to use quotas

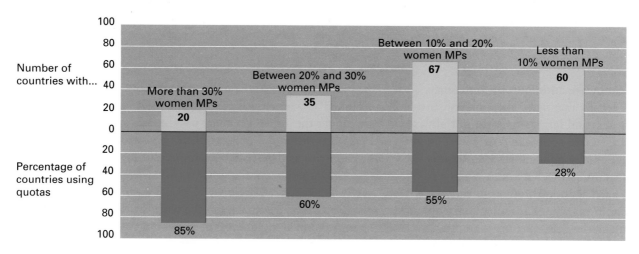

Note: Quotas include constitutional quotas, election law quotas and political party quotas for electoral candidates.

Sources: Women in parliament from the Inter-Parliamentary Union database on 'Women in National Parliaments', <http://www.ipu.org/wmn-e/classif.htm>, accessed May 2006. The figures for those legislatures using quotas are derived from the Global Database of Quotas for Women, <www.quotaproject.org/country.cfm>, also accessed May 2006.

women and children. Involving women in the early stages of policy development help ensure that programmes will be designed with the needs of women and children in mind.

Grass-roots women's movements are vocal and active champions of women's equality and empowerment and have campaigned successfully for CEDAW and other conventions mandated to improve the situation of women and girls at the international level. The benefit of women's groups is even more evident at the local level, where they are working to improve the quality of life for their families.

Engaging men and boys

Men can make a crucial contribution to ending gender discrimination. Globally, men continue to dominate decision-making processes in households, economies and governments. In addition, men's participation in initiatives to promote gender mainstreaming and gender equality remains low. Such initiatives may be perceived as a threat to their status and power.

By making child-friendly choices and supporting women in their capacities as decision-makers, men can be powerful allies in the struggle for women's equality. Evidence shows that men are more likely to be active, hands-on fathers when they feel positive about themselves and their relationship with the child's mother, when they have support for active involvement in their children's lives from family and friends, and when they are in employment.[47]

Involving men

Men are often the dominant household decision-makers, yet they tend to be overlooked by programmes that improve conditions for women and children.[48] In one Indian state, for instance, researchers discovered that advocacy campaigns on nutrition were targeted to women, even though approximately 20 per cent of fathers made the decisions regarding children's nutrition.[49]

UNICEF's experience shows that programmes that focus on males provide ways to promote positive gender socialization. Programmes that

Women's participation in community-based initiatives across the developing world

Across the developing world, studies show that women's participation in community initiatives can have long-lasting benefits for women and children. Women who are empowered to take action, whether through programmes led by governments, non-governmental organizations or those driven by the community, often have a positive influence on the lives of other women.

Bangladesh. One example is the Food for Education (FFE) programme in Bangladesh, which focused on female-headed households. Lessons learned from the FFE programme, which ran from 1993 to 2002, were applied in a follow-up project by the World Bank. About 40 per cent of the 5.2 million students enrolled in schools with FFE received food grains, primarily wheat. The programme successfully increased primary school enrolment, promoted school attendance and reduced drop-out rates. While boys' school enrolment increased by nearly 30 per cent, the increase for girls was even more remarkable, at over 40 per cent. In addition, there is some evidence that the programme also enabled girls to stay in school longer, thus delaying marriage and improving their income-earning potential.

Guatemala. Families with working mothers in need of childcare were the focus of Programa de Hogares Comunitarios, in Guatemala. Under this government-sponsored initiative, a group of parents was given the opportunity to designate a woman from their community as their childcare provider. The success of the programme, which began in 1991, was reinforced by the positive outcomes for the children, who consumed, on average, 20 per cent more energy, proteins and iron and 50 per cent more vitamin A than children in the control group. Programme evaluations also revealed that mothers involved were more likely to receive work-related social and medical benefits than other non-participating working mothers.

Indonesia. Non-governmental organizations are actively involved in the campaign for women's rights in Indonesia. Since 1986, the Centre for the Development of Women's Resources has been a leader in the movement to end violence against women. The centre trains community-based groups on women's issues, including survival strategies and skills for building support networks to cope with violence against women. The groups are then equipped with modules to conduct succession training until the information reaches village level.

According to the Asian Development Bank, the organization's campaign and training has increased the number of women requesting legal assistance from the Indonesia Women's Association for Justice, another leading non-governmental organization.

Uzbekistan. In Uzbekistan, the women of Angren City Municipality have given young disabled children and their mothers a new source of hope. Developed by women in the community who wanted to improve the social services available to the families of disabled children, the Sunday School Programme provides an educational environment for children who are excluded from traditional classrooms.

Women play a crucial role in the school's success, organizing the programmes and encouraging mothers, many of whom rarely participate in social events outside of the household, to enrol their children. By providing a safe and supportive environment in which disabled children and their parents can learn and socialize, the programme caters to the emotional and practical needs of families.

See References, page 88.

encourage the participation of both men and women can help to increase communication between the sexes and encourage a more even division of childcare responsibilities. In Viet Nam, for example, UNICEF has mobilized men to promote the use of oral rehydration salts to treat diarrhoea and to increase immunization coverage. Throughout Afghanistan, Bangladesh, India, Nepal, Pakistan and Sri Lanka, male and female activists are campaigning against gender-based violence. In Uganda and Zimbabwe, UNICEF programmes are attempting to foster the socialization of girls and boys as a means of stemming the spread of HIV/AIDS.[50]

© UNICEF/HQ06-0656/Josh Estey

Another strategy for increasing men's support for gender equality involves policies that aim to redistribute benefits to men and women more equitably. Evidence from the 'Nordic experiment' illustrates how this works. In Scandinavian countries, a combination of government and non-government initiatives contributed to a dramatic increase in the availability of paternity leave for men. In Sweden, for instance, fathers now assume responsibility for 45 per cent of childcare responsibilities, thanks in large part to the growing popularity of paternal leave.[51]

Challenging gender stereotypes and changing attitudes

Advocacy initiatives designed to educate men and women on the benefits of gender equality and joint decision-making can help nurture a more cooperative relationship between men and women. Evidence shows that fathers are more likely to stop abusive treatment towards mothers if they have been exposed to information on how gender-based violence adversely affects their children.[52]

Research and data on the situation of women and girls

There is broad recognition of the impact that discrimination has on the lives of women. But an overwhelming lack of sex-disaggregated statistics often results in scant or weak quantitative research on the issues that affect women and, in turn, children. This report has shown that there is sufficient data and research on women and girls to outline where their rights are violated and illustrate the negative impacts these violations can have on children. Nonetheless, much more needs to be known about many of the most important aspects of women's lives and the impact discrimination has on those around them. Research and data are sorely lacking in several key areas listed below.

- **Maternal mortality:** While 111 countries produced data based on registration systems and other surveys, for 62 countries no recent national data were available and estimates therefore had to be based on models.

Program H: Challenging gender stereotypes and changing attitudes in Brazil and other countries

Advocacy initiatives designed to educate men and women on the benefits of gender equality and joint decision-making can help nurture a more cooperative relationship between them.

A Brazilian non-governmental organization, Instituto Promundo, is implementing one such gender-sensitive programme, with positive results for women, men and children. Program H (the H refers to *homens*, or men in Portuguese) encourages young men to respect their partners, to avoid using violence against women, and to take precautions to avoid HIV and other sexually transmitted infections.

Through a creative blend of radio announcements, billboards and dances, Promundo challenges traditional male attitudes by promoting the idea that it is 'cool and hip' to be a more gender-equitable man.

Evaluations of the group meetings, where young men discuss the consequences of high-risk lifestyle choices, show that men who complete the programme are less likely to support traditional gender norms (for example, the belief that childcare is a woman's job and that there are times when a woman deserves to be beaten). The number of young male participants (aged 15 to 28) who supported the statement that "a

woman's most important role is to take care of the home and cook" declined from 41 per cent in the pretest to 29 per cent after completion of the programme.

The success of the Program H initiative in Brazil has inspired similar programmes in other countries in the region, as well as in Asia, sub-Saharan Africa and the United States. In India, for example, where programmes modelled on the Program H approach have been adopted, preliminary findings suggest that men's attitudes towards women have changed.

See References, page 88.

UNICEF has joined with other UN agencies and institutions to create a partnership dedicated to producing more comprehensive and accurate data.[53]

- **Violence against women:** Only 38 countries in the world have conducted at least one national survey on violence against women since 1995. A further 30 countries have surveys completed that cover parts of the country.[54]

- **Enrolment, school attendance and literacy:** While there are significant data disaggregated by sex on school enrolment, sex-disaggregated data on literacy and school attendance are available for only 112 and 96 countries, respectively. Efforts to compile and release sex-disaggregated data on female completion rates at the primary, secondary and tertiary levels of education must also be strengthened.[55]

- **Labour force, unemployment and occupational distribution:** Just over half the world's 204 countries and territories provided sex-

disaggregated data on these fundamental areas of work, with only 105 providing data on occupational segregation by sex.[56]

- **Wage statistics:** This is a vital area where discrimination affects women and their children, and yet just under half (52) of the 108 countries or territories that reported wage data were also able to provide disaggregation by sex. Europe and Asia account for almost three quarters of these countries.[57]

- **Informal employment:** Even with an internationally agreed-upon definition of informal employment, only 60 countries have produced data on informal employment, and in many cases these statistics are not fully comparable.[58]

- **Unpaid work and time use:** Since 1995, 67 countries or areas have conducted time use surveys, with again the vast majority in CEE/CIS and South and East Asia. Only seven countries in Africa and three in South America have collected such data.[59]

- **Women's participation in national and local governments:** The Inter-Parliamentary Union collects data on the number of women in parliaments and how the numbers have changed over time.[60] Data on women's participation in local government are relatively scarce, however, although United Cities and Local Governments has collected data in more than 70 countries.[61]

- **Women in peace negotiations and peace-building:** No systematic data are available on women participating as parties to peace negotiations. With the exception of the statistics made available by the UN Department of Peacekeeping Operations, no systematic data are available about women involved in different dimensions of peace-building.

In some areas, collection of data is much more difficult than in others. Collecting data on violence and trafficking, for example, poses more methodological problems than data on women in national parliaments. However, the lack of data in many key areas reflects not the difficulties of data collection, but rather the significant discrepancy between the resources invested in the excellent and careful collection of data in some areas, and lack of data in others. In other words, it is not only a question of capacity but also one of political will to invest in data collection.

When statistics are a priority, even if difficult to collect, they are there. Financial statistics such as inflation, for example, are not easy to collect as they require detailed and rapidly updated economic information, yet they are available almost universally – even in the poorest countries. But many countries, particularly poorer ones, do not currently have the statistical capacity to regularly collect the most basic disaggregated statistical series, let alone in areas such as informal employment, time use and wages.

While country-led censuses and surveys are the centrepiece of statistical collection, other approaches can rapidly produce data even where statistical capacity is limited. The Multiple Indicator Cluster Survey, a household survey programme developed by UNICEF to

Figure 5.3 In many countries sex-disaggregated data are not available for key indicators

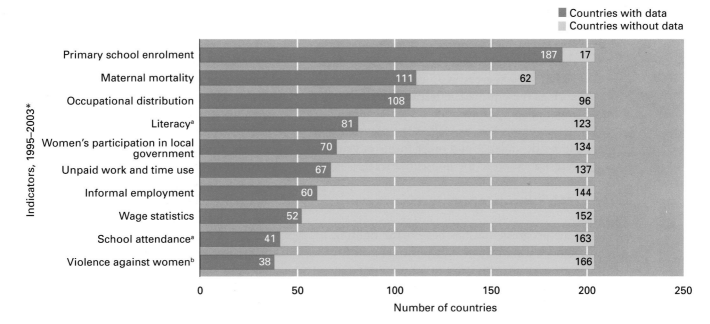

*Data refer to the most recent year available during the period specified.

Note: 'Countries with data' includes only countries where data are based on censuses, surveys or other sources, not countries where data are derived from modelled estimates. [a]Data from censuses only. [b]Includes only data from national surveys. An additional 30 countries have surveys covering part of the country.

Source: United Nations, Department of Social and Economic Affairs, *The World's Women 2005: Progress in statistics,* United Nations, New York, 2006.

Partnering to provide improved estimates of maternal mortality

Each year, over 500,000 women die as a result of pregnancy-related causes, and many others suffer life-long health complications. Reducing maternal mortality is one of the eight Millennium Development Goals, but it is also among the most difficult to monitor owing to difficulties in measuring maternal mortality. In some cases, measurement is complicated by a lack of data; maternal deaths often go unrecorded in countries that lack reliable civil registration of births and deaths, or where the cause of death is not adequately classified or reported. Even in those countries with robust civil registration systems, maternal deaths are often misclassified or attributed to other causes – particularly if the pregnancy status of the woman is not known or recorded.

UNICEF is collaborating with the World Health Organization (WHO) and the United Nations Population Fund (UNFPA) to improve the information base on maternal mortality. Building on more than a decade of inter-agency collaboration and cooperation, UNICEF, WHO and UNFPA are pooling their expertise to pioneer a new approach to estimating the number of women dying from causes related to or aggravated by pregnancy. The methodology developed for the project will correct existing data discrepancies and generate estimates for countries that currently lack data.

The group's joint work will also enhance data collection and dissemination by compiling and reviewing country concerns to ensure widespread acceptance of final estimates on maternal mortality, obtaining the most recently reported national data from their country and regional offices and organizing interregional consultations to discuss underlying statistical issues.

See References, page 88.

assist countries in filling data gaps for monitoring the situation of children and women, is capable of producing statistically sound, internationally comparable estimates of key indicators. One of the three questionnaires focuses on women aged 15–49 and currently includes questions on assets and security of tenure. Another valuable source of household data is the Demographic and Health Surveys, which include 200 surveys in 75 countries. Surveys such as these provide effective vehicles for getting in-depth information on the economic situation of women, as well as the prevalence of domestic violence and other forms of gender discrimination at the household level.

The time is now

The progress that has been made fighting gender discrimination is positive: girls are catching up with boys in school attendance and performance, and in a few developing countries and regions have surpassed them; more women are economically active and in higher level positions than ever before; and the number of women in parliament is increasing year after year. But, in addition to showing how far we have come, the assessment of this report underlines how far there is to go.

Eliminating gender discrimination will produce a double dividend, fulfilling the rights of women and going a long way towards realizing those of children as well. With concerted efforts, real progress, based on respect, universal human rights and equal opportunities for women and men alike, can be made towards transforming discriminatory attitudes behaviours, customs, laws, institutions and practices in society. Effective partnerships involving governments, donors and international agencies, can support this process through the design and implementation of human-rights-based development strategies.

Tackling gender discrimination requires a different approach to policymaking. Generally, the key actors in policy decisions are governments. In areas such as debt or trade, for example, economists, members of the public and business leaders may be influential, but the decision to act rests with the governing authorities. Although governments and donors

have a key role in addressing gender discrimination and inequality through legislation, policies and funding for key programmes, the core agents of change are an altogether more diverse group that includes all members of society, and women and girls themselves. These are the individuals and groups who hold the power to eliminate gender discrimination and inequalities through everyday attitudes, behaviours and practices.

The challenge to achieve such change is as exhilarating as it is daunting. It is not simply a question of producing a big decision by an important body, which would be in many ways a simpler task to conceptualize and approach. It requires societies to examine openly and honestly the extent of gender discrimination and rights violations suffered by women and girls, and commit themselves to eliminating its root causes. Although challenging at times, this process will be worth the

reward. Every person who argues that women have an equal place in decision-making forums, every community that demands girls go to school, and every government committed to ensuring that violence, abuse, exploitation and discrimination against women have no place in society brings the double dividend of gender equality a step closer for this and future generations of women and children.

REFERENCES

CHAPTER 1

[1] Preparation of the text of the Convention on the Elimination of All Forms of Discrimination against Women began in 1976.

[2] King, Elizabeth M., and Andrew D. Mason, 'Engendering Development Through Gender Equality in Rights, Resources, and Voice', World Bank and Oxford University Press, Washington, D.C., January 2001, pp. 78-83.

[3] Information derived from United Nations, 'Multilateral Treaties Deposited with the Secretary-General', <http://untreaty.un.org/English/Bible/englishinternetbible/partI/chapterIV/treaty10.asp>, accessed September 2006.

[4] Lawn, Joy E., Simon Cousens and Jelka Zupan, '4 Million Neonatal Deaths: When? Where? Why?, Series on Neonatal Survival 1, The Lancet.com, March 2005, p. 5. Information on population by sex in Asia derived from United Nations Population Division, 'World Population Prospects: The 2004 Revision Database', <http://esa.un.org/unpp>, accessed September 2006.

[5] World Health Organization, WHO Multi-Country Study on Women's Health and Domestic Violence against Women: Initial results of prevalence, health outcomes and women's responses, Summmary Report, WHO, Geneva, 2005, p. xiii.

[6] United Nations Population Fund, The State of the World's Population, UNFPA, New York, 2005, p. 66.

[7] Derived from websites of national governments and from Inter-Parliamentary Union, 'Women in Politics: 60 years in retrospect', IPU, Geneva, February 2006, Data Sheet No. 4. Note: The figure for total women Heads of State and Government in 2006 includes of the Government of the Netherlands Antilles, which is an autonomous country within the Netherlands. Queens and Governor Generals are not included in the figure cited.

[8] Information derived from Inter-Parliamentary Union, 'Women in Politics: 60 years in retrospect', op. cit.

[9] United Nations International Research and Training Institute for the Advancement of Women, 'Beijing at 10: Putting policy into practice', in Women and Poverty: New challenge, INSTRAW, <www.un-instraw.org/en/images/stories/Beijing/womenandpoverty.pdf>.

[10] UNESCO Institute for Statistics, 'Literacy Estimates, International Literacy Day 2005, <www.uis.unesco.org>.

[11] Otunnu, Olara A., 'Special Comment' on Children and Security, Disarmament Forum, No. 3, United Nations Institute for Disarmament Research, Geneva, 2002, pp. 3-4.

[12] Waring, Marilyn, et al., Politics: Women's insights, Inter-Parliamentary Union, Geneva, 2000, p. 134.

CHAPTER 1 PANELS

Gender discrimination across the life cycle

Information derived from:

Gorman, Mark, Age and Security: How social pensions can deliver effective aid to poor older people and their families, HelpAge International, London, 2004, p. 5.

CHAPTER 1 FIGURES

Figure 1.2 Men's discriminatory attitudes towards women vary across regions but are significant everywhere

Technical note: Methodology used to derive regional and country aggregates from the World Values Survey

The World Values Survey <www.worldvaluessurvey.org> is a worldwide investigation of socio-cultural and political change. It is conducted by a network of social scientists at leading universities around the world. Interviews have been carried out with nationally representative samples of the public in more than 80 societies on all six inhabited continents. A total of four waves have been carried out since 1981, with the latest wave being carried out between 1999 and 2004. All the data used in this Report come from the latest wave (1999–2004).

Data for key questions regarding attitudes towards gender relations used for the report were accessed on 1 June 2006 for all countries with available data in the latest phase <www.worldvaluessurvey.org/services/index.html>. The data were then extracted using the World Values Survey data extraction tool (cross-tabs) and aggregated. In cases of countries with two surveys, the most recent survey was used. In the rare case of countries with two surveys for the same dates, an average of the two surveys was used. Data were compiled for a series of questions relevant to the Report. For each question the World Values Survey provides data for 'Men', 'Women' and 'Total'. The data used in the Report vary according to the context, but are clearly labelled in each case.

In some figures and occasions in the text, data from countries within the same regional group were compiled as averages. Regions are based on UNICEF classification with the exceptions of clustering 'countries in transition' and 'high-income countries' separately, in order to separate opinions from these groupings of countries. In each case in the text or figure, the full list of countries used from each region is listed.

Countries with data from the World Values Survey (year of survey indicated in parentheses):

South Asia: Bangladesh (2002), India (2001), Pakistan (2001). **Latin America and the Caribbean:** Argentina (1999), Bolivarian Republic of Venezuela (2000), Chile (2000), Mexico (2000), Peru (2001). **Middle East and North Africa:** Algeria (2002), Egypt (2000),

Gupta, Neeru, and Mary Mahy, Adolescent Child-Bearing in Sub-Saharan Africa: Can increased schooling alone raise ages at first birth?', Demographic Research, vol. 8, 14 February 2003.

Joint United Nations Programme on HIV/AIDS, 2006 Report on the global AIDS epidemic, UNAIDS, Geneva, 2006, pp. 505-506. Based on 2005 estimates.

Islamic Republic of Iran (2000), Iraq (2004), Jordan (2001), Morocco (2001), Saudi Arabia (2003). **East Asia and Pacific:** China (2001), Indonesia (2001), Philippines (2001), Republic of Korea (2001), Singapore (2002), Viet Nam (2001). **Sub-Saharan Africa:** Nigeria (2000), South Africa (2001), Uganda (2001), United Republic of Tanzania (2001). **Higher income countires:** Austria (1999), Belgium (1999), Canada (2000), Denmark (1999), Finland (2000), France (1999), Greece (1999), Iceland (1999), Ireland (1999), Israel (2001), Italy (1999), Japan (2000), Luxembourg (1999), Malta (1999), Netherlands (1999), Portugal (1999), Spain (2000), Sweden (1999), United Kingdom (1999), United States (1999). **Countries in transition:** Albania (2002), Belarus (2000), Bosnia and Herzegovina (2001), Bulgaria (1999), Croatia (1999), Czech Republic (1999), Estonia (1999), Hungary (1999), Kyrgyzstan (2003), Latvia (1999), Lithuania (1999), Montenegro (2001), Poland (1999), Republic of Moldova (2002), Romania (1999), Russian Federation (1999), Serbia (2001), Slovakia (1999), Slovenia (1999), The former Yugoslav Republic of Macedonia (2001).

The percentages refer to the proportion of respondents who agreed or strongly agreed with the following statements:

- "University is more important for a boy than for a girl."

- "When jobs are scarce, men should have more right to a job than a woman."

- "Husbands and wives should both contribute to income."

- "Men make better political leaders than women do."

Figure 1.4 More than 1 our of every 4 births to an adolescent mother (aged 15-19) occurs in the least developed countries

Country composition of regional groups: More developed regions comprise all regions of Europe plus Northern America, Australia/New Zealand and Japan. Less developed regions comprise all regions of Africa, Asia (excluding Japan), Latin America and the Caribbean plus Melanesia, Micronesia and Polynesia. The list of least developed countries can be found in Summary indicators, p. 136. These countries are also included in the less developed regions. For the full breakdown of these regions, see United Nations Population Division, ' World Population Prospects; The 2004 Revision Database', <http://esa.un.org/unpp>.

Joint United Nations Programme on HIV/AIDS, The Global Coalition on Women and AIDS, *The Female AIDS Epidemic: 2005 statistics*, UNAIDS, Geneva, 2005.

King, Elizabeth M., and Andrew D. Mason, 'Engendering Development Through Gender Equality in Rights, Resources, and Voice', World Bank and Oxford University Press, Washington, D.C., January 2001, pp. 78-83.

Lawn, Joy E., Simon Cousens and Jelka Zupan, '4 Million Neonatal Deaths: When? Where? Why?', op. cit.

Malhotra, Anju, Rohini Pande and Caren Grown, *Impact of Investments in Female Education on Gender Equality*, paper commissioned by the World Bank Gender and Development Group, International Center for Research on Women, Washington, D.C., 27 August 2003 (rev.).

United Nations Children's Fund, *Progress for Children: A report card on gender parity and primary education, Number 2*, UNICEF, New York, April 2005, pp. 2, 4 and 5.

United Nations Children's Fund, *Child Protection Information Sheets*, UNICEF, New York, 2006, pp. 17 and 25.

United Nations Children's Fund, 'Early Marriage: Child spouses', *Innocenti Digest No. 7*, UNICEF Innocenti Research Centre, Florence, 2001, p. 11.

United Nations Population Division, 'World Population Prospects: The 2004 Revision Database', <http://esa.un.org/unpp>, accessed September 2006.

United Nations Population Fund, *The State of World Population 2005: The promise of equality, gender equity, reproductive health and the Millennium Development Goals*, UNFPA, New York, 2005, pp. 34-38.

United Nations Population Fund and University of Aberdeen, *Maternal Mortality Update 2004: Delivering into good hands*, UNFPA, New York, 2004.

United Nations, Report of the Independent Expert for the United Nations Study on Violence against Children, United Nations, New York, 2006, pp. 12 and 17.

World Health Organization, United Nations Children's Fund, and United Nations Population Fund, *Maternal Mortality in 2000: Estimates developed by WHO, UNICEF and UNFPA*, WHO, Geneva, 2005. Based on 2000 estimates of maternal deaths.

Gender discrimination and inequalities across regions

For the methodology and questions used to derive the aggregates from the World Values Survey, see page 88 of this report. Methodology used to derive regional and country aggregates from the World Values Survey.

Gallup Poll, 'Latin American Women Leadership Study: A look at changing attitudes of Latin Americans toward gender and women's leadership capabilities', Report for the Inter-American Development Bank, Washington, D.C., November 2000, pp. 7-8.

United Nations Development Programme, *Human Development Report 2005: International cooperation at a crossroads: Aid, trade and security in an unequal world*, Oxford University Press for UNDP, New York, 2005, pp. 303-306. See p. 345 of the report for a full explanation of the methodology used to calculate the gender empowerment measure.

CHAPTER 2

[1] Vadnais, Daniel, Adrienne Kols and Noureddine Abderrahim, *Women's Lives and Experiences: Changes in the past ten years*, ORC Macro and US Agency for International Development, Maryland, 2006, pp. 75-76. Data refer to women who do not participate in all four areas of household decision-making assessed from the Demographic and Health Surveys. These included decisions regarding a woman's own health care, major household purchases, purchases for daily household needs, and timing of visits to friends and relatives. The 10 countries (out of 30 assessed) where more than half the women surveyed participated in all four areas of decision-making were Armenia, Bolivia, Colombia, Eritrea, Indonesia, Madagascar, Peru, Philippines, Rwanda and Turkmenistan.

[2] UNICEF calculations based on Demographic and Health Survey (DHS) data. All data available from STATcompiler at <www.measuredhs.com>, accessed June 2006.

[3] Quisumbing, Agnes, 'What Have We Learned from Research on Intrahousehold Allocation?', Chapter 1 in Agnes Quisumbing, ed., *Household Decisions, Gender and Development: A synthesis of recent research*, International Food Policy Institute, Washington, D.C., 2003, pp. 1-6. Also see Chant, Sylvia, 'Poverty begins at home? Questioning some (mis)conceptions about children, poverty and privation in female-headed households', background paper written for *The State of the World's Children 2007*, UNICEF, New York, 2006.

[4] Frankenberg, Elizabeth, and Duncan Thomas, 'Measuring Power', Chapter 4 in Agnes Quisumbing, ed., *Household Decisions, Gender and Development: A synthesis of recent research*, International Food Policy Research Institute, Washington, D.C., 2003, pp. 29-36.

[5] Agarwal, Bina, '"Bargaining" and Gender Relations', op. cit., pp. 11-12. Also see Nosseir, Nazek, 'Family in the New Millennium: Major trends affecting families in North Africa', Chapter 7 in United Nations, *Major Trends Affecting Families: A background document*, UN, New York, 2003, p. 189.

[6] Smith, Lisa C., et al., *The Importance of Women's Status for Child Nutrition in Developing Countries*, Research Report 131, International Food Policy Research Institute, Washington D.C., 2003, p. 22.

[7] United Nations Children's Fund, *Early Marriage: A harmful traditional practice*, UNICEF, New York, 2005, p. 1.

[8] Smith, Lisa C., et al., *The Importance of Women's Status for Child Nutrition in Developing Countries*, op. cit., p. 21.

[9] United Nations Population Fund, *The State of World Population 2005*, UNFPA, New York, 2005, p. 65.

[10] Chant, Sylvia, 'Poverty begins at home?', op. cit., p. 14.

[11] United Nations Children's Fund, *Early Marriage*, op. cit., 2005, p. 23.

[12] United Nations Development Fund for Women, *Not a Minute More: Ending violence against women*, UNIFEM, New York, 2003, p. 8.

[13] World Health Organization, *WHO Multi-Country Study on Women's Health and Domestic Violence against Women: Initial results on prevalence, health outcomes and women's responses*, Summary Report, WHO, Geneva, 2005, p. 6.

[14] World Health Organization, *The World Report on Violence and Health*, WHO, Geneva, 2002, p. 93.

[15] United Nations Development Fund for Women, *Not a Minute More*, op. cit., p. 8.

[16] Desai, Sonalde, and Kiersten Johnson, 'Women's Decisionmaking and Child Health: Familial and social hierarchies', in Sunitor Kishor, ed., *A Focus on Gender: Collected papers on gender using DHS data*, ORC Macro and US Agency for International Development, Maryland, USA, 2005, p. 56.

[17] Smith, Lisa C., et al., *The Importance of Women's Status for Child Nutrition in Developing Countries*, op. cit., pp. 127-128.

[18] UNICEF defines undernutrition as the outcome of insufficient food intake (hunger) and repeated infectious diseases. Undernutrition includes being underweight for one's age, too short for one's age (stunted), dangerously thin (wasted), and deficient in vitamins and minerals (micronutrient malnutrition). United Nations Children's Fund, *Progress for Children: A report card on nutrition, Number 4*, UNICEF, New York, May 2006, pp. 1 and 3.

[19] Ibid., p. 6.

[20] Ibid., pp. 4 and 10.

[21] Smith, Lisa C., et al., *The Importance of Women's Status for Child Nutrition in Developing Countries*, op. cit., pp. 126-131.

[22] Ibid., p. 3; and United Nations Standing Committee on Nutrition, 5th Report on the World Nutrition Situation, United Nations, Geneva, March 2004, p. 42.

[23] The underlying data can be found in the Statistical Tables of this report, *Table 2. Nutrition*, p. 106.

[24] Smith, Lisa C., et al., *The Importance of Women's Status for Child Nutrition in Developing Countries*, op. cit., pp. 15-34. Within the study, women's influence is measured by the differences between men's and women's ages, levels of education and control over assets and income.

[25] Ibid., p. xi.

[26] It is also important to note that in all the regions studied, improving a woman's social status – ability to influence decision-making processes –

corresponded to a reduction in breastfeeding, which is harmful to child nutrition. Efforts to improve women's status, therefore, must be accompanied by efforts to protect, support and promote breastfeeding. See Smith, Lisa C., et al., *The Importance of Women's Status for Child Nutrition in Developing Countries*, op. cit., p. xii.

27 Ibid., p. 127.

28 Floro, Maria Sagrario, and Stephanie Seguino, 'Gender Effects on Aggregate Saving: A theoretical and empirical analysis', *Policy Research Report on Gender and Development, Working Paper Series No. 23*, World Bank, Washington, D.C., 2000, p. 9.

29 Duflo, Esther, and Christopher R. Udry, 'Intrahousehold Resource Allocation in Côte d'Ivoire: Social norms, separate accounts and consumption choices', *Yale University Economic Growth Center Discussion Paper No. 857*, Social Science Research Network, June 2003, p. 31; and Doss, Cheryl R., 'Do households fully share risks? Evidence from Ghana', Department of Applied Economics, University of Minnesota, St. Paul, July 1996, p. 18.

30 Alderman, Harold, et al., 'Gender Differentials in Farm Productivity: Implications for household efficiency and agricultural policy', *Food Consumption and Nutrition Division Discussion Paper No. 6*, International Food Policy Research Institute, Washington, D.C., 1995, pp. 9-12.

31 Ibid., p. 22.

32 Visaria, Leela, 'Female Autonomy and Fertility Behaviour: An exploration of Gujarat data,' in *Proceedings of the International Population Conference, Montreal 1993, volume 4*, International Union for the Scientific Study of Population, Liege (Belgium), 1993, pp. 263-275, in Sonalde Desai and Kiersten Johnson, 'Women's Decisionmaking and Child Health: familial and social hierarchies,' op. cit., p. 56.

33 Desai, Sonalde, and Kiersten Johnson, 'Women's Decisionmaking and Child Health', op. cit., p. 66. Effects are the weakest in sub-Saharan Africa, with Latin America and the Caribbean falling in between.

34 'Gender Perspective in Malaria Management', Malaria Knowledge Programme, Policy Brief, Liverpool School of Tropical Medicine, Liverpool, undated.

35 Desai, Sonalde, and Kiersten Johnson, 'Women's Decisionmaking and Child Health', op. cit., p. 56.

36 Emerson, Patrick M., and Andre Portela Souza, 'Bargaining over Sons and Daughters: Child labor, school attendance and intra-household gender bias in Brazil', Working Paper No. 02-W13, Vanderbilt University, Nashville, 2002, p. 14.

37 United Nations Children's Fund, *Progress for Children: A report card on gender parity and primary education, Number 2*, UNICEF, New York, 2005, p. 7.

38 Gibbons, Elizabeth, Friedrich Huebler and Edilberto Loaiza, 'Child Labor, Education, and the Principle of Non-Discrimination', Chapter 10 in Philip Alston and Mary Robinson, eds., *Human Rights and Development: Towards mutual rein-*

forcement, Oxford University Press, Oxford, 2005, p. 214.

39 Ibid., p. 222.

40 Delamonica, Enrique, Asmaa Donahue and Alberto Minujin, 'Children Living Only with their Mothers: Are they disadvantaged?' in Alberto Minujin, Enrique Dalamonica and Marina Komareci, eds., *Human Rights and Social Policies for Children and Women: The Multiple Indicator Cluster Survey (MICS) in practice*, New School University and UNICEF, New York, 2005, p. 201.

41 Bongaarts, John, 'Household Size and Composition in the Developing World', Working Paper No. 144, Population Council, New York, 2001, p. 14.

42 Chant, Sylvia, 'Poverty Begins at Home?', op. cit., p. 1.

43 Quisumbing, Agnes, Lawrence Haddad and Christine Peña, 'Are Women Over-Represented Among the Poor? An analysis of poverty in ten developing countries', *Journal of Development Economics*, vol. 66, no. 1, 2001, pp. 225-269; and *FCND Discussion Paper No. 115*, Food Consumption and Nutrition Division, International Food Policy Research Institute, Washington, D.C., 2001, pp. 8-9.

44 Helen Keller International, 'Female Decision-Making Power and Nutritional Status within Bangladesh's Economic Context', Nutritional Surveillance Project, Bulletin No. 20, Dhaka, August 2006, p. 2.

45 Chant, Sylvia, 'Poverty Begins at Home?', op. cit., p.10.

46 Delamonica, Enrique, Asmaa Donahue and Alberto Minujin, 'Children Living Only with their Mothers', op. cit., p.201.

47 Ibid., p. 220.

48 Chant, Sylvia, 'Poverty Begins at Home?', op. cit., p. 11.

49 Expenditure patterns, rather than the total per capita amount, differed between female-headed households and male-headed households. The expenditures of female-headed and male-headed households, disaggregated by expenditure quintiles, did not differ except in the wealthiest quintile, where female-headed households had higher expenditures.

50 Helen Keller International, 'Female Decision-Making Power and Nutritional Status within Bangladesh's Economic Context,' op. cit., p. 2.

51 United Nations Children's Fund, *Role of Men in the Lives of Children: A study of how improving knowledge about men in families helps strengthen programming for children and women*, UNICEF, New York, 1997, p. 9.

52 Barker, Gary, et al., *Supporting Fathers: Contributions from the International Fatherhood Summit 2003*, Early Childhood Development: Practice and Reflections, no. 20, Bernard van Leer Foundation, The Hague, April 2004, p. 12.

53 US Department of Health and Human Services, Child Care Bureau, 'Promoting Responsible Fatherhood through Child Care', National Child

Care Information Center, Vienna (Virginia), April 2004, p. 1.

54 Christian Children's Fund, 'Children in Poverty: Shaping a Reponse to Poverty: A conceptual overview and implications for responding to children living in poverty', *Children and Poverty Series, Part III*, CCF, Richmond, 2003, p 7.

55 Brown, Janet, and Gary Barker, 'Global Diversity and Trends in Patterns of Fatherhood,'in Supporting Fathers, op. cit., p. 17

56 Barker, Gary, et al., *Supporting Fathers*, op. cit., p. 1.

57 Renk, Kimberly, et al., 'Mothers, Fathers, Gender Role, and Time Parents Spend with their Children', *Sex Roles: A Journal of Research*, vol. 48, nos. 7-8, April 2003. pp. 1-2.

58 Cliquet, Robert, 'Major trends affecting families in the new millennium: Western Europe and North America', *Major Trends Affecting Families (background document)*, Division for Social Policy and Development, United Nations, New York, 2003-2004, p. 5. These numbers are even higher when the separation figures of unmarried cohabitant couples and divorce rates are combined.

59 Brown, Janet, and Gary Barker, 'Global Diversity and Trends in Patterns of Fatherhood', op. cit., p. 22.

60 Joseph Rowntree Foundation, 'A Man's Place in the Home: Fathers and families in the UK', *Foundations*, No. 440, April 2000, <www.jrf.org.uk/knowledge/findings/foundations/440.asp>, accessed September 2006.

61 El-Haddad, Yahya, 'Major Trends Affecting Families in the Gulf Countries', *Major Trends Affecting Families*, United Nations, New York, 2003, p. 225.

62 Nosseir, Nazek, 'Major trends affecting families in North Africa,', op. cit., p. 194.

63 Badran, Hoda, 'Major Trends Affecting Families in El Mashrek El Araby', *Major Trends Affecting Families*, United Nations, New York, 2003, p. 206.

64 Kabeer, Naila, 'The Conditions and Consequences of Choice: Reflections on the measurement of women's empowerment' *UNRISD Discussion Paper No. 108*, United Nations Research Institute for Social Development, Geneva, August 1999, p. 55.

65 Desai, Sonalde, and Kiersten Johnson, 'Women's Decisionmaking and Child Health', op. cit., p. 66.

66 Malombe, Joyce, 'Women's Groups and Shelter Improvement in Kenya,' in Ann Schlyter, ed., *A Place to Live: Gender research on housing in Africa*, Nordiska Afrikainstitutet, Uppsala, 1996, p. 167.

67 Desai, Sonalde, and Kiersten Johnson, 'Women's Decisionmaking and Child Health', op. cit., p. 66.

68 Karl, Marilee, *Women and Empowerment: Participation and Decision-Making*, Zed Books, London, 1995, p. 19.

69 Agarwal, Bina, '"Bargaining" and Gender Relations', op. cit., p. 32.

CHAPTER 2 FIGURES

Figures 2.1, 2.2 and 2.3

Technical note: Methodology used to derive regional and country aggregates from the Demographic and Health Surveys

The data on household decision-making (used in Chapter 2) come from the Demographic and Health Surveys (DHS), which are nationally-representative household surveys with large sample sizes (usually between 5,000 and 30,000 households). DHS surveys provide data for a wide range of monitoring and impact evaluation indicators in the areas of population, health and nutrition.

Data for the following questions were extracted from the DHS STATcompiler <www.measuredhs .com> in June 2006. The data used covered women who were married or living with a partner, and their ability to participate in four key areas of household decision-making: own health care; large household purchases; daily household purchases; visits to family or relatives. There was one answer out of three possible responses for each question: decision made by wife alone; decision made jointly with husband; decision made by husband alone.

The countries included in the survey were (year of survey in parenthesis):

CEE/CIS: Armenia (2000), Turkmenistan (2000). **East Asia and Pacific:** Indonesia (2002-2003), Philippines (2003). **Latin America and Caribbean:** Bolivia (2003), Colombia (2005), Haiti (2000), Nicaragua (2001), Peru (2000). **Middle East and North Africa:** Egypt (2000), Jordan (2002), Morocco (2003-2004). **South Asia:** Bangladesh (2004), Nepal (2001). **Sub-Saharan Africa:** Benin (2001), Burkina Faso (2003), Cameroon (2004), Eritrea (2002), Ghana (2003), Kenya (2003), Madagascar (2003-2004), Malawi (2000), Mali (2001), Mozambique (2003), Nigeria (2003), Rwanda (2000), Uganda (2000-2001), United Republic of Tanzania (2004), Zambia (2001/2002), Zimbabwe (1999).

70 United Nations Children's Fund, *Role of Men in the Lives of Children*, op. cit., p. 9.

71 McNulty, Stephanie, 'Women's Organizations During and After War: From service delivery to policy advocacy', Research and Reference Services Project, United States Agency for International Development Center for Development Information and Evaluation, Washington, D.C., October 1998, p. 3.

CHAPTER 2 PANELS

Domestic violence against children

Information derived from:

Jaffe, P., and M. Sudermann, 'Child Witness of Women Abuse: Research and community responses' in Sandra M. Stith and Murray A. Straus, *Understanding Partner Violence: Prevalence, causes, consequences, and solutions*, Families in Focus Services, vol. II, Minneapolis, National Council on Family Relations, 1995.

Strauss, Murray A., Richard J. Gelles and Christine Smith, 'Physical Violence in American Families: Risk factors and adaptations to violence in 8,145 families', Transaction Publishers, New Brunswick, 1990.

United Nations, Report of the Independent Expert for the United Nations Study on Violence against Children, United Nations, New York, August 2006.

United Nations Children's Fund, 'Domestic Violence against Women and Girls' UNICEF Innocenti Research Centre, Florence, 2000, pp. 9-12

Wolfe, D.A., et al., 'Strategies to Address Violence in the Lives of High Risk Youth' in Peled, E., P.G. Jaffe and J.L. Edleson, eds., *Ending the Cycle of Violence: Community responses to children of battered women*, Sage Publications, New York, 1995

Grandmothers and HIV/AIDS

Information derived from:

HelpAge International, 'Age and Security: How social pensions can deliver effective aid to poor older people and their families', HelpAge International, London, 2004, pp. 7- 8.

United Nations Children's Fund, *Africa's Orphaned and Vulnerable Generations: Children affected by AIDS*, UNICEF, New York, 2006, pp. 10, 14-16, 27 and 29-31.

United Nations Children's Fund, *Africa's Orphaned Generations*, UNICEF, New York, 2003, pp. 15 and 17.

Mother Centres in Central and Eastern Europe and the Gambia

Information derived from:

Jaffe, P., and Sudermann, M., 'Child Witness of Women Abuse: Research and community responses', op. cit.

Mothers Centres in Central and Eastern Europe: Mother Centres International Network for Empowerment (MINE), and Laux, Andrea, and Rut Kolinska, 'Mother Centres International Network Empowerment', Case Study for Workshop and Networking Event 'Building Bridges with the Grassroots: Scaling up through knowledge sharing', World Urban Forum, Barcelona, 12-17 September 2004.

Information on *Mothers Clubs in the Gambia* provided by UNICEF West and Central Regional Office.

CHAPTER 3

1 Grown, Caren, Geeta Rao Gupta and Aslihan Kes, *Taking Action: Achieving gender equality and empowering women*, Earthscan, London/Virginia, for the UN Millennium Project Task Force on Education and Gender Equality, 2005, p. 77.

2 Ibid., p. 89.

3 UNICEF calculations based on data derived from United Nations Development Programme, *Human Development Report 2006: Beyond scarcity: Power, poverty and the global water crisis*, Oxford University Press for UNDP, New York, 2006, p. 379.

4 Machinea, José Luis, Alicia Bárcena and Arturo León, *The Millennium Development Goals: A Latin American and Caribbean perspective*, United Nations, Santiago, 2005, p. 128.

5 De Ferranti, David, *Inequality in Latin America and the Caribbean: Breaking with history?*, World Bank, Mexico, 2004, p. 19.

6 Unni, Jeemol, 'Gender and Informality in Labour Market in South Asia', in *Economic and Political Weekly*, vol. 36, no. 26, 30 June 2001, p. 2370.

7 United Nations Development Programme, *Human Development Report 2005: International cooperation at a crossroads: Aid, trade and security in an unequal world*, Oxford University Press for UNDP, New York, 2005, p. 315.

8 UNICEF calculations based on the World Values Survey database, accessed June 2006. The results are based on the respondents who agreed or strongly agreed that a "Husband and wife should both contribute to income." (Note on the methodology employed to calculate regional aggregates can be found on p. 88.

9 International Labour Office, *Global Employment Trends Brief, January 2006*, International Labour Organization, Geneva, 2006, p. 3.

10 United Nations Development Programme, *Human Development Report 2005*, op. cit., p. 314. The female economic activity rate is calculated on the basis of data on the economically active population and the total population.

11 Ibid. The gender parity activity rate is calculated as the female economic activity rate as a percentage of the male rate.

12 Son, Hyun H., and Nanak Kakwani, 'The Gender Pay Gap over Women's Working Lifetime', International Poverty Centre, United Nations Development Programme, June 2006, <www.undp-povertycentre.org/newsletters/ OnePager20.pdf>.

13 UNICEF calculations based on United Nations Development Programme, *Human Development Report 2005*, op. cit., table 25, pp. 299-302. Aggregates weighed and based on UNICEF regions.

14 International Labour Organization, 'National Report for Promoting the Linkages Between Women's Employment and the Reduction of Child Labour', ILO Area Office, Dar es Salaam, 1994, p. 6; and Baidya, Bal Gopal, Madhup Dhungana and Rojee Kattel, 'The Linkages Between Women's Employment, Family Welfare and Child Labour in Nepal', *GENPROM Working Paper No. 12*, International Labour Organization, Gender Promotion Programme, Geneva, 2002, p. 1.

15 Grown, Caren, Geeta Rao Gupta and Aslihan Kes, *Taking Action*, op. cit., p. 78.

16 Steinzor, Nadia, *Women's Property and Inheritance Rights: Improving lives in changing times*, Women in Development Technical Assistance Projects, Washington, D.C., March 2003, p. 6.

17 Grown, Caren, Geeta Rao Gupta and Aslihan Kes, *Taking Action*, op. cit., p. 78.

18 Ibid., p. 78.

19 Ibid.

20 Quisumbing, Agnes R., ed., *Household Decisions, Gender and Development: A synthesis of recent research*, Johns Hopkins University Press for International Food Policy Research Institute, Washington D.C., 2003, p. 118.

21 Alderman, H., et al., 'Gender Differentials in Farm Productivity: Implications for Household Efficiency and Agricultural Policy,' *FCND Discussion Paper No. 6*, Food Consumption and Nutrition Division, International Food Policy Research Institute, Washington, D.C., 1995, p. 22.

22 Quisumbing, Agnes R., 'What Have We learned from Research on Intra-household Allocation?', op. cit., p. 54.

23 Hallman, Kelly, David Lewis and Suraiya Begum, 'An Integrated Economic and Social Analysis to Assess the Impact of Vegetable and Fishpond Technologies on Poverty in Rural Bangladesh', Environment and Production Technology Division; Food Consumption and Nutrition Division, *EPTD Discussion Paper No. 112/FCND Discussion Paper 163*, International Food Policy Research Institute, October 2003, p .50; and International Food Policy Research Institute, 'Women: Still the key to food and nutrition security', IFPRI, Washington, D.C., 2005, p. 1.

24 Hallman, Kelly, David Lewis and Suraiya Begum, 'An Integrated Economic and Social Analysis to Assess the Impact of Vegetable and Fishpond Technologies on Poverty in Rural Bangladesh', op. cit., pp. 42-43.

25 United Nations Development Fund for Women, *Progress of the World's Women 2005: Women, work and poverty*, UNIFEM, New York, 2005, p. 9.

26 United Nations, *The World's Women 2005: Progress in statistics*, ST/ESA/STAT/SER.K/17, Department of Economic and Social Affairs, Statistics Division, United Nations, New York, 2006, p. 55.

27 Chen, M. et al., *Progress of the World's Women 2005: Women, work and poverty*, United Nations Development Fund for Women, New York, 2005, p. 39.

28 Ibid., pp. 63-64.

29 Ibid., pp. 27-29. Also Engle, Patrice L., 'Urban Women: Balancing work and childcare', Chapter 3 in *2020 Focus*, Number 3, Brief 08, International Food Policy Research Institute, Washington, D.C., August 2000.

30 Ibid., p. 33.

31 International Labour Organization, *Global Employment Trends for Women 2004*, ILO, Geneva, 2004, p. 9. The reference is based on the increasing ratio of employment to population ratio for women. This ratio indicates the capacity of economies to create employment opportunities for their population. Information on industrialized countries is derived from Eileen Appelbaum, et al., *Shared work, Valued Care: New norms for organizing market work and unpaid care work*, Economic Policy Institute, Washington, D.C., 2002, p. vii.

32 Gospel, Howard, 'Quality of Working Life: A review on changes in work organization, conditions of employment and work-life arrangements', *Conditions of Work and Employment Series No. 1*, International Labour Organization, Geneva, 2003, p. 17.

33 Heyman, Jody, 'Social Transformations and their Implications for the Global Demand for ECCE', *Policy Brief on Early Childhood No. 8*, United Nations Educational, Scientific and Cultural Organisation, Paris, November/December 2002, pp. 1-2.

34 Chen, M. et al., *Progress of the World's Women 2005*, op. cit., p. 29.

35 International Labour Office, *Breaking Through the Glass Ceiling: Women in management*, International Labour Organization, Geneva, 2004 update, p. 29.

36 Organisation for Economic Co-operation and Development, *OECD Employment Outlook 2001: Reconciling social and employment goals*, OECD, Paris, p. 132.

37 International Labour Office, *Breaking Through the Glass Ceiling*, op. cit., p. 29.

38 Ibid, p. 32.

39 Whiteford, Peter, 'Reconciling Work and Family Life: A comparative analysis of OECD countries', Organisation for Economic Co-operation and Development, Paris, 2005, p. 5.

40 Gospel, Howard, 'Quality of Working Life', op. cit., p.17.

41 Dodson, Lisa, Tiffany Manuel and Ellen Bravo, 'Keeping Jobs and Raising Families in Low-Income America: It just doesn't work' – A Report of the Across the Boundaries Project, The Radcliffe Public Policy Center and 9to5 National Association of Working Women, Cambridge, Massachusetts, 2002, p. 1.

42 Ibid.

43 Peisner-Feinberg, Ellen S. et al., 'The Children of the Cost, Quality, and Outcomes Study Go To School: Technical report', University of North Carolina at Chapel Hill, Frank Porter Graham Child Development Center, Chapel Hill, NC, 2000, p. 1; and Loeb, Susanna et al., 'Child Care in Poor Communities: Early learning effects of type, quality and stability', *Child development*, vol. 75, no. 1, 2004, pp. 47-65.

44 Dodson, Lisa, Tiffany Manuel and Ellen Bravo, 'Keeping Jobs and Raising Families in Low-Income America: It just doesn't work', op. cit., pp. 6-7; and Lindars, Helen, 'How Can Suitable, Affordable Child Care Be Provided For All Parents Who Need To Work', Equal Opportunities Commission submission to the Work and Pensions Select Committee Inquiry, Equal Opportunities Commission, Manchester, United Kingdom, February 2003, p. 2, 3-5.

45 Aubel, Judi, 'Grandmothers: A learning institution', United States Agency for International Development, Washington, D.C., August 2005, p. 81.

46 King, Elizabeth M., and Andrew D. Mason, 'Engendering Development 2001' – A World Bank Policy Research Report', World Bank, Washington, D.C., January 2001, pp. 24 and 170.

47 Appelbaum, Eileen, et al., *Shared Work, Valued Care*, op. cit., pp. 29-30.

48 Ministry of Social Affairs and Employment, The Netherlands, 'Work/family arrangements' and 'Childcare Act', <http://internationalezaken.szw.nl/index.cfm?fuseaction=dsp_rubriek&rubriek_id=13039>, accessed September 2006.

49 Gospel, Howard, 'Quality of Working Life', op. cit., p. 17.

50 Dodson, Lisa, Tiffany Manuel and Ellen Bravo, 'Keeping Jobs and Raising Families in Low-Income America', op. cit., p. 1.

51 International Organization for Migration, *World Migration 2005: Costs and Benefits of International Migration*, IOM, Geneva, 2005, p. 13.

52 Cortés, Rosalía, 'Remittances and Children's Rights: An overview of academic and policy literature', internal document, United Nations Children's Fund, New York, February 2006, p. 4.

53 Bryant, John, 'Children of International Migrants in Indonesia, Thailand, and the Philippines: A review of evidence and policies', *Innocenti Working Paper 2005-05*, UNICEF Innocenti Research Centre, Florence, April 2005, p. iii.

54 Ibid, p. 23.

55 Cortés, Rosalía, 'Remittances and Children's Rights', op. cit., p. 8.

56 United Nations Development Fund for Women, 'Claim and Celebrate Women Migrants' Human Rights through CEDAW – A UNIFEM Briefing Paper', UNIFEM, Geneva, 2005, p. 36.

57 Cortés, Rosalía, 'Remittances and Children's Rights', op. cit., p. 4.

58 Ibid.

59 Ibid, p. 14.

60 Scalabrini Migration Center, 'Filipino families in motion', in *Hearts Apart: Migration in the eyes of Filipino children*, Scalabrini Migration Center, Manila, 2003, p. 50, <http://www.smc.org.ph/heartsapart/pdfs/Hearts%20Apart.pdf>.

61 Cortes, Rosalia, 'Remittances and Children's Rights', op. cit., p. 4.

62 United Nations High Commissioner for Refugees, *Refugee Children: Guidelines on protection and care*, UNHCR, Geneva, 1994, p. 10.

63 United Nations High Commissioner for Refugees, 'Refugee Children', Global Consultations on International Protection, 4th Meeting, EC/GC/02/9, 25 April 2002.

64 United Nations Development Fund for Women, *Claim and Celebrate Women Migrants' Human Rights through CEDAW*, op. cit., p. 36.

65 Waldorf, Lee, 'Human Rights Protections Applicable to Women Migrant Workers', UNIFEM-CEDAW Panel on Addressing Women Migrant Workers' Concerns', United Nations

Development Fund for Women, New York, July 2003, p. 30.

[66] Bryant, John, 'Children of International Migrants in Indonesia, Thailand, and the Philippines', op. cit., p. 10.

[67] UNIFEM East and Southeast Asia Regional Office, *Empowering Women Migrant Workers in Asia*, Bangkok, United Nations Development Fund for Women, 2004, pp. 3-5.

[68] United Nations, Convention on the Elimination of All Forms of Discrimination against Women, <www.unhchr.ch/html/menu3/b/e1cedaw.htm>.

[69] United Nations, Commission on the Status of Women, Report on the forty-ninth session (28 February-11 and 22 March 2005), E/2005/27 and E/CN.6/2005/11, United Nations, New York, pp. 24-28.

[70] Ibid, pp. 27-28.

[71] Grown, Caren, Geeta Rao Gupta and Ashlihan Kes, *Taking Action*, op. cit., p. 48.

[72] Ibid.

[73] United Nations, Commission on the Status of Women, Report on the forty-ninth session, op. cit., pp. 24-27.

[74] United Nations Development Fund for Women, *Gender Budget Initiatives*, UNIFEM (New York), Commonwealth Secretariat (London), and International Development Research Centre (Ottawa), p. 1, <www.idrc.ca/gender-budgets/ev-66716-201-1-DO_TOPIC.html>.

CHAPTER 3 PANELS

Do girls risk missing out on school when women work?

Information derived from:

Assaad, Ragui, Deborah Levison and Nadia Zibani, 'The Effect of Child Work on School Enrollment in Egypt', Humphrey Institute of Public Affairs, University of Minnesota, Minneapolis, 2001 rev., p. 23.

Baidya, Bal Gopal, Madhup Dhungan and Rojee Kattel, 'The Linkages Between Women's Employment, Family Welfare and Child Labour in Nepal', *GENPROM Working Paper No. 12*, International Labour Office/International Labour Organization, Geneva, 2002, p. 1.

Ilhai, Nadeem, 'Children's Work and Schooling: Does gender matter? Evidence from Peru LSMS Panel Data', *World Bank Policy Research Working Paper No. 2745*, World Bank, Washington, D.C., 2001, p. 4.

International Labour Organization, 'National Report for Promoting the Linkages Between Women's Employment and the Reduction of Child Labour', Gender Promotion Programme, International Labour Organization Area Office, Dar es Salaam, 2001, p. 101.

Kamerman, Sheila B., 'Early Childhood Care and Education and Other Family Policies and Programs in South-East Asia', *Early Childhood and Family Policy Series, No.4*, United Nations Educational, Cultural and Scientific Organization, Paris, 2002, p. 23.

The impact of family-friendly workplaces in industrialized countries

Information derived from:

Appelbaum, Eileen et al., *Shared Work*, Valued Care, op. cit., pp. 28-29.

Datta Gupta, Nabanita, Nina Smith, and Mette Verner, 'Childcare and Parental Leave in the Nordic countries: A model to aspire to?', IZA, Institute for the Study of Labor, *IZA Discussion Paper No. 2014*, Bonn, March 2006, Introduction; and United Nations Population Fund, *The State of the World's Population*, UNFPA, New York, 2005, p. 15.

Dean, Hartley, 'Business versus Families: Whose side is New Labour on?', *Social Policy and Society*, vol. 1, no. 1, Cambridge University Press, 2002, pp. 7-8.

Gauthier, Anne H., ''Trends in Policies for Family-Friendly Societies', in Miroslav Macura, Alphonese L. MacDonald and Werner Haug, eds., *The New Demographic Regime: Population, challenges and policy responses*, United Nations, New York and Geneva, 2005, pp. 98 and 107.

Henry, Collen, Misha Werschkul and Manita C. Rao, 'Child Care Subsidies Promote Mothers' Employment and Children's Development', IWPR Publication # G714, Institute for Women's Policy Research, Washington, D.C., October 2003, p. 1.

Organisation for Economic Co-operation and Development, 'Babies and Bosses: Reconciling work and family life, Volume 1, Australia, Denmark and the Netherlands', OECD, Paris, 2002, pp. 182-184 and 191-193.

Organisation for Economic Co-operation and Development, 'Babies and Bosses: Reconciling work and family life, Volume 4, Canada, Finland, Sweden and the United Kingdom', OECD, Paris, 2002, p. 28.

Peus, Claudia, 'Work-Family Balance? The case of Germany', Working Paper WPC#0025, MIT Workplace Center, Sloan School of Management, Cambridge, Massachusetts, 2006.

Study of Work and Family Life commissioned by Novartis together with the Federation of Migros Cooperatives, the Raiffeisen Group, the Swiss Post Office and the Swiss Federal Department of Economic Affairs. ETH Zürich. Nestlé Switzerland and Victorinox also took part in the study.

Child labour: Are girls affected differently from boys?

Information derived from:

Various publication of the International Labour Organization, Geneva (years and page numbers cited only for ease of reference): *Child domestic labour in Southeast and East Asia: Emerging good practices to combat it*, 2006, p. 18. *Every Child Counts*, 2002, p. 25. *Promotion of Gender Equality in Action Against Child Labour and Trafficking: A practical guide for organizations*, May 2003, pp. 15 and 17. *Gender, Education and Child Labour in Egypt*, 2004, p. 9-10. *Gender, Education and Child Labour in Turkey*, 2004, p. 112-113. *Global Child Labour Data Review: A gender perspective*, 2004, pp. 7 and 157-158. *Helping Hands or Shackled Lives?*, 2004, pp. ii, 2, 20, 22 and 37.

United Nations Children's Fund, *Child Domestic Work*, UNICEF Innocenti Research Centre, Florence, 1999, p. 4.

CHAPTER 4

[1] UNICEF calculations based on data from the Inter-Parliamentary Union database, <www.ipu.org/wmn-e/world.htm>, accessed July 2006.

[2] Beaman, Lori, et al., 'Women Politicians, Gender Bias, and Policy-making in Rural India', background paper written for *The State of the World's Children 2007*, UNICEF, 2006, pp. 4 and 5.

[3] See, for example, Susan J. Carroll, ed., *The Impact of Women in Public Office*, Indiana University Press, Bloomington, Indiana, 2001.

[4] See, for example, Jones, Mark P., 'Legislator Gender and Legislator Policy Priorities in the Argentine Chamber of Deputies and the United States House of Representatives', *Policy Studies Journal*, vol. 5, no.4, 1997, p. 615. See also Mala Htun, 'Women in Political Power in Latin America', *International IDEA*, Women in Parliament, International Idea, Stockholm, 2002, p. 9.

[5] Jones, Mark P., 'Legislator Gender and Legislator Policy Priorities in the Argentine Chamber of Deputies and the United States House of Representatives', op. cit., p. 618.

[6] Ibid., p. 621.

[7] Schwindt-Bayer, Leslie, 'Female Legislators and the Promotion of Women, Children, and Family Policies in Latin America', background paper written for *The State of the World's Children 2007*, UNICEF, New York, 2006, pp. 15.

[8] Ibid., p. 14.

[9] Grey, Sandra, 'Women and Parliamentary Politics: Does Size Matter? Critical Mass and Women MPs in the New Zealand House of Representatives', Political Science Program, Research School of Social Sciences, Australian National University, paper for the 51st Political Studies Association Conference, Manchester, UK, 10-12 April 2001, pp. 5-6.

[10] Childs, Sarah, Joni Lovenduski and Rosie Campbell, *Women at the Top 2005: Changing numbers, changing politics?*, Hansard Society, London, 2005, p. 56.

[11] Karam, Azza, and Joni Lovenduski, 'Women in Parliament: Making a difference', Chapter 5 in Julie Ballington and Azza Karam, eds., *Women in Parliament: Beyond numbers, A Revised Edition*, International Institute for Democracy and Electoral Assistance, Stockholm, 2005, p. 194. For the inclusion of Rwanda, see Elizabeth Powley, 'Rwanda: The impact of women legislators on policy outcomes affecting children and families,' background paper written for *The State of the World's Children 2007*, UNICEF, New York, 2006, p. 5.

[12] Shevchenko, Iulia, 'Who Cares about Women's Problems? Female legislators in the 1995 and 1999 Russian State Dumas', *Europe-Asia Studies*, vol. 54, no. 8, 1 December 2002, p. 1208.

13 Powley, Elizabeth, 'Rwanda: The Impact of Women Legislators on Policy Outcomes Affecting Children and Families', op. cit., pp. 10-11 and 15.

14 Vetten, Lisa, 'Addressing Domestic Violence in South Africa: Reflections on strategy and practice', expert paper prepared for the Expert Group Meeting on 'Violence against Women: Good practices in combating and eliminating violence against women', United Nations Division for the Advancement of Women, Vienna, 2005, pp. 3-4.

15 Stéphane Oertel, Governance Profile of Namibia: Measuring and monitoring progress towards good governance in Africa, United Nations Economic Commission for Africa, Addis Ababa, September 2004, p. 4. Government of Namibia, 'Government Gazette of the Republic of Namibia, Government Notice, No. 126, Promulgation of Act of Parliament', Windhoek, 24 June 2003.

16 Schwindt-Bayer, Leslie, 'Female Legislators and the Promotion of Women, Children, and Family Policies in Latin America', op. cit., p. 10.

17 'Gender-Sensitizing Commonwealth Parliaments: The report of a Commonwealth Parliamentary Association study group', Commonwealth Parliamentary Association Secretariat, London, 2001, <www.cpahq.org/uploadstore/docs/gendersensitizingcwparliaments.pdf>, accessed September 2006.

18 Wangnerud, Lena, 'Case Study: Sweden: A step-wise development' in Women in Parliament, op. cit., p. 246

19 Karam, Azza, and Joni Lovenduski, 'Women in Parliament: Making a difference', op. cit., p. 198.

20 Data drawn from the Inter-Parliamentary Union database, 'Women in National Parliaments', <www.ipu.org/wmn-e/classif.htm>, accessed July 2006.

21 Data drawn from the Inter-Parliamentary Union poster 'Women in Politics, 2005', <www.ipu.org/pdf/publications/wmnmap05_en.pdf>, accessed July 2006.

22 Derived from websites of national governments and from Inter-Parliamentary Union, 'Women in Politics: 60 years in retrospect', IPU, Geneva, February 2006, Data Sheet No. 4. Note: The countries cited as examples of women Heads of State and Government in 2006 includes the Government of the Netherlands Antilles, which is an autonomous country within the Netherlands. Queens and Governor-Generals are not included in the figure cited.

23 Derived from websites of national governments and from the Inter-Parliamentary Union poster 'Women in Politics, 2005', op. cit.

24 Budlender, Debbie, and Guy Hewittt, Gender Budgets Make More Cents: Country studies and good practice, The Commonwealth Secretariat, London, August 2002, p. 11.

25 Weldon, S. Laurel, Protest, Policy, and the Problem of Violence Against Women: A cross-national comparison, University of Pittsburgh Press, Pittsburgh, 2002, pp. 19, 23, 88 and 103.

26 Matland, Richard E., 'Enhancing Women's Political Participation: Legislative recruitment and electoral systems', in Women in Parliament: Beyond numbers, A Revised Edition, Chapter 3, International Institute for Democracy and Electoral Assistance, Stockholm, 2005, pp. 96.

27 Bratton, Kathleen A., and Leonard P. Ray, 'Descriptive Representation, Policy Outcomes, and Municipal Day-Care Coverage in Norway', American Journal of Political Science, vol. 46, no. 2, April 2002, p. 435.

28 Davis, Matthew M., and Amy M. Upston, 'State Legislator Gender and Other Characteristics Associated With Sponsorship of Child Health Bills', Ambulatory Pediatrics, vol. 4, no. 4, July-August 2004, pp. 295-302.

29 Caiazza, Amy, 'Does Women's Representation in Elected Office Lead to Women-Friendly Policy?, Institute for Women's Policy Research, Washington, D.C., May 2002, pp. 2, 4.

30 Chattopadhyay, Raghabendra, and Esther Duflo, 'Women as Policy Makers: Evidence from a randomized policy experiment in India', Econometrica, vol. 72, no. 5, September 2004, pp. 1409-1443.

31 Beaman, Lori, et al., 'Women Politicians, Gender Bias, and Policy-making in Rural India', op. cit., pp. 11, 15 and 16.

32 Mbatha, Likhapha, 'Democratising Local Government: Problems and opportunities in the advancement of gender equality in South Africa', in Anne Marie Goetz and Shireen Hassim, eds., No Shortcuts to Power: African women in politics and policy making, Chapter 7, Zed Books, London and New York, 2003, pp. 196 and 201.

33 Drage, Jean, 'Women in Local Government in Asia and the Pacific: A comparative analysis of thirteen countries', (based on country reports prepared for the United Nations Economic and Social Commission for Asia and the Pacific, and LOGOTRI (Network of Local Government Training and Research Institutes in Asia and the Pacific) prior to the Asia-Pacific Summit of Women Mayors and Councilors, Thailand, 19-22 June 2001), Victoria University of Wellington, New Zealand, 2001, p. 22.

34 Ibid.

35 United Cities and Local Governments, Statistics, World, <www.cities-localgovernments.org/uclg/index.asp?pag=wldmstatistics.asp&type=&L=EN&pon=1>.

36 Chattopadhyay, Raghabendra, and Esther Duflo, 'Women as Policy Makers', op. cit, p. 1427.

37 International Crisis Group, 'Beyond Victimhood: Women's Peacebuilding in Sudan, Congo and Uganda', Africa Report No. 112, International Crisis Group, 28 June 2006, p. i.

38 Chinkin, Christine, Peace Agreements as a Means for Promoting Gender Equality and Ensuring the Participation of Women, EGM/PEACE/2003/BP.1, Division for the Advancement of Women, United Nations, New York, 31 October 2003, p. 1.

39 Ibid., p. 2.

40 Francesc, Maria Cañadas, et al., 'Alert 2005: Report on conflicts, human rights and peace-building', School for Peace Culture , Bellaterra, Spain, January 2005, p. 124.

41 Interview with Donald Steinberg, Vice President for Multilateral Affairs, International Crisis Group, and former United States Ambassador to Angola. Steinberg and The State of the World's Children 2007 research and editorial team discussed the peace process in Angola on 12 June 2006.

42 Anderlini, Sanam Naraghi, 'Women at the Peace Table: Making a difference', United Nations Development Fund for Women, New York, 2000, p. 17.

43 Rhen, Elisabeth, and Ellen Johnson Sirleaf, Women, War and Peace: The Independent Experts' assessment on the impact of armed conflict on women and women's role in peace-building, United Nations Development Fund for Women, New York, 2002, p. 79.

For a more detailed discussion of women's role in the peace process in Northern Ireland, see Fionnuala Ni Aoláin, 'Peace Agreements as Means for Promoting Gender Equality and Ensuring the Participation of Women', Northern Ireland Case Study, EGM/PEACE/2003/EP.4, written for United Nations Division for the Advancement of Women, Expert Group Meeting, Ottawa, Canada, November 2003.

44 Sultan, Masuda, 'From Rhetoric to Reality: Afghan women on the agenda for peace', Women Waging Peace Policy Commission, Hunt Alternatives Fund, Cambridge, Massachusetts, February 2005, pp. 6-7.

45 Conaway, Camille Pampell, and Kelly Fish, 'Children's Security', Inclusive Security, Sustainable Peace: A toolkit for advocacy and action, International Alert (London) and Women Waging Peace (Cambridge, Massachusetts and Washington, D.C.), 2004, p. 59.

46 Quintos-Deles, Teresita, 'Corridors of Peace in the Corridors of Power: Bridging spaces for women in governance for peace', presented at the Sixth Asia Pacific Congress of Women in Politics and Decision-Making, Makati City, Philippines, 10-12 February 2006, p. 13.

47 Mazurana, Dyan, and Khristopher Carlson, 'From Combat to Community: Women and girls of Sierra Leone', Women Waging Peace, Cambridge, Massachusetts and Washington, D.C., January 2004, p. 16.

48 Anderlini, Sanam Naraghi, 'Women at the Peace Table', op. cit., p. 21.

49 Ibid., p. 20.

50 Rhen, Elisabeth, and Ellen Johnson Sirleaf, Women, War and Peace, op. cit., p. 78.

51 WomenWarPeace.org, <www.womenwarpeace.org/sri_lanka/sri_lanka.htm>, accessed October 2006.

52 Jain, Devaki, Women, Development and the UN: A sixty-year quest for equality and justice, United Nations Intellectual History Project, Indiana University Press, Bloomington, Indiana, 2005, p. 71.

53 Camille Conaway and Anne-Marie Goetz, 'Beyond Numbers: Supporting women's political participation and promoting gender equality in post-

conflict governance in Africa, A review of the role of the United Nations Development Fund for Women', UNIFEM, New York, January 2006, p. 6.

[54] Pippa Norris and Donald Ingelhart, 'Cultural Barriers to Women's Leadership: A worldwide comparison', written for Special Session 16 'Social Cleavages and Elections', International Political Science Association World Congress, Quebec City, Canada, 3 August 2000, p. 8.

[55] Powley, Elizabeth, 'Rwanda: The impact of women legislators on policy outcomes affecting children and families', op. cit., p. 8.

[56] Jayal, Niraja Gopal, 'From Representation to Participation: Women in local government', EGM/EPWD/2005/EP.3, written for the Expert Group Meeting on Equal Participation of Women and Men in Decision-Making Processes, with Particular Emphasis on Political Participation and Leadership, United Nations, Addis Ababa, Ethiopia, 24-27 October 2005, p. 8.

[57] Drage, Jean, 'Women in Local Government in Asia and the Pacific, op. cit, p. 44.

[58] United Cities and Local Governments, Statistics, World, op. cit.

CHAPTER 4 PANELS

Women and politics: Realities and myths

Information derived from:

Beaman, Lori, et al., 'Women Politicans, Gender Bias and Policy-making in Rural India, op. cit., pp. 5 and 16.

Goetz, Anne-Marie Goetz, 'Political Cleaners: How women are the new anti-corruption force. Does the evidence wash?', paper prepared for the international workshop 'Feminist Fables and Gender Myths: Repositioning gender in development policy and practice', 2-4 July 2003, Institute of Development Studies, Sussex, 2003, p. 4.

Goetz, Anne-Marie, "Women's political effectiveness: A conceptual framework," in Anne-Marie Goetz and Shireen Hassim, eds., *No Shortcuts to Power African Women in politics and policy making*, Zed Books, London and New York, 2003, p. 36.

Human Rights Watch, 'Between Hope and Fear: Intimidation and attacks against women in public life in Afghanistan', Human Rights Watch Briefing Paper, October 2004, p. 29; Inter-Parliamentary Union. 'Politics: Women's insight', IPU Survey, Geneva, 2000, pp. 1, 7, 30 and 31.

Inter-Parliamentary Union, 'Women in Politics', <www.IPU.org/wmne-e/suffrage.htm>, accessed July 2006.

Jones, Mark P., 'Legislator Gender and Legislator Policy Priorities in the Argentine Chamber of Deputies and the United States House of Representatives', *Policy Studies Journal*, vol. 5, no. 4, 1997, pp. 613-629.

Lawless, Jennifer L. and Richard L. Fox, *It Takes a Candidate: Why women don't run for office*, Cambridge University Press, New York, 2005, pp. 84-85.

Lawless, Jennifer L. and Richard L. Fox, 'Why Don't Women Run for Office?', Brown Policy Report, Taubman Center for Public Policy, Brown University, Providence, Rhode Island, January 2004, pp. 1-7.

Poll conducted by Bangkok University and United Nations Development Programme, 'Women's Right to a Political Voice in Thailand', UNDP, New York, 2006, p. 18.

Rheingold, Beth, 'Concepts of Representation among Female and Male State Legislators' *Legislative Studies Quarterly*, vol. 17, no. 4, November 1992, pp. 509-537; and Galligan, Yvonne, 'Public Attitudes towards Women's Political Participation in Northern Ireland', Economic and Social Research Council Research Report, 2004.

World Values Survey, <www.worldvaluessurvey.org>, accessed July 2006.

Women's groups: A force for political change

Information derived from:

Afghan Women's Network, 'Afghan Parliamentary Elections: Report of Paghman Province' and 'Women's Participation in the Democratic Processes in Iraq and Afghanistan: Achievements and challenges', Position Paper, Independent Women's Forum, Washington, D.C., June 2006.

Powley, Elizabeth, 'Strengthening Governance: The role of women in Rwanda's transition,' The Initiative for Inclusive Security, Hunt Alternatives Fund, Women Waging Peace, Washington, D.C., 2003.

Submission to the National Inquiry into Children in Immigration Detention from the University of New South Wales Centre for Refugee Research and the Australian National Committee on Refugee Women, Human Rights and Equal Opportunity Commission, Government of Australia.

United Nations Children's Fund, 'National Situational Analysis of Children and Women', UNICEF Mozambique, 2006.

United Nations Development Fund for Women, *Progress of Arab Women*, UNIFEM Arab Regional States Office, Amman, p. 62.

United Nations Development Fund for Women, 'Tajikistan: Women demand law to criminalize domestic violence', *Voices from the Field*, UNIFEM, New York, November 2005, <www.unifem.org/gender_issues/voices_from_the_field/story.php?StoryID=366>.

Women and the Darfur Peace Agreement

Information derived from:

African Union, Report of the Chairperson of the Commission on the Situation in Darfur (the Sudan), African Union Peace and Security Council 45th meeting, Addis Ababa, 12 January 2006, p. 9.

Darfur Peace Agreement, signed at Abuja, Nigeria, 5 May 2006.

International Crisis Group, *Beyond Victimhood: Women's peacebuilding in Sudan, Congo and Uganda*, ICG, Washington, D.C., pp. 6 and 7.

'Women's Priorities in the Peace Process and Reconstruction in Darfur', 7th round of the Inter-Sudanese peace talks on the conflict in Darfur, Abuja (Nigeria), 30 December 2005, <www.peacewomen.org/resources/Sudan/Womens_Priorities.doc>.

Women as mediators and peacekeepers

Information derived from:

For a discussion of children's vulnerability to exploitation and abuse during delivery of assistance

in Liberia, see Save the Children, 'From Camp to Community: Liberia study on exploitation of children', Save the Children, Monrovia, May 2006, p. 11. Also see United Nations, Special Measures for Protection from Sexual Exploitation and Sexual Abuse, Report of the Secretary General, A/59/782, United Nations, New York, 15 April 2005.

Potter, Antonia, 'We the Women: Why conflict mediation is not just a job for men', *Opinion*, Center for Humanitarian Dialogue, Geneva, 2005.

United Nations Department of Peacekeeping Operations, Policy Dialogue to Review Strategies for Enhancing Gender Balance among Uniformed Personnel in Peacekeeping Missions, Final Report, United Nations, New York, 28-29 March 2006.

United Nations, A Comprehensive Strategy to Eliminate Further Sexual Exploitation and Abuse in United Nations Peacekeeping Operations, A/59/710, United Nations, New York, 24 March 2005, pp. 18-19.

CHAPTER 5

[1] In 1945, 3 per cent of members of Parliament in single or lower houses were women (Inter-Parliamentary Union, 'Women in Parliaments 1945-1995', *Reports and documents No. 23*, IPU, Geneva, 1995, p. 28). In 2006, 16.8 per cent of members of Parliament in single or lower houses were women ('Women in National Parliaments', <www.ipu.org/wmn-e/world.htm>, accessed August 2006).

[2] United Nations Children's Fund, *Progress for Children: A report card on gender parity and primary education, Number 2*, UNICEF, April 2005, p. 2.

[3] See, for example, Population Council and International Center for Research on Women, 'Involving Young Men in HIV Prevention Programs: Operations research on gender-based approaches in Brazil, Tanzania, and India', *Horizons Report*, HIV/AIDS Operations Research, Population Council, Washington, D.C., December 2004.

[4] World Bank, 'Education and Development', Education Advisory Service, World Bank, Washington, D.C., <http://siteresources.worldbank.org/EDUCATION/Resources/278200-1099079877269/547664-1099080118171/EducationBrochure.pdf>, accessed September 2006.

[5] Ibid.

[6] Ibid.

7 World Bank, 'Engendering Change in the Classroom', 11 November 2004, <http://web.worldbank.org/WBSITE/EXTERNAL/TOPICS/EXTEDUCATION/0,,contentMDK:20279910~menuPK:617572~pagePK:148956~piPK:216618~theSitePK:282386,00.html>, accessed 4 October 2006.

8 United Nations Children's Fund and World Bank, 'Building on what we know and defining sustained support', School Fee Abolition Initiative Workshop, organized by UNICEF and the World Bank, Nairobi, 5-7 April 2006, p. 3.

9 Ibid.

10 United Nations Children's Fund, *The State of the World's Children 2004: Girls' education and development*, UNICEF, New York, 2003, pp. 23-24.

11 United Nations Children's Fund and World Bank, 'Building on what we know and defining sustained support', op. cit., p. 3.

12 United Nations Children's Fund, *The State of the World's Children 2004*, op. cit., p. 23.

13 World Bank, 'Engendering Change in the Classroom', op. cit.

14 Ibid.

15 Ibid.

16 United Nations Millennium Project, *Investing in Development: A practical plan to achieve the Millennium Development Goals*, Earthscan, London/Sterling, Virginia., 2005, pp. 239-256.

17 Vandemoortele, Jan, and Rathin Roy, 'Making Sense of MDG Costing', Bureau for Development Policy, New York, August 2004, p. 3.

18 Grown, Caren, et al., 'The Financial Requirements of Achieving Gender Equality and Women's Empowerment', *The Levy Economics Institute of Bard College Working Paper No. 467*, August 2006, p. 2.

19 Figures derived from Ibid., p. 17.

20 Ibid., p. 3.

21 Grown, Caren, Geeta Rao Gupta and Aslihan Kes, *Taking Action: Achieving gender equality and empowering women*, UN Millennium Project, Earthscan, London/Sterling, Virginia, 2005, p. 29.

22 Grown, Caren, et al., 'The Financial Requirements of Achieving Gender Equality and Women's Empowerment', op. cit., p. 17.

23 Ibid., p. 21.

24 International Helsinki Federation for *Human Rights, Human Rights in the OSCE Region: Europe, Central Asia and North America, Report 2006 (Events of 2005)*, IHF, Vienna, 2006, p. 429.

25 Intergovernmental Authority on Development, 'Declaration of the 4th Regular Meeting of IGAD Ministers in Charge of Gender/Women Affairs', Nairobi, 21-22 February 2006, <www.igad.org/gender/nairobi_gender_decl.htm>, accessed 4 October 2006.

26 African Union, 'Symposium on the African Union's Protocol on the Rights of Women in Africa', keynote address by H.E. Mrs. Julia Dolly Joiner, Commissioner for Political Affairs,

Commission of the African Union, Khartoum, 21 January 2006, <www.oxfam.org.uk/what_we_do/issues/panafrica/>, accessed 4 October 2006.

27 United Nations Development Fund for Women, *Not a Minute More: Ending violence against women*, UNIFEM, New York, pp. 8-15

28 United Nations, Report of the independent expert for the United Nations study on violence against children, Provisional version, UN A/61/150 and Corr. 1, United Nations, New York, 23 August 2005.

29 United Nations Development Fund for Women, *Not a minute more*, op. cit., p. 39.

30 Ibid., p. 40.

31 United Nations Office for the Coordination of Humanitarian Affairs/Integrated Regional Information Networks, 'Sexual Violence in Times of War', Chapter 13 in *Broken Bodies, Broken Dreams: Violence against women exposed*, OCHA/IRIN, New York, 2005, pp. 179-205.

32 United Nations, General Assembly, 58th session, Special Measures for Protection from Sexual Exploitation and Sexual Abuse, Report of the Secretary-General (A/58/777), United Nations, New York, 23 April 2004, para. 3.

33 United Nations, Security Council Resolution 1325, para. 10, adopted by the Security Council at its 4213th Meeting, United Nations, New York, 31 October 2000.

34 United Nations Office for the Coordination of Humanitarian Affairs/Integrated Regional Information Networks, 'Sexual Violence in Times of War', op. cit., p. 197.

35 King, Elizabeth M., and Andrew D. Mason, 'Engendering Development Through Gender Equality in Rights, Resources, and Voice', World Bank and Oxford University Press, Washington, D.C., January 2001, p. 120.

36 Ibid., pp. 117-122.

37 Inter-Parliamentary Union, 'Women's Suffrage', <www.ipu.org/wmn-e/suffrage.htm>, accessed September 2006.

38 Inter-Parliamentary Union database, 'Women in National Parliaments', <www.ipu.org/wmn-e/world.htm>, accessed September 2006.

39 Ibid.

40 Inter-Parliamentary Union, 'The Participation of Women and Men in Decision-Making: The parliamentary dimension', Data Sheet No. 6 in *Women in Politics: 60 years in retrospect*, IPU, Geneva, 2006.

41 Inter-Parliamentary Union, 'Women in Parliaments: World classification', <www.ipu.org/wmn-e/classif.htm>; and International Institute for Democracy and Electoral Assistance and Stockholm University, 'Global Database of Quotas for Women', <www.quotaproject.org/country.cfm?SortOrder=LastLowerPercentage%20DESC>, accessed 28 September 2006.

42 United Nations Development Fund for Women, 'On the Agenda: Women's essential role in peace-building', UNIFEM 2005 World Summit, 2005, UNIFEM, New York, p. 1.

43 Gobodo-Madikizela, Pumla, 'Women's Contribution to South Africa's Truth and Reconciliation Commission', Women Waging Peace Policy Commission, Cambridge, Massachusetts and Washington, D.C., February 2005, p. 9.

44 Dahlerup, Drude, 'Quotas are Changing the History of Women', paper presented at the IDEA/EISA/SADC Parliamentary Forum Conference, Pretoria, November 2003.

45 McNulty, Stephanie, 'Women's Organizations During and After War: From service delivery to policy advocacy', Research and Reference Services Project, United States Agency for International Development Center for Development Information and Evaluation, Washington, D.C., 2 October 1998, p. 3.

46 Maluccio, John A., Lawrence Haddad and Julian May, 'Social capital and gender in South Africa, 1993-98', in Agnes R. Quisumbing, ed., *Household Decisions, Gender, and Development: A synthesis of recent research*, International Food Policy Research Institute, Washington, D.C., 2003, p. 147.

47 Cowan, Carolyn Pape, et al., 'Encouraging Strong Relationships Between Fathers and Children', *Working Strategies*, vol. 8, no. 4, Summer 2005, p. 2.

48 Engle, Patrice, Tom Beardshaw and Craig Loftin, 'Local and International Policies and Programmes', in Linda Richter and Robert Morrell, eds., *Baba: Men and fatherhood in South Africa*, Human Sciences Research Council, Cape Town, 2006, p. 294.

49 Ibid.

50 United Nations Children's Fund, *Role of Men in the Lives of Children: A study of how improving knowledge about men in families helps strengthen programming for children and women*, UNICEF, New York, 1997, p. 9.

51 Fathers Direct, 'Sweden may be leading Europe in developing father-friendly policies and practices', *FatherWorld*, vol. 3, no. 2, Fathers Direct, London, <www.fathersdirect.com/download.php?pID=2655.3>, accessed 24 April 2006; and Holter, Oystein Gullvag, *Can Men Do It? Men and Gender Equality: The Nordic experience*, Nordic Council of Ministers, Copenhagen, 2003, p. 126 cited in R.W. Connell, 'The Role of Men and Boys in Achieving Gender Equality', paper prepared for UN Division for the Advancement of Women, ILO, UNAIDS, UNDP Expert Groups Meeting (21-24 October 2003, Brasilia), 7 October 2003, p. 8.

52 Tonkin, Bernard, 'Men Reinventing Themselves: Recovery from hegemonic masculinity', *Working Paper No. 4*, UN International Research and Training Institute for the Advancement of Women, Santo Domingo, 2001, p. 5 and 18, <www.un-instraw.org/en/docs/mensroles/Tonkin.pdf>, accessed 4 October 2006.

53 United Nations, *The World's Women 2005: Progress in statistics*, United Nations Division of Economic and Social Affairs, New York, 2006, p. 26.

54 Ibid., p. 71.

55 Ibid., p. 44.

56 Ibid., p. 64.

57 Ibid., p. 55.

58 Ibid.

59 Ibid., p. 57.

60 Inter-Parliamentary Union database, <www.ipu.org/wmn-e/classif.htm>.

61 United Cities and Local Government statistics, <www.cities-localgovernments.org/uclg/index.asp?pag=wldmstatistics.asp&type=&L=EN&pon=1>.

CHAPTER 5 PANELS

Partnerships for girls' education

Information derived from:

Campaign for Female Education, <www.camfed.org>, accessed September 2006.

Forum for African Women Educationalists, <www.fawe.org/content/aboutfawe.html>, accessed September 2006.

Forum for African Women Educationalists, *The ABC of Gender Responsive Education Policies: Guidelines for developing Education for All policies*, FAWE, Nairobi, 2002.

Global Campaign for Education, <www.campaign foreducation.org>, accessed September 2006

Oxfam, *Partnerships for Girls' Education*, Oxfam, Oxford, 2005, pp. 23-38, 49-65 and 131-143.

Swainson, Nicola, and Global Campaign for Education, *A Fair Chance: Attaining gender equality in basic education by 2005*, Global Campaign for Education, Johannesburg, April 2003, pp. 43-49.

United Nations Girls' Education Initiative, <www.ungei.org>, accessed September 2006.

Monitoring government's commitments to women's empowerment through gender-responsive budgets

Information derived from:

Budlender, Debbie, and Guy Hewit, eds., *Gender Budgets Make More Cents: Country studies and good practice*, Commonwealth Secretariat, London, pp. 13, 23-42, 84-97 and 117-132.

Kingdom of Morocco, Ministry of Finance and Privatization, Direction of Studies and Financial Preview, 'Gender Report', translated by Dr. Ibrahim Moussabbir, 2006, <www.idrc.ca/gender-budgets/ev-104427-201-1-DO_TOPIC.html>.

Leadbetter, Helen, 'Gender Budgeting', in *Spectrum: Policy and technical perspective for CIPFA members and students*, Issue Number 4, The Charted Institute of Public Finance and Accountancy, London, March 2004, pp. 3-4.

United Nations Development Fund for Women, *Gender Budget Initiatives*, UNIFEM (New York), Commonwealth Secretariat (London), and International Development Research Centre (Ottawa), p. 1, <www.idrc.ca/gender-budgets/ev-66716-201-1-DO_TOPIC.html>; and International

Development Research Centre, 'Moroccan National Budget includes Gender Report', <www.idrc.ca/gender-budgets/ev-91685-201-1-DO_TOPIC.html>.

Partnering to promote child rights and gender equality in political agendas

Information derived from:

Inter-Parliamentary Union and United Nations Children's Fund, *Child Protection: A handbook for parliamentarians*, IPU, Geneva, 2004.

Inter-Parliamentary Union and United Nations Children's Fund, *Combating Child Trafficking: A handbook for parliamentarians*, IPU/UNICEF, Geneva and New York, March 2005.

Quotas: One size does not fit all

Information derived from:

Dahlerup, Drude, 'Increasing Women's Political Representation: New trends in gender quotas', in Julie Ballington and Azza Karam, eds., *Women in Parliament: Beyond the numbers, A Revised Edition*, International Institute for Democracy and Electoral Assistance, Stockholm, 2005, pp. 141-143.

Dahlerup, Drude, ed., *Women, Quotas and Politics*, Routledge Research in Comparative Politics Series, Routledge, London/New York, 2006, Introduction.

Women's participation in community initiatives around the world

Information derived from:

Amhed, Akhter U., and Carlo del Ninno, 'Food for Education in Bangladesh', in Agnes Quisumbing, ed., *Household Decisions, Gender and Development: A synthesis of recent research*, International Food Policy Research Institute, Washington D.C., pp. 202-203.

Amhed, Akhter U., 'Comparing Food and Cash for Schooling in Bangladesh', in *Linking Research and Action: Strengthening food assistance and food policy research*, Policy Brief of International Food Policy Research Institute and World Food Programme, Washington, D.C., and Rome, 2005.

Asian Development Bank, 'Gender Activities', Workshop on Violence against Women for Grassroots Women's Groups, Centre for Women's Resource Development, <http://209.225.62.100/gender/working/ino002.asp>. Asian Development Bank, 'Ending Violence Against Women', *ADB Review*, February 2004, p. 36.

Hallman, Kelly, et al., 'Childcare, Mothers' Work, and Earnings: Findings from the urban slums of Guatemala City', Policy Research Division Woking Papers No. 165, Population Council, New York, 2002, pp. 25-26.

Information on the Sunday school programme is derived from UNICEF Uzbekistan.

Smith, Lisa C., et al., 'The Importance of Women's Status for Child Nutrition in Developing Countries', Research Report 131, International Food Policy Research Institute, Washington, D.C., 2003, p. 135.

World Bank, 'Social Safety Nets in Banglandesh: An assessment', *Bangladesh Development Series Paper No. 9*, World Bank Office, Dhaka, January 2006, pp. 14, 21-22.

Program H: Challenging gender stereotypes and changing attitudes in Brazil and other countries

Information derived from:

Population Council, 'Promoting Healthy Relationships and HIV/STI Prevention for Young Men: Positive findings from an intervention study in Brazil, *Horizons Research Update*, Population Council/Horizons, Washington, D.C., April 2004.

Population Council, 'Reducing HIV Risk Behaviors among Key Populations by Increasing Community Involvement and Building Social Capital: Baseline findings from Andhra Pradesh, India', *Horizons Research Update*, Population Council/Horizons, New Delhi, April 2006.

Partnering to provide improved estimates of maternal mortality

Information derived from:

AbouZahr, C., and Tessa Wardlaw, 'Maternal Mortality at the End of the Decade: Sign of progress?', *Bulletin of the World Health Organization*, vol. 79, no. 6, Geneva, June 2001, pp. 561-573.

World Health Organization, United Nations Children's Fund and United Nations Population Fund, *Maternal Mortality in 2000: Estimates developed by WHO, UNICEF and UNFPA*, WHO, Geneva, 2004, pp. 1-10.

Research commissioned for *The State of the World's Children 2007*

Background papers

Lori Beaman and Rohini Pande, Yale University; Esther Duflo, Jameel Poverty Action Lab, Massachusetts Institute of Technology; and Petia Topalova, International Monetary Fund, 'Women Politicians, Gender Bias, and Policy-making in Rural India', 2006.

Sylvia Chant, London School of Economics, 'Poverty Begins at Home? Questioning some (mis)conceptions about children, poverty and privation in female-headed households', 2006.

Elizabeth Powley, Women Waging Peace, 'Rwanda: The impact of women legislators on policy outcomes affecting children and families', 2006.

Leslie Schwindt-Bayer, University of Mississippi, 'Female Legislators and the Promotion of Women, Children, and Family Policies in Latin America', 2006.

STATISTICAL TABLES

Economic and social statistics on the countries and territories of the world, with particular reference to children's well-being.

STATISTICAL TABLES

Economic and social statistics on the countries and territories of the world, with particular reference to children's well-being.

General note on the data

The data presented in the following statistical tables are accompanied by definitions, sources and explanations of symbols. Data from the responsible United Nations organization have been used wherever possible. Where such internationally standardized estimates do not exist, the tables draw on other sources, particularly data received from the appropriate UNICEF field office. Wherever possible, only comprehensive or representative national data have been used. More detailed information on methodology and sources of the data presented are available at <www.childinfo.org>.

Data quality is likely to be adversely affected for countries that have recently suffered from human-caused or natural disasters. This is particularly true where basic country infrastructure has been fragmented or major population movements have occurred.

Several of the indicators, such as the data for life expectancy, total fertility rates and crude birth and death rates, are part of the regular work on estimates and projections undertaken by the United Nations Population Division. These and other internationally produced estimates are revised periodically, which explains why some data will differ from earlier UNICEF publications.

Mortality estimates

Each year, UNICEF includes in *The State of the World's Children* mortality estimates, such as the infant mortality rate, under-five mortality rate, under-five deaths and, beginning this year, neonatal mortality rate, for at least two reference years. These figures represent the best estimates available at the time the report is produced and are based on the work of the Interagency Group for Mortality Estimation, which includes UNICEF, the World Health Organization, the World Bank and the UN Population Division. This Group updates these estimates every year, undertaking a detailed review of all newly available data points. At times, this review will result in adjustments to previously reported estimates. Therefore, estimates published in consecutive editions of *The State of the World's Children* may not be comparable and should not be used for analyzing mortality trends over time. It is important to note that comparable under-five mortality estimates for the period 1970 to present are available for all countries at <www.childinfo.org>, and that this time series is based on the most recent estimates produced by the Interagency Group for Mortality Estimation.

Revisions

Several statistical tables have been revised this year.

Table 1. Basic Indicators: A new indicator – neonatal mortality rate – has been added to the Basic Indicators table. Estimates for this indicator are presented for the year 2000.

Table 3. Health: There are three major changes in this year's child health indicators.

• *Improved drinking water and adequate sanitation:* Data have been updated to include the latest estimates from the World Health Organization/UNICEF Joint Monitoring Programme on Water Supply and Sanitation, which now refer to the year 2004.

• *Immunization:* Coverage estimates, specifically for hepatitis B (HepB) and *Haemophilus influenzae* type b (Hib), are now also presented for countries where these vaccines have been dispensed in only parts of the country (such as India). In previous reports, no values were provided for countries with only partial coverage from these vaccines.

• *Suspected pneumonia:* The term 'suspected pneumonia' is employed in place of 'acute respiratory infections (ARI)', which was used in previous editions. However, the data collection methodology has not changed, and estimates presented in previous reports are comparable to those in this year's edition. The change in terminology was initially proposed and supported at an inter-agency meeting in 2004.

The term 'suspected pneumonia' is a more accurate description of the data collected, as these data refer to children under five with cough and fast or difficult breathing, which are the key symptoms of pneumonia. 'Acute respiratory infections' is a more general term and refers to infections of either the upper or lower respiratory tract. Pneumonia is a severe infection of the lungs that accounts for a significant proportion of the ARI disease burden.

Table 4. HIV/AIDS: Estimates of adults, children and women living with HIV have changed due to revisions by the Joint United Nations Programme on HIV/AIDS (UNAIDS) to the estimates of HIV prevalence. These revisions are based on better and more precise information newly available from countries on the number of infections. UNAIDS also adjusted its reporting on the estimated

STATISTICAL TABLES

Economic and social statistics on the countries and territories of the world, with particular reference to children's well-being.

General note on the data (continued)

number of adults infected with HIV from 15–49 to 15+. This was done to reflect the increasing number of older adults who are infected.

The changes in HIV prevalence, and to some extent changes in adult mortality estimates from the UN Population Division, have also affected the estimates of the numbers of orphans due to AIDS and to all causes. In addition, there have been changes to the organization of Table 4 in this year's report. The columns have been reordered to reflect the priorities of the global campaign *Unite for Children. Unite against AIDS*, which focuses on prevention of mother-to-child transmission of HIV, prevention among young people, paediatric HIV, and protection and support for children affected by AIDS (the 'Four Ps'). An additional indicator was included in the table that reports HIV prevalence among young people (aged 15–24). Finally, the 'comprehensive knowledge of HIV' indicator was changed to exclude two components previously included.

Multiple Indicator Cluster Surveys (MICS)

UNICEF supports countries in collecting statistically robust and internationally comparable data through the Multiple Indicator Cluster Surveys (MICS). MICS are a major data source for monitoring important international goals and targets, such as the Millennium Development Goals, 'A World Fit for Children' Plan of Action, the UN General Assembly Special Session on HIV/AIDS targets and the Abuja targets for malaria. Around 50 countries conducted MICS in 2005–2006. However, while these surveys were conducted in 2005-2006, the results were not available in time for inclusion in this edition of *The State of the World's Children*. These data will be included in the next edition, and will also be published at <www.childinfo.org>.

Explanation of symbols

Because the aim of these statistical tables is to provide a broad picture of the situation of children and women worldwide, detailed data qualifications and footnotes are seen as more appropriate for inclusion elsewhere. The following symbols are common across all tables; symbols specific to a particular table are included in the table footnotes.

-     Data are not available.

x   Data refer to years or periods other than those specified in the column heading, differ from the standard definition, or refer to only part of a country. Such data are not included in the regional averages or totals.

y   Data differ from the standard definition or refer to only part of a country but are included in the calculation of regional and global averages.

*   Data refer to the most recent year available during the period specified in the column heading.

‡   Due to the cession in June 2006 of Montenegro from the State Union of Serbia and Montenegro and its subsequent admission to the UN on 28 June 2006, disaggregated data for Montenegro and Serbia as separate States are not yet available. Aggregated data presented are for Serbia and Montenegro pre-cession.

§   Includes territories within each country category or regional group. Countries and territories in each country category or regional group are listed on page 136.

Under-five mortality rankings

The following list ranks countries and territories in descending order of their estimated 2005 under-five mortality rate (U5MR), a critical indicator of the well-being of children. Countries and territories are listed alphabetically in the tables that follow.

	Under-5 mortality rate (2005)			Under-5 mortality rate (2005)			Under-5 mortality rate (2005)	
	Value	Rank		Value	Rank		Value	Rank
Sierra Leone	282	1	Guyana	63	66	Bulgaria	15	129
Angola	260	2	Namibia	62	67	Dominica	15	129
Afghanistan	257	3	Timor-Leste	61	68	Mauritius	15	129
Niger	256	4	Marshall Islands	58	69	Serbia and Montenegro (pre-cession)‡	15	129
Liberia	235	5	Korea, Democratic People's Republic of	55	70	Syrian Arab Republic	15	129
Somalia	225	6	Mongolia	49	71	Uruguay	15	129
Mali	218	7	Georgia	45	72	Saint Lucia	14	137
Chad	208	8	Guatemala	43	73	Sri Lanka	14	137
Congo, Democratic Republic of the	205	9	Maldives	42	74	Seychelles	13	139
Equatorial Guinea	205	9	Micronesia (Federated States of)	42	74	Antigua and Barbuda	12	140
Rwanda	203	11	Honduras	40	76	Barbados	12	140
Guinea-Bissau	200	12	Morocco	40	76	Belarus	12	140
Côte d'Ivoire	195	13	Algeria	39	78	Costa Rica	12	140
Nigeria	194	14	Suriname	39	78	Malaysia	12	140
Central African Republic	193	15	Tuvalu	38	80	Oman	12	140
Burkina Faso	191	16	Vanuatu	38	80	Bahrain	11	146
Burundi	190	17	Nicaragua	37	82	Kuwait	11	146
Zambia	182	18	Indonesia	36	83	Latvia	11	146
Ethiopia	164	19	Iran (Islamic Republic of)	36	83	Palau	11	146
Swaziland	160	20	Cape Verde	35	85	Chile	10	150
Benin	150	21	Brazil	33	86	Brunei Darussalam	9	151
Guinea	150	21	Egypt	33	86	Lithuania	9	151
Cameroon	149	23	Philippines	33	86	United Arab Emirates	9	151
Mozambique	145	24	Dominican Republic	31	89	Hungary	8	154
Cambodia	143	25	Lebanon	30	90	Slovakia	8	154
Togo	139	26	Nauru	30	90	Croatia	7	156
Gambia	137	27	Armenia	29	92	Cuba	7	156
Senegal	136	28	Samoa	29	92	Estonia	7	156
Uganda	136	28	Solomon Islands	29	92	Poland	7	156
Djibouti	133	30	Turkey	29	92	United States	7	156
Lesotho	132	31	China	27	96	Australia	6	161
Zimbabwe	132	31	El Salvador	27	96	Canada	6	161
Iraq	125	33	Mexico	27	96	Ireland	6	161
Malawi	125	33	Peru	27	96	Israel	6	161
Mauritania	125	33	Jordan	26	100	Malta	6	161
Tanzania, United Republic of	122	36	Saudi Arabia	26	100	New Zealand	6	161
Botswana	120	37	Ecuador	25	102	United Kingdom	6	161
Haiti	120	37	Panama	24	103	Austria	5	168
Kenya	120	37	Tonga	24	103	Belgium	5	168
Madagascar	119	40	Tunisia	24	103	Cyprus	5	168
Sao Tome and Principe	118	41	Occupied Palestinian Territory	23	106	Denmark	5	168
Ghana	112	42	Paraguay	23	106	France	5	168
Congo	108	43	Colombia	21	108	Germany	5	168
Myanmar	105	44	Grenada	21	108	Greece	5	168
Turkmenistan	104	45	Qatar	21	108	Korea, Republic of	5	168
Yemen	102	46	Thailand	21	108	Luxembourg	5	168
Pakistan	99	47	Venezuela (Bolivarian Republic of)	21	108	Monaco	5	168
Gabon	91	48	Cook Islands	20	113	Netherlands	5	168
Sudan	90	49	Jamaica	20	113	Portugal	5	168
Azerbaijan	89	50	Saint Kitts and Nevis	20	113	Spain	5	168
Lao People's Democratic Republic	79	51	Saint Vincent and the Grenadines	20	113	Switzerland	5	168
Eritrea	78	52	Libyan Arab Jamahiriya	19	117	Czech Republic	4	182
Bhutan	75	53	Romania	19	117	Finland	4	182
India	74	54	Trinidad and Tobago	19	117	Italy	4	182
Nepal	74	54	Viet Nam	19	117	Japan	4	182
Papua New Guinea	74	54	Albania	18	121	Liechtenstein	4	182
Bangladesh	73	57	Argentina	18	121	Norway	4	182
Kazakhstan	73	57	Fiji	18	121	Slovenia	4	182
Comoros	71	59	Russian Federation	18	121	Sweden	4	182
Tajikistan	71	59	Belize	17	125	Andorra	3	190
South Africa	68	61	The former Yugoslav Republic of Macedonia	17	125	Iceland	3	190
Uzbekistan	68	61	Ukraine	17	125	San Marino	3	190
Kyrgyzstan	67	63	Moldova, Republic of	16	128	Singapore	3	190
Bolivia	65	64	Bahamas	15	129	Holy See	-	-
Kiribati	65	64	Bosnia and Herzegovina	15	129	Niue	-	-

‡ Due to the cession in June 2006 of Montenegro from the State Union of Serbia and Montenegro, and its subsequent admission to the UN on 28 June 2006, disaggregated data for Montenegro and Serbia as separate States are not yet available. Aggregated data presented are for Serbia and Montenegro pre-cession.

TABLE 1. BASIC INDICATORS

Countries and territories	Under-5 mortality rank	Under-5 mortality rate 1990	Under-5 mortality rate 2005	Infant mortality rate (under 1) 1990	Infant mortality rate (under 1) 2005	Neonatal mortality rate 2000	Total population (thousands) 2005	Annual no. of births (thousands) 2005	Annual no. of under-5 deaths (thousands) 2005	GNI per capita (US$) 2005	Life expectancy at birth (years) 2005	Total adult literacy rate 2000-2004*	Net primary school enrolment/ attendance (%) 2000-2005*	% share of household income 1994-2004* lowest 40%	% share of household income 1994-2004* highest 20%
Afghanistan	3	260	257	168	165	60	29863	1441	370	250x	47	28	53s	-	-
Albania	121	45	18	37	16	12	3130	53	1	2580	74	99	52s	23	37
Algeria	78	69	39	54	34	20	32854	684	27	2730	72	70	97	19	43
Andorra	190	-	3	-	3	4	67	1	0	d	-	-	89	-	-
Angola	2	260	260	154	154	54	15941	767	199	1350	41	67	58s	-	-
Antigua and Barbuda	140	-	12	-	11	8	81	2	0	10920	-	-	-	-	-
Argentina	121	29	18	26	15	10	38747	687	12	4470	75	97	99	10	57
Armenia	92	54	29	46	26	17	3016	34	1	1470	72	99	94	21	43
Australia	161	10	6	8	5	3	20155	250	2	32220	81	-	96	18	41
Austria	168	10	5	8	4	3	8189	74	0	36980	79	-	-	22	38
Azerbaijan	50	105	89	84	74	36	8411	134	12	1240	67	99	91s	28	31
Bahamas	129	29	15	22	13	10	323	6	0	14920x	71	-	84	-	-
Bahrain	146	19	11	15	9	11	727	13	0	10840x	75	87	86s	-	-
Bangladesh	57	149	73	100	54	36	141822	3747	274	470	64	-	84s	22	41
Barbados	140	17	12	15	11	8	270	3	0	9270x	76	-	97	-	-
Belarus	140	19	12	16	10	5	9755	91	1	2760	68	100	90	22	38
Belgium	168	10	5	8	4	3	10419	110	1	35700	79	-	99	22	41
Belize	125	42	17	34	15	18	270	7	0	3500	72	-	95	-	-
Benin	21	185	150	111	89	38	8439	348	52	510	55	35	54s	19	45
Bhutan	53	166	75	107	65	38	2163	64	5	870	64	-	70s,y	-	-
Bolivia	64	125	65	89	52	27	9182	265	17	1010	65	87	78s	7	63
Bosnia and Herzegovina	129	22	15	18	13	11	3907	36	1	2440	74	97	93s	24	36
Botswana	37	58	120	45	87	40	1765	45	5	5180	34	81	82	7x	70x
Brazil	86	60	33	50	31	15	186405	3726	123	3460	71	89	96s,y	9	62
Brunei Darussalam	151	11	9	10	8	4	374	8	0	24100x	77	93	-	-	-
Bulgaria	129	18	15	15	12	8	7726	67	1	3450	73	98	95	22	38
Burkina Faso	16	210	191	113	96	36	13228	617	118	400	48	22	32s	18	47
Burundi	17	190	190	114	114	41	7548	347	66	100	44	59	47s	15	48
Cambodia	25	115	143	80	98	40	14071	429	61	380	57	74	65s	18	48
Cameroon	23	139	149	85	87	40	16322	563	84	1010	46	68	79s	15	51
Canada	161	8	6	7	5	4	32268	327	2	32600	80	-	99	20	40
Cape Verde	85	60	35	45	26	10	507	15	1	1870	71	-	92	-	-
Central African Republic	15	168	193	102	115	48	4038	150	29	350	39	49	43s	7x	65x
Chad	8	201	208	120	124	45	9749	471	98	400	44	26	36s	-	-
Chile	150	21	10	18	8	6	16295	249	2	5870	78	96	-	10	62
China	96	49	27	38	23	21	1315844	17310	467	1740	72	91	99	14	50
Colombia	108	35	21	26	17	14	45600	968	20	2290	73	93	91s	9	63
Comoros	59	120	71	88	53	29	798	28	2	640	64	-	31s	-	-
Congo	43	110	108	83	81	32	3999	177	19	950	53	-	-	-	-
Congo, Democratic Republic of the	9	205	205	129	129	47	57549	2873	589	120	44	67	52s	-	-
Cook Islands	113	32	20	26	17	12	18	0	0	-	-	-	77	-	-
Costa Rica	140	18	12	16	11	7	4327	79	1	4590	78	95	-	12	55
Côte d'Ivoire	13	157	195	103	118	65	18154	665	130	840	46	49	56	14	51
Croatia	156	12	7	11	6	5	4551	41	0	8060	75	98	87	21	40
Cuba	156	13	7	11	6	4	11269	134	1	1170x	78	100	96	-	-
Cyprus	168	12	5	10	4	4	835	10	0	17580x	79	97	96	-	-
Czech Republic	182	13	4	11	3	2	10220	91	0	10710	76	-	-	25	36
Denmark	168	9	5	8	4	4	5431	62	0	47390	78	-	100	23	36
Djibouti	30	175	133	116	88	38	793	27	4	1020	53	-	33	-	-
Dominica	129	17	15	15	13	7	79	2	0	3790	-	-	88	-	-
Dominican Republic	89	65	31	50	26	19	8895	211	7	2370	68	87	86	12	57
Ecuador	102	57	25	43	22	16	13228	295	7	2630	75	91	98	11	58
Egypt	86	104	33	76	28	21	74033	1909	63	1250	70	71	83s	21	44
El Salvador	96	60	27	47	23	16	6881	166	4	2450	71	-	92	10	56
Equatorial Guinea	9	170	205	103	123	40	504	22	5	c	42	87	61s	-	-
Eritrea	52	147	78	88	50	25	4401	170	13	220	55	-	67s	-	-
Estonia	156	16	7	12	6	6	1330	13	0	9100	72	100	94	19	43
Ethiopia	19	204	164	131	109	51	77431	3104	509	160	48	-	31s	22	39
Fiji	121	22	18	19	16	9	848	19	0	3280	68	-	96	-	-
Finland	182	7	4	6	3	2	5249	55	0	37460	79	-	99	24	37
France	168	9	5	7	4	3	60496	742	4	34810	80	-	99	20	40
Gabon	48	92	91	60	60	31	1384	42	4	5010	54	-	94s	-	-
Gambia	27	151	137	103	97	46	1517	52	7	290	57	-	53s	14	53

102   THE STATE OF THE WORLD'S CHILDREN 2007

	Under-5 mortality rank	Under-5 mortality rate		Infant mortality rate (under 1)		Neonatal mortality rate 2000	Total population (thousands) 2005	Annual no. of births (thousands) 2005	Annual no. of under-5 deaths (thousands) 2005	GNI per capita (US$) 2005	Life expectancy at birth (years) 2005	Total adult literacy rate 2000-2004*	Net primary school enrolment/ attendance (%) 2000-2005*	% share of household income 1994-2004*	
		1990	2005	1990	2005									lowest 40%	highest 20%
Georgia	72	47	45	43	41	25	4474	49	2	1350	71	-	93	16	46
Germany	168	9	5	7	4	3	82689	679	3	34580	79	-	-	22	37
				75	68	27	22113	683	76	450	57	58	65	16	47
				10	4	4	11120	101	1	19670	78	96	99	19	42
				30	17	13	103	2	0	3920	-	-	84	-	-
				60	32	19	12599	437	19	2400	68	69	93	10	60
				145	98	48	9402	387	58	370	54	29	57s	17	47
				153	124	48	1586	79	16	180	45	-	39s	14x	53x
				64	47	25	751	15	1	1010	64	-	97s	-	-
				102	84	34	8528	255	31	450	52	-	55s	9	63
				-	-	-	1	0	-	-	-	-	-	-	-
				44	31	18	7205	206	8	1190	68	80	91	11	58
				15	7	6	10098	94	1	10030	73	-	89	23	37
				6	2	2	295	4	0	46320	81	-	99	-	-
				84	56	43	1103371	25926	1919	720	64	61	76s	21	43
				60	28	18	222781	4495	162	1280	68	90	94	20	43
				54	31	22	69515	1348	49	2770	71	77	89	15	50
				40	102	63	28807	978	122	2170x	60	74	78s	-	-
				8	5	4	4148	64	0	40150	78	-	96	20	42
				10	5	4	6725	134	1	18620	80	97	98	16	45
				9	4	3	58093	528	2	30010	80	98	99	19	42
				17	17	10	2651	52	1	3400	71	80	91	17	46
				5	3	2	128085	1162	5	38980	82	-	100	25x	36x
				33	22	17	5703	150	4	2500	72	90	99s	18	46
				53	63	32	14825	237	17	2930	64	100	93	19	42
				64	79	29	34256	1361	163	530	48	74	76	16	49
				65	48	27	99	2	0	1390	-	-	97x	-	-
				42	42	22	22488	342	19	a	64	-	-	-	-
				8	5	3	47817	457	2	15830	78	-	99	22	38
				14	9	6	2687	51	1	16340x	77	93	86	-	-
				68	58	31	5264	116	8	440	67	99	90	22	39
				120	62	35	5924	205	16	440	55	69	62s	20	43
				14	9	7	2307	21	0	6760	72	100	-	18	45
				32	27	20	3577	66	2	6180	72	-	93	-	-
				81	102	28	1795	50	7	960	34	82	65s	6	67
				157	157	66	3283	167	39	130	42	-	66	-	-
				35	18	11	5853	136	3	5530	74	-	-	-	-
				9	3	-	35	0	0	d	-	-	88	-	-
				10	7	5	3431	31	0	7050	73	100	89	18	43
				7	4	4	465	6	0	65630	79	-	91	-	-
				103	74	33	18606	712	85	290	56	71	76s	13	54
				131	79	40	12884	555	69	160	40	64	82s,y	13	56
				16	10	5	25347	547	7	4960	74	89	93	13	54
				79	33	37	329	10	0	2390	67	96	90	-	-
				140	120	55	13518	661	144	380	48	19	39s	13	56
				9	5	5	402	4	0	13590	79	88	94	-	-
				63	51	26	62	2	0	2930	-	-	90	-	-
				85	78	70	3069	126	16	560	53	51	44s	17	46
				21	13	12	1245	20	0	5260	73	84	95	-	-
				37	22	15	107029	2172	59	7310	76	91	98	13	55
				45	34	12	110	3	0	2300	68	-	-	-	-
				29	14	16	4206	43	1	880	69	98	86	20	41
				7	4	3	35	0	0	d	-	-	-	-	-
				78	39	26	2646	58	3	690	65	98	84	16	51
				-	-	-	-	-	-	-	-	-	-	-	-
				69	36	21	31478	717	29	1730	70	52	86	17	47
				158	100	48	19792	773	112	310	42	-	60s	17	47
				91	75	40	50519	976	102	220x	61	90	84s	-	-
				60	46	25	2031	56	3	2990	46	85	74	4x	79x
				-	25	14	14	0	0	-	-	-	-	-	-
				100	56	40	27133	787	58	270	62	49	78	15	55

TABLE 1. BASIC INDICATORS

	Under-5 mortality rank	Under-5 mortality rate		Infant mortality rate (under 1)		Neonatal mortality rate 2000	Total population (thousands) 2005	Annual no. of births (thousands) 2005	Annual no. of under-5 deaths (thousands) 2005	GNI per capita (US$) 2005	Life expectancy at birth (years) 2005	Total adult literacy rate 2000-2004*	Net primary school enrolment/ attendance (%) 2000-2005*	% share of household income 1994-2004*	
		1990	2005	1990	2005									lowest 40%	highest 20%
Netherlands	168	9	5	7	4	4	16299	187	1	36620	79	77	99	21	39
New Zealand	161	11	6	8	5	4	4028	54	0	25960	79	-	99	18	44
Nicaragua	82	68	37	52	30	18	5487	154	6	910	70	-	80s	15	49
Niger	4	320	256	191	150	43	13957	750	192	240	45	29	30s	10	53
Nigeria	14	230	194	120	100	53	131530	5377	1043	560	44	-	60	15	49
Niue	-	-	-	-	-	13	1	0	-	-	-	-	99x	-	-
Norway	182	9	4	7	3	3	4620	54	0	59590	80	-	99	24	37
Occupied Palestinian Territory	106	40	23	34	21	-	3702	138	3	1110x	73	92	92s,y	-	-
Oman	140	32	12	25	10	6	2567	64	1	7830x	75	81	78	-	-
Pakistan	47	130	99	100	79	57	157935	4773	473	690	64	50	56s	22	40
Palau	146	21	11	18	10	14	20	0	0	7630	-	-	96	-	-
Panama	103	34	24	27	19	11	3232	70	2	4630	75	92	98	9	60
Papua New Guinea	54	94	74	69	55	32	5887	174	13	660	56	57	-	12	57
Paraguay	106	41	23	33	20	16	6158	177	4	1280	71	-	96s	9	61
Peru	96	78	27	58	23	16	27968	628	17	2610	71	88	97	10	59
Philippines	86	62	33	41	25	15	83054	2018	67	1300	71	93	88s	14	52
Poland	156	18	7	19	6	6	38530	365	3	7110	75	-	97	19	42
Portugal	168	14	5	11	4	3	10495	111	1	16170	78	-	99	17	46
Qatar	108	26	21	21	18	5	813	14	0	12000x	73	89	95	-	-
Romania	117	31	19	27	16	9	21711	211	4	3830	72	97	92	21	39
Russian Federation	121	27	18	21	14	9	143202	1540	28	4460	65	99	91	17	47
Rwanda	11	173	203	103	118	45	9038	375	76	230	44	65	73	23x	39x
Saint Kitts and Nevis	113	36	20	30	18	12	43	1	0	8210	-	-	94	-	-
Saint Lucia	137	21	14	20	12	10	161	3	0	4800	73	-	98	-	-
Saint Vincent and the Grenadines	113	25	20	22	17	11	119	2	0	3590	71	-	94	-	-
Samoa	92	50	29	40	24	13	185	5	0	2090	71	-	90	-	-
San Marino	190	14	3	13	3	2	28	0	0	d	-	-	-	-	-
Sao Tome and Principe	41	118	118	75	75	38	157	5	1	390	63	-	84s	-	-
Saudi Arabia	100	44	26	35	21	12	24573	671	17	11770	72	79	59	-	-
Senegal	28	148	136	90	77	31	11658	423	58	710	56	39	66	17	48
Serbia‡	-	-	-	-	-	-	-	-	-	-	-	-	-	-	-
Seychelles	139	19	13	17	12	9	81	3	0	8290	-	92	96	-	-
Sierra Leone	1	302	282	175	165	56	5525	252	71	220	41	35	41s	3x	63x
Singapore	190	9	3	7	3	1	4326	39	0	27490	79	93	-	14	49
Slovakia	154	14	8	12	7	5	5401	51	0	7950	74	-	-	24	35
Slovenia	182	10	4	8	3	4	1967	17	0	17350	77	-	98	23	36
Solomon Islands	92	38	29	31	24	12	478	15	0	590	63	-	80	-	-
Somalia	6	225	225	133	133	49	8228	366	82	130x	47	-	12s	-	-
South Africa	61	60	68	45	55	21	47432	1082	74	4960	46	82	89	10	62
Spain	168	9	5	8	4	3	43064	454	2	25360	80	-	99	19	42
Sri Lanka	137	32	14	26	12	11	20743	329	5	1160	74	91	99	21	42
Sudan	49	120	90	74	62	29	36233	1166	105	640	57	61	58s	-	-
Suriname	78	48	39	35	30	18	449	9	0	2540	70	90	92	-	-
Swaziland	20	110	160	78	110	38	1032	29	5	2280	30	80	77	9	64
Sweden	182	7	4	6	3	2	9041	96	0	41060	80	-	99	23	37
Switzerland	168	9	5	7	4	3	7252	67	0	54930	81	-	94	20	41
Syrian Arab Republic	129	39	15	31	14	9	19043	532	8	1380	74	80	95	-	-
Tajikistan	59	115	71	91	59	38	6507	185	13	330	64	99	89s	20	41
Tanzania, United Republic of	36	161	122	102	76	43	38329	1408	172	340	46	69	73s	19	42
Thailand	108	37	21	31	18	13	64233	1009	21	2750	71	93	-	16	49
The former Yugoslav Republic of Macedonia	125	38	17	33	15	9	2034	23	0	2830	74	96	92	17	46
Timor-Leste	68	177	61	133	52	40	947	49	3	750	56	-	75s,y	-	-
Togo	26	152	139	88	78	40	6145	236	33	350	55	53	70s	-	-
Tonga	103	32	24	26	20	10	102	2	0	2190	73	99	91x	-	-
Trinidad and Tobago	117	33	19	28	17	13	1305	19	0	10440	70	-	92	16x	46x
Tunisia	103	52	24	41	20	14	10102	166	4	2890	74	74	97	16	47
Turkey	92	82	29	67	26	22	73193	1500	44	4710	69	87	89	15	50
Turkmenistan	45	97	104	80	81	35	4833	108	11	1340x	63	99	76s	16	48
Tuvalu	80	54	38	42	31	22	10	0	0	-	-	-	-	-	-
Uganda	28	160	136	93	79	32	28816	1468	200	280	49	67	87s	16	50
Ukraine	125	26	17	19	13	9	46481	392	7	1520	66	99	82	23	38

	Under-5 mortality rank	Under-5 mortality rate		Infant mortality rate (under 1)		Neonatal mortality rate 2000	Total population (thousands) 2005	Annual no. of births (thousands) 2005	Annual no. of under-5 deaths (thousands) 2005	GNI per capita (US$) 2005	Life expectancy at birth (years) 2005	Total adult literacy rate 2000-2004*	Net primary school enrolment/ attendance (%) 2000-2005*	% share of household income 1994-2004*	
		1990	2005	1990	2005									lowest 40%	highest 20%
United Arab Emirates	151	15	9	13	8	5	4496	69	1	18060x	79	-	71	-	-
United Kingdom	161	10	6	8	5	4	59668	659	4	37600	79	-	99	18	44
United States	156	12	7	9	6	5	298213	4165	29	43740	78	-	92	16	46
Uruguay	129	23	15	21	14	7	3463	57	1	4360	76	-	-	14	51
Uzbekistan	61	79	68	65	57	27	26593	615	42	510	67	-	95s	23	36
Vanuatu	80	62	38	48	31	19	211	6	0	1600	69	74	94	-	-
Venezuela (Bolivarian Republic of)	108	33	21	27	18	12	26749	593	12	4810	73	93	92	14	49
Viet Nam	117	53	19	38	16	15	84238	1648	31	620	71	90	94	19	45
Yemen	46	139	102	98	76	37	20975	845	86	600	62	-	75	20	41
Zambia	18	180	182	101	102	40	11668	472	86	490	38	68	57s	16	49
Zimbabwe	31	80	132	53	81	33	13010	384	51	340	37	-	82	13	56

MEMORANDUM

Serbia and Montenegro (pre-cession)	129	28	15	24	12	9	10503	121	2	3280	74	96	96	-	-

SUMMARY INDICATORS

Sub-Saharan Africa		188	169	112	101	44	713457	28715	4853	764	46	62	61	11	59
Eastern and Southern Africa		166	146	104	93	40	356126	13575	1982	1043	46	73	66	10	61
West and Central Africa		209	190	119	108	48	357331	15140	2877	491	46	49	56	14	51
Middle East and North Africa		81	54	59	43	26	378532	9743	526	2627	69	72	80	16	47
South Asia		129	84	89	63	44	1483358	37077	3114	691	64	59	74	22	41
East Asia and Pacific		58	33	43	26	20	1952656	29820	984	2092	71	91	96	17	48
Latin America and Caribbean		54	31	43	26	15	555853	11651	361	4078	72	90	94	13	53
CEE/CIS		53	35	43	29	18	404322	5595	196	3433	67	97	90	22	39
Industrialized countries§		10	6	9	5	4	961191	10848	65	35410	79	-	96	21	40
Developing countries§		105	83	71	57	33	5238533	120128	9971	1801	65	79	81	17	48
Least developed countries§		182	153	115	97	43	759389	28258	4323	383	53	60	62	11	57
World		95	76	65	52	30	6449371	133449	10142	7002	68	80	82	20	42

‡ Due to the cession in June 2006 of Montenegro from the State Union of Serbia and Montenegro, and its subsequent admission to the UN on 28 June 2006, disaggregated data for Montenegro and Serbia as separate States are not yet available. Aggregated data presented are for Serbia and Montenegro pre-cession (see Memorandum item).

§ Also includes territories within each country category or regional group. Countries and territories in each country category or regional group are listed on page 136.

DEFINITIONS OF THE INDICATORS

Under-five mortality rate – Probability of dying between birth and exactly five years of age expressed per 1,000 live births.

Infant mortality rate – Probability of dying between birth and exactly one year of age expressed per 1,000 live births.

Neonatal mortality rate – Probability of dying during the first 28 completed days of life expressed per 1,000 live births.

GNI per capita – Gross national income (GNI) is the sum of value added by all resident producers, plus any product taxes (less subsidies) not included in the valuation of output, plus net receipts of primary income (compensation of employees and property income) from abroad. GNI per capita is gross national income divided by midyear population. GNI per capita in US dollars is converted using the World Bank Atlas method.

Life expectancy at birth – The number of years newborn children would live if subject to the mortality risks prevailing for their cross section of the population at the time of their birth.

Adult literacy rate – Percentage of the population aged 15 and older who can read and write.

Net primary school enrolment/attendance ratios – Derived from net primary school enrolment rates as reported by UNESCO Institute for Statistics and from national household survey reports of attendance at primary school or higher. The net primary school attendance ratio is defined as the percentage of children in the age group that officially corresponds to primary schooling eligibility who attend primary school or higher.

Income share – Percentage of income received by the 20 per cent of households with the highest income and by the 40 per cent of households with the lowest income.

MAIN DATA SOURCES

Under-five and infant mortality rates – UNICEF, World Health Organization, United Nations Population Division and United Nations Statistics Division.

Neonatal mortality rate – World Health Organization using vital registration systems and household surveys.

Total population – United Nations Population Division.

Births – United Nations Population Division.

Under-five deaths – UNICEF.

GNI per capita – World Bank.

Life expectancy – United Nations Population Division.

Adult literacy – United Nations Educational, Scientific and Cultural Organization (UNESCO) and UNESCO Institute for Statistics (UIS), including the Education for All 2000 Assessment.

School enrolment/attendance – UIS, Multiple Indicator Cluster Surveys (MICS) and Demographic and Health Surveys (DHS).

Household income – World Bank.

NOTES

a: Range low income ($875 or less).
b: Range lower-middle income ($876 to $3,465).
c: Range upper-middle income ($3,466 to $10,725).
d: Range high income ($10,726 or more).

- Data not available.
s National household survey data.
x Data refer to years or periods other than those specified in the column heading, differ from the standard definition, or refer to only part of a country.
y Data differ from the standard definition or refer to only part of a country, but are included in the calculation of regional and global averages.
* Data refer to the most recent year available during the period specified in the column heading.

TABLE 2. NUTRITION

Countries and territories	% of infants with low birthweight 1998-2005*	% of children (1996-2005*) who are:			% of under-fives (1996-2005*) suffering from:						Vitamin A supplementation coverage rate (6-59 months) 2004	% of households consuming iodized salt 1998-2005*
		exclusively breastfed (<6 months)	breastfed with complementary food (6-9 months)	still breastfeeding (20-23 months)	underweight		wasting	stunting				
					moderate & severe	severe	moderate & severe	moderate & severe				
Afghanistan	-	-	29	54	39	12	7	54	96t	28
Albania	5	6	24	6	14	1	11	34	-	62
Algeria	7	13	38	22	10	3	8	19	-	69
Andorra	-	-	-	-	-	-	-	-	-	-
Angola	12	11	77	37	31	8	6	45	77	35
Antigua and Barbuda	8	-	-	-	-	-	-	-	-	-
Argentina	8	-	-	-	4	-	1	4	-	90x
Armenia	7	33	57	15	4	0	5	13	-	97
Australia	7	-	-	-	-	-	-	-	-	-
Austria	7	-	-	-	-	-	-	-	-	-
Azerbaijan	12	7	39	16	7	1	2	13	14	26
Bahamas	7	-	-	-	-	-	-	-	-	-
Bahrain	8	34x,k	65x	41x	9x	2x	5x	10x	-	-
Bangladesh	36	36	69	90	48	13	13	43	83t	70
Barbados	11	-	-	-	-	-	-	-	-	-
Belarus	5	-	-	-	-	-	-	-	-	55
Belgium	8x	-	-	-	-	-	-	-	-	-
Belize	6	24k	54	23	-	-	-	-	-	90x
Benin	16	38	66	62	23	5	8	31	94t	72
Bhutan	15	-	-	-	19	3	3	40	-	95
Bolivia	7	54	74	46	8	1	1	27	42	90
Bosnia and Herzegovina	4	6	-	-	4	1	6	10	-	62
Botswana	10	34	57	11	13	2	5	23	62w	66
Brazil	8	-	30	17	6	1	2	11	-	88
Brunei Darussalam	10	-	-	-	-	-	-	-	-	-
Bulgaria	10	-	-	-	-	-	-	-	-	98
Burkina Faso	19	19	38	81	38	14	19	39	95t	45
Burundi	16	62	46	85	45	13	8	57	94	96
Cambodia	11	12	72	59	45	13	15	45	72t	14
Cameroon	13	24	79	29	18	4	5	32	81	88
Canada	6	-	-	-	-	-	-	-	-	-
Cape Verde	13	57k	64	13	-	-	-	-	-	0x
Central African Republic	14	17	77	53	24	6	9	39	79	86
Chad	22	2	77	65	37	14	14	41	84t	56
Chile	6	63	47	-	1	-	0	1	-	100
China	4	51	32	15	8	-	-	14	-	93
Colombia	9	47	65	32	7	1	1	12	-	92x
Comoros	25	21	34	45	25	-	8	44	7	82
Congo	-	19	78	21	15	3	7	26	94	-
Congo, Democratic Republic of the	12	24	79	52	31	9	13	38	81t	72
Cook Islands	3	19k	-	-	-	-	-	-	-	-
Costa Rica	7	35x,k	47x	12x	5	0	2	6	-	97x
Côte d'Ivoire	17	5	73	38	17	5	7	21	60	84
Croatia	6	23	-	-	1	-	1	1	-	90
Cuba	5	41	42	9	4	0	2	5	-	88
Cyprus	-	-	-	-	-	-	-	-	-	-
Czech Republic	7	-	-	-	-	-	-	-	-	-
Denmark	5	-	-	-	-	-	-	-	-	-
Djibouti	16	-	-	-	27	8	18	23	-	-
Dominica	11	-	-	-	-	-	-	-	-	-
Dominican Republic	11	10	41	16	5	1	2	9	-	18
Ecuador	16	35	70	25	12	-	-	26	-	99
Egypt	12	38	67	37	6	1	4	18	-	78
El Salvador	7	24	76	43	10	1	1	19	-	62
Equatorial Guinea	13	24	-	-	19	4	7	39	-	33
Eritrea	14	52	43	62	40	12	13	38	50	68
Estonia	4	-	-	-	-	-	-	-	-	-
Ethiopia	15	49	54	86	38	11	11	47	52	28
Fiji	10	47x,k	-	-	-	-	-	-	-	31x
Finland	4	-	-	-	-	-	-	-	-	-
France	7	-	-	-	-	-	-	-	-	-

	% of infants with low birthweight 1998-2005*	% of children (1996-2005*) who are:			% of under-fives (1996-2005*) suffering from:						Vitamin A supplementation coverage rate (6-59 months) 2004	% of households consuming iodized salt 1998-2005*
		exclusively breastfed (<6 months)	breastfed with complementary food (6-9 months)	still breastfeeding (20-23 months)	underweight		wasting	stunting				
					moderate & severe	severe	moderate & severe	moderate & severe				
Gabon	14	6	62	9	12	2	3	21		-	36
Gambia	17	26	37	54	17	4	8	19		27	8
Georgia	7	18k	12	12	3	0	2	12		-	68
Germany	7	-	-	-	-	-	-	-		-	-
Ghana	16	53	62	67	22	5	7	30		95	28
Greece	8	-	-	-	-	-	-	-		-	-
Grenada	8	39k	-	-	-	-	-	-		-	-
Guatemala	12	51	67	47	23	4	2	49		18w	67
Guinea	16	27	41	71	26	7	9	35		95t	68
Guinea-Bissau	22	37	36	67	25	7	10	30		64	2
Guyana	13	11	42	31	14	3	11	11		-	-
Haiti	21	24	73	30	17	4	5	23		-	11
Holy See	-	-	-	-	-	-	-	-		-	-
Honduras	14	35	61	34	17	2	1	29		40	80
Hungary	9	-	-	-	-	-	-	-		-	-
Iceland	4	-	-	-	-	-	-	-		-	-
India	30	37k	44	66	47	18	16	46		51w	57
Indonesia	9	40	75	59	28	9	-	-		73t	73
Iran (Islamic Republic of)	7x	44	-	0	11	2	5	15		-	94
Iraq	15	12	51	27	12	3	8	23		-	40
Ireland	6	-	-	-	-	-	-	-		-	-
Israel	8	-	-	-	-	-	-	-		-	-
Italy	6	-	-	-	-	-	-	-		-	-
Jamaica	10	-	-	-	4	-	4	3		-	100
Japan	8	-	-	-	-	-	-	-		-	-
Jordan	12	27	70	12	4	1	2	9		-	88
Kazakhstan	8	36	73	17	4	0	2	10		-	83
Kenya	10	13	84	57	20	4	6	30		63	91
Kiribati	5	80x,k	-	-	-	-	-	-		58	-
Korea, Democratic People's Republic of	7	65	31	37	23	8	7	37		95t	40
Korea, Republic of	4	-	-	-	-	-	-	-		-	-
Kuwait	7	12k	26	9	10	3	11	24		-	-
Kyrgyzstan	7x	24	77	21	11	2	3	25		95	42
Lao People's Democratic Republic	14	23	10	47	40	13	15	42		48	75
Latvia	5	-	-	-	-	-	-	-		-	-
Lebanon	6	27k	35	11	4	-	5	11		-	92
Lesotho	13	36	79	60	20	4	4	38		71	91
Liberia	-	35	70	45	26	8	6	39		95	-
Libyan Arab Jamahiriya	7x	-	-	23x	5x	1x	3x	15x		-	90x
Liechtenstein	-	-	-	-	-	-	-	-		-	-
Lithuania	4	-	-	-	-	-	-	-		-	-
Luxembourg	8	-	-	-	-	-	-	-		-	-
Madagascar	17	67	78	64	42	11	13	48		89t	75
Malawi	16	53	78	80	22	5	5	48		57	49
Malaysia	9	29k	-	12	11	1	-	-		-	-
Maldives	22	10	85	-	30	7	13	25		-	44
Mali	23	25	32	69	33	11	11	38		97	74
Malta	6	-	-	-	-	-	-	-		-	-
Marshall Islands	12	63x,k	-	-	-	-	-	-		24	-
Mauritania	-	20	78	57	32	10	13	35		95t	2
Mauritius	14	21k	-	-	15x	2x	14x	10x		-	0x
Mexico	8	-	-	-	8	1	2	18		-	91
Micronesia (Federated States of)	18	60k	-	-	-	-	-	-		74	-
Moldova, Republic of	5	46	66	2	4	1	4	8		-	59
Monaco	-	-	-	-	-	-	-	-		-	-
Mongolia	7	51	55	57	7	1	3	20		93t	75
Montenegro‡	-	-	-	-	-	-	-	-		-	-
Morocco	15	31	66	15	10	2	9	18		-	59
Mozambique	15	30	80	65	24	6	4	41		26	54
Myanmar	15	15k	66	67	32	7	9	32		96t	60
Namibia	14	19	57	37	24	5	9	24		-	63

TABLE 2. NUTRITION

	% of infants with low birthweight 1998-2005*	% of children (1996-2005*) who are:			% of under-fives (1996-2005*) suffering from:						Vitamin A supplementation coverage rate (6-59 months) 2004	% of households consuming iodized salt 1998-2005*
		exclusively breastfed (<6 months)	breastfed with complementary food (6-9 months)	still breastfeeding (20-23 months)	underweight		wasting	stunting				
					moderate & severe	severe	moderate & severe	moderate & severe				
Nauru	-	-	-	-	-	-	-	-			-	-
Nepal	21	68	66	92	48	13	10	51			97t	63
Netherlands	-	-	-	-	-	-	-	-			-	-
New Zealand	6	-	-	-	-	-	-	-			-	83
Nicaragua	12	31	68	39	10	2	2	20			98	97
Niger	13	1	56	61	40	14	14	40			-	15
Nigeria	14	17	64	34	29	9	9	38			85t	97
Niue	0	-	-	-	-	-	-	-			-	-
Norway	5	-	-	-	-	-	-	-			-	-
Occupied Palestinian Territory	9	29k	78	11	5	1	3	10			-	64
Oman	8	-	92	73	18	1	7	10			95w	61
Pakistan	19x	16x,k	31x	56x	38	13	13	37			95t	17
Palau	9	59x,k	-	-	-	-	-	-			-	-
Panama	10	25x	38x	21x	8	1	1	18			-	95
Papua New Guinea	11x	59	74	66	-	-	-	-			32	-
Paraguay	9	22	60	-	5	-	1	14			-	88
Peru	11	64	81	41	8	0	1	24			-	91
Philippines	20	34	58	32	28	-	6	30			85t	56
Poland	6	-	-	-	-	-	-	-			-	-
Portugal	8	-	-	-	-	-	-	-			-	-
Qatar	10	12k	48	21	6x	-	2x	8x			-	-
Romania	8	16	41	-	3	0	2	10			-	53
Russian Federation	6	-	-	-	3x	1x	4x	13x			-	35
Rwanda	9	90	69	77	23	4	4	45			95t	90
Saint Kitts and Nevis	9	56k	-	-	-	-	-	-			-	100
Saint Lucia	10	-	-	-	-	-	-	-			-	-
Saint Vincent and the Grenadines	10	-	-	-	-	-	-	-			-	-
Samoa	4x	-	-	-	-	-	-	-			-	-
San Marino	-	-	-	-	-	-	-	-			-	-
Sao Tome and Principe	20	56	53	42	13	2	4	29			76t	74
Saudi Arabia	11x	31k	60	30	14	3	11	20			-	-
Senegal	18	34	61	42	17	3	8	16			95	41
Serbia‡	-	-	-	-	-	-	-	-			-	-
Seychelles	-	-	-	-	-	-	-	-			-	-
Sierra Leone	23	4	51	53	27	9	10	34			95t	23
Singapore	8	-	-	-	3	0	2	2			-	-
Slovakia	7	-	-	-	-	-	-	-			-	-
Slovenia	6	-	-	-	-	-	-	-			-	-
Solomon Islands	13x	65k	-	-	-	-	-	-			-	-
Somalia	-	9	13	8	26	7	17	23			6	-
South Africa	15	7	46	-	12	2	3	25			37	62
Spain	6x	-	-	-	-	-	-	-			-	-
Sri Lanka	22	53	-	73	29	-	14	14			57w	94
Sudan	31	16	47	40	41	15	16	43			70	1
Suriname	13	9	25	11	13	2	7	10			-	-
Swaziland	9	24	60	25	10	2	1	30			86	59
Sweden	4	-	-	-	-	-	-	-			-	-
Switzerland	6	-	-	-	-	-	-	-			-	-
Syrian Arab Republic	6	81k	50	6	7	1	4	18			-	79
Tajikistan	15	41	91	55	-	-	5	36			98t	28
Tanzania, United Republic of	10	41	91	55	22	4	3	38			94t	43
Thailand	9	4x,k	71x	27x	18x	2x	5x	13x			-	63
The former Yugoslav Republic of Macedonia	6	37	8	10	6	1	4	7			-	94
Timor-Leste	12	31	82	35	46	15	12	49			43	72
Togo	18	18	65	65	25	7	12	22			95t	67
Tonga	0	62k	-	-	-	-	-	-			-	-
Trinidad and Tobago	23	2	19	10	6	1	4	4			-	1
Tunisia	7	47	-	22	4	1	2	12			-	97
Turkey	16	21	38	24	4	1	1	12			-	64
Turkmenistan	6	13	71	27	12	2	6	22			-	100
Tuvalu	5	-	-	-	-	-	-	-			-	-

	% of infants with low birthweight 1998-2005*	% of children (1996-2005*) who are:			% of under-fives (1996-2005*) suffering from:					Vitamin A supplementation coverage rate (6-59 months) 2004	% of households consuming iodized salt 1998-2005*
		exclusively breastfed (<6 months)	breastfed with complementary food (6-9 months)	still breastfeeding (20-23 months)	underweight		wasting	stunting			
					moderate & severe	severe	moderate & severe	moderate & severe			
Uganda	12	63	75	50	23	5	4	39	68	95
Ukraine	5	22	-	-	1	0	0	3	-	32
United Arab Emirates	15x	34x,k	52x	29x	14x	3x	15x	17x	-	-
United Kingdom	8	-	-	-	-	-	-	-	-	-
United States	8	-	-	-	2	0	6	1	-	-
Uruguay	8	-	-	-	5x	1x	1x	8x	-	-
Uzbekistan	7	19	49	45	8	2	7	21	86t	57
Vanuatu	6	50k	-	-	-	-	-	-	-	-
Venezuela (Bolivarian Republic of)	9	7k	50	31	5	1	4	13	-	90
Viet Nam	9	15	-	26	27	4	8	31	95t,w	83
Yemen	32x	12	76	-	46	15	12	53	20	30
Zambia	12	40	87	58	20	-	6	50	50	77
Zimbabwe	11	33	90	35	17	3	5	26	20	93

MEMORANDUM

Serbia and Montenegro (pre-cession)	4	11k	33	11	2	0	4	5	-	73

SUMMARY INDICATORS

Sub-Saharan Africa	14	30	67	55	28	8	9	37	73	67
Eastern and Southern Africa	13	40	69	63	27	7	7	40	60	60
West and Central Africa	15	20	65	48	28	9	10	35	85	73
Middle East and North Africa	15	30	59	24	16	4	8	24	-	65
South Asia	29	38	47	69	45	16	14	44	62	54
East Asia and Pacific	7	43	43	27	15	-	-	19	81**	85
Latin America and Caribbean	9	-	49	26	7	1	2	15	-	86
CEE/CIS	9	22	47	28	5	1	3	14	-	50
Industrialized countries§	7	-	-	-	-	-	-	-	-	-
Developing countries§	16	36	52	46	27	10	10	31	68**	71
Least developed countries§	19	34	64	65	35	10	10	42	75	53
World	15	36	52	46	25	9	9	30	68**	70

‡ Due to the cession in June 2006 of Montenegro from the State Union of Serbia and Montenegro, and its subsequent admission to the UN on 28 June 2006, disaggregated data for Montenegro and Serbia as separate States are not yet available. Aggregated data presented are for Serbia and Montenegro pre-cession (see Memorandum item).

§ Also includes territories within each country category or regional group. Countries and territories in each country category or regional group are listed on page 136.

DEFINITIONS OF THE INDICATORS

Low birthweight – Infants who weigh less than 2,500 grams.

Underweight – Moderate and severe – below minus two standard deviations from median weight for age of reference population; severe – below minus three standard deviations from median weight for age of reference population.

Wasting – Moderate and severe – below minus two standard deviations from median weight for height of reference population.

Stunting – Moderate and severe – below minus two standard deviations from median height for age of reference population.

Vitamin A – Percentage of children aged 6-59 months who have received at least one high dose of vitamin A capsules in 2004.

Iodized salt consumption – Percentage of households consuming adequately iodized salt (15 ppm or more).

MAIN DATA SOURCES

Low birthweight – Demographic and Health Surveys (DHS), Multiple Indicator Cluster Surveys (MICS), other national household surveys and data from routine reporting systems.

Breastfeeding – DHS, MICS and UNICEF.

Underweight, wasting and stunting – DHS, MICS, World Health Organization (WHO) and UNICEF.

Salt iodization – MICS, DHS and UNICEF.

Vitamin A – UNICEF and WHO.

NOTES
- Data not available.
- x Data refer to years or periods other than those specified in the column heading, differ from the standard definition, or refer to only part of a country.
- k Refers to exclusive breastfeeding for less than four months.
- * Data refer to the most recent year available during the period specified in the column heading.
- t Identifies countries that have achieved a second round of vitamin A coverage greater than or equal to 70 per cent.
- ** Excludes China.
- w Identifies countries with vitamin A supplementation programmes that do not target children all the way up to 59 months of age.

TABLE 3. HEALTH

Countries and territories	% of population using improved drinking water sources 2004 total	urban	rural	% of population using adequate sanitation facilities 2004 total	urban	rural	% of routine EPI vaccines financed by government 2005 total	TB BCG	DPT DPT1[β]	DPT3[β]	Polio polio3	Measles measles	HepB HepB3	Hib Hib3	% new-borns protected against tetanus	% under-fives with suspected pneumonia[±] 1999-2005	% under-fives with suspected pneumonia taken to health-care provider[±] 1999-2005*	% under-fives with diarrhoea receiving oral rehydration and continued feeding 1998-2005*	Malaria 1999-2005* % under-fives sleeping under a mosquito net	% under-fives sleeping under a treated mosquito net	% under-fives with fever receiving anti-malarial drugs
Afghanistan	39	63	31	34	49	29	0	73	88	76	76	64	-	-	55	19	28	48	-	-	-
Albania	96	99	94	91	99	84	80	98	98	98	97	97	98	-	-	1	83	51	-	-	-
Algeria	85	88	80	92	99	82	100	98	94	88	88	83	83	-	-	9	52	-	-	-	-
Andorra	100	100	100	100	100	100	-	-	98	98	98	94	79	97	-	-	-	-	-	-	-
Angola	53	75	40	31	56	16	50	61	62	47	46	45	-	-	75	8	58	32	10	2	63
Antigua and Barbuda	91	95	89	95	98	94	100	-	99	99	98	99	99	99	-	-	-	-	-	-	-
Argentina	96	98	80	91	92	83	100	99	90	92	92	99	87	92	-	-	-	-	-	-	-
Armenia	92	99	80	83	96	61	35	94	96	90	92	94	91	-	-	8	28	48	-	-	-
Australia	100	100	100	100	100	100	100	-	97	92	92	94	94	94	-	-	-	-	-	-	-
Austria	100	100	100	100	100	100	-	-	91	86	86	75	86	86	-	-	-	-	-	-	-
Azerbaijan	77	95	59	54	73	36	100	98	95	93	97	98	96	-	-	3	36	40	12	1	1
Bahamas	97	98	86	100	100	100	100	-	99	93	90	85	93	93	-	-	-	-	-	-	-
Bahrain	-	100	-	-	100	-	100	-	99	98	98	99	98	98	-	-	-	-	-	-	-
Bangladesh	74	82	72	39	51	35	16	99	96	88	88	81	62	-	89	21	20	52	-	-	-
Barbados	100	100	100	100	99	100	94	-	97	92	91	93	92	92	-	-	-	-	-	-	-
Belarus	100	100	100	84	93	61	100	99	99	99	98	99	99	-	-	-	-	-	-	-	-
Belgium	-	100	-	-	-	-	-	-	98	97	97	88	78	95	-	-	-	-	-	-	-
Belize	91	100	82	47	71	25	100	96	97	96	96	95	97	96	-	-	66	-	-	-	-
Benin	67	78	57	33	59	11	47	99	99	93	93	85	92	35	69	12	35	42	32	7	60
Bhutan	62	86	60	70	65	70	0	99	97	95	95	93	95	-	-	-	-	-	-	-	-
Bolivia	85	95	68	46	60	22	40	93	94	81	79	64	81	81	-	22	52	54	-	-	-
Bosnia and Herzegovina	97	99	96	95	99	92	80	95	95	93	95	90	93	50	-	2	80	23	-	-	-
Botswana	95	100	90	42	57	25	100	99	98	97	97	90	85	-	-	40	14	7	-	-	-
Brazil	90	96	57	75	83	37	100	-	99	99	98	99	92	96	-	24x	46x	28x	-	-	-
Brunei Darussalam	-	-	-	-	-	-	100	96	99	99	99	97	99	99	-	-	-	-	-	-	-
Bulgaria	99	100	97	99	100	96	100	98	97	96	97	96	96	-	-	-	-	-	-	-	-
Burkina Faso	61	94	54	13	42	6	100	99	99	96	94	84	-	-	75	9	36	47	20	2	50
Burundi	79	92	77	36	47	35	70	84	86	74	64	75	74	74	45	13	40	16	3	1	31
Cambodia	41	64	35	17	53	8	7	87	85	82	82	79	-	-	53	20	37	59	-	-	-
Cameroon	66	86	44	51	58	43	34	77	85	80	79	68	79	-	65	11	40	43	12	1	53
Canada	100	100	99	100	100	99	100	-	97	94	89	94	-	83	-	-	-	-	-	-	-
Cape Verde	80	86	73	43	61	19	80	78	75	73	72	65	69	-	-	-	-	-	-	-	-
Central African Republic	75	93	61	27	47	12	0	70	65	40	40	35	-	-	56	10	32	47	31	2	69
Chad	42	41	43	9	24	4	78	40	45	20	36	23	-	-	39	9	12	27	56	-	44
Chile	95	100	58	91	95	62	100	95	92	91	92	90	-	91	-	-	-	-	-	-	-
China	77	93	67	44	69	28	100	86	95	87	87	86	84	-	-	-	-	-	-	-	-
Colombia	93	99	71	86	96	54	100	87	95	87	87	89	87	87	-	10	57	39	27	-	-
Comoros	86	92	82	33	41	29	15	90	85	80	85	80	80	-	65	10	49	31	36	9	63
Congo	58	84	27	27	28	25	70	-	73	65	65	56	-	-	65	-	-	-	-	-	-
Congo, Democratic Republic of the	46	82	29	30	42	25	0	84	82	73	73	70	-	-	66	11	36	17	12	1	45
Cook Islands	94	98	88	100	100	100	11	99	99	99	99	99	99	-	-	-	-	-	-	-	-
Costa Rica	97	100	92	92	89	97	100	88	DPT1 91	91	89	90	89	-	-	-	-	-	-	-	-
Côte d'Ivoire	84	97	74	37	46	29	53	-	71	56	56	51	56	-	73	4	38	34	14	4	58
Croatia	100	100	100	100	100	100	100	98	96	96	96	96	99	96	-	-	-	-	-	-	-
Cuba	91	95	78	98	99	95	99	99	99	99	99	98	99	94	-	-	-	-	-	-	-
Cyprus	100	100	100	100	100	100	25	-	99	98	98	86	98	58	-	-	-	-	-	-	-
Czech Republic	100	100	100	98	99	97	100	99	98	97	96	97	99	97	-	-	-	-	-	-	-
Denmark	100	100	100	-	-	-	100	-	93	93	95	95	-	93	-	-	-	-	-	-	-
Djibouti	73	76	59	82	88	50	85	52	73	71	71	65	-	-	-	19	44	54	12	4	4
Dominica	97	100	90	84	86	75	70	98	98	98	98	98	-	-	-	-	-	-	-	-	-
Dominican Republic	95	97	91	78	81	73	65	99	92	77	73	99	77	77	-	20	63	42	-	-	-
Ecuador	94	97	89	89	94	82	100	99	99	94	93	93	94	94	-	-	-	-	-	-	-
Egypt	98	99	97	70	86	58	100	98	98	98	98	98	98	-	80	9	73	29	-	-	-
El Salvador	84	94	70	62	77	39	100	84	89	89	89	99	89	89	-	42	62	-	-	-	-
Equatorial Guinea	43	45	42	53	60	46	100	73	65	33	39	51	-	-	48	-	-	36	15	1	49
Eritrea	60	74	57	9	32	3	0	91	91	83	83	84	83	-	-	19	44	54	12	4	4
Estonia	100	100	99	97	97	96	-	99	99	96	96	96	95	37	-	-	-	-	-	-	-
Ethiopia	22	81	11	13	44	7	0	67	78	69	66	59	-	-	45	24	16	38	2	1	3
Fiji	47	43	51	72	87	55	100	90	80	75	80	70	75	75	-	-	-	-	-	-	-
Finland	100	100	100	100	100	100	-	98	99	97	97	97	-	98	-	-	-	-	-	-	-
France	100	100	100	-	-	-	-	84	98	98	98	87	29	87	-	-	-	-	-	-	-

	% of population using improved drinking water sources 2004			% of population using adequate sanitation facilities 2004			% of routine EPI vaccines financed by government 2005	Immunization 2005[λ] 1-year-old children immunized against:							% new-borns protected against tetanus	% under-fives with suspected pneumonia[±]	% under-fives with suspected pneumonia taken to health-care provider[±]	% under-fives with diarrhoea receiving oral rehydration and continued feeding 1998-2005*	Malaria 1999-2005*		
								TB	DPT		Polio	Measles	HepB	Hib					% under-fives sleeping under a mosquito net	% under-fives sleeping under a treated mosquito net	% under-fives with fever receiving anti-malarial drugs
									corresponding vaccines:							1999-2005*					
	total	urban	rural	total	urban	rural	total	BCG	DPT1[β]	DPT3[β]	polio3	measles	HepB3	Hib3	tetanus				net	net	drugs
Gabon	88	95	47	36	37	30	100	89	69	38	31	55	55	-	60	13	48	44	-	-	-
Gambia	82	95	77	53	72	46	60	89	94	88	90	84	88	88	-	8	75	38	42	15	55
Georgia	82	96	67	94	96	91	20	95	94	84	84	92	74	-	-	4	99	-	-	-	-
Germany	100	100	100	100	100	100	-	-	96	90	94	93	84	92	-	-	-	-	-	-	-
Ghana	75	88	64	18	27	11	55	99	88	84	85	83	84	84	84	10	44	40	15	4	63
Greece	-	-	-	-	-	-	-	88	96	88	87	88	88	88	-	-	-	-	-	-	-
Grenada	95	97	93	96	96	97	100	-	93	99	99	99	99	99	-	-	-	-	-	-	-
Guatemala	95	99	92	86	90	82	100	96	93	81	81	77	27	27	-	18	64	22	6	1	-
Guinea	50	78	35	18	31	11	10	90	90	69	70	59	-	-	76	15	33	44	25	4	56
Guinea-Bissau	59	79	49	35	57	23	0	80	86	80	80	80	-	-	54	10	64	23	67	7	58
Guyana	83	83	83	70	86	60	60	96	93	93	93	92	93	93	-	5	78	40	67	6	3
Haiti	54	52	56	30	57	14	10	71	76	43	43	54	-	-	52	39	26	41	-	-	12
Holy See	-	-	-	-	-	-	-	-	-	-	-	-	-	-	-	-	-	-	-	-	-
Honduras	87	95	81	69	87	54	100	91	97	91	91	92	91	91	-	-	-	-	-	-	-
Hungary	99	100	98	95	100	85	99	99	99	99	99	99	-	99	-	-	-	-	-	-	-
Iceland	100	100	100	100	100	100	-	-	95	95	95	90	-	95	-	-	-	-	-	-	-
India	86	95	83	33	59	22	100	75	81	59	58	58	8	-	80	19	67	22	-	-	12
Indonesia	77	87	69	55	73	40	100	82	88	70	70	72	70	-	70	8	61	56	-	26	1
Iran (Islamic Republic of)	94	99	84	-	-	-	100	99	97	95	95	94	94	-	-	24	93	-	-	-	-
Iraq	81	97	50	79	95	48	95	93	93	81	87	90	81	-	70	7	76	54	7	0	1
Ireland	-	100	-	-	-	-	100	93	96	90	90	84	-	90	-	-	-	-	-	-	-
Israel	100	100	100	-	100	-	100	61	98	95	93	95	95	96	-	-	-	-	-	-	-
Italy	-	-	-	-	-	-	-	-	97	96	97	87	96	95	-	-	-	-	-	-	-
Jamaica	93	98	88	80	91	69	100	95	91	88	83	84	87	89	-	3	39	21	-	-	-
Japan	100	100	100	100	100	100	100	-	99	99	97	99	-	-	-	-	-	-	-	-	-
Jordan	97	99	91	93	94	87	100	89	98	95	95	95	95	95	-	6	78	44	-	-	-
Kazakhstan	86	97	73	72	87	52	100	69	99	98	99	99	94	-	-	3	48	22	-	-	-
Kenya	61	83	46	43	46	41	80	85	85	76	76	69	76	76	72	18	49	33	15	5	27
Kiribati	65	77	53	40	59	22	100	94	75	62	61	56	67	99	-	-	-	-	-	-	-
Korea, Democratic People's Republic of	100	100	100	59	58	60	0	94	83	79	97	96	92	-	-	12	93	-	-	-	-
Korea, Republic of	92	97	71	-	-	-	100	97	98	96	96	99	99	-	-	-	-	-	-	-	-
Kuwait	-	-	-	-	-	-	100	-	99	99	99	99	99	-	-	-	-	-	-	-	-
Kyrgyzstan	77	98	66	59	75	51	30	96	98	98	98	99	97	-	-	4x	48x	16x	-	-	-
Lao People's Democratic Republic	51	79	43	30	67	20	0	65	68	49	50	41	49	-	30	1	36	37	82	18	9
Latvia	99	100	96	78	82	71	100	99	98	99	99	95	98	94	-	-	-	-	-	-	-
Lebanon	100	100	100	98	100	87	100	-	98	92	92	96	88	92	-	4	74	-	-	-	-
Lesotho	79	92	76	37	61	32	9	96	95	83	80	85	83	-	-	19	54	53	-	-	-
Liberia	61	72	52	27	49	7	0	82	92	87	77	94	-	-	72	39	70	-	-	-	-
Libyan Arab Jamahiriya	-	-	-	97	97	96	100	99	98	98	98	97	97	-	-	-	-	-	-	-	-
Liechtenstein	-	-	-	-	-	-	-	-	-	-	-	-	-	-	-	-	-	-	-	-	-
Lithuania	-	-	-	-	-	-	100	99	98	94	93	97	95	61	-	-	-	-	-	-	-
Luxembourg	100	100	100	-	-	-	100	-	99	99	99	95	95	98	-	-	-	-	-	-	-
Madagascar	50	77	35	34	48	26	29	72	71	61	63	59	61	-	45	9	48	47	-	-	34
Malawi	73	98	68	61	62	61	20	-	99	93	94	82	93	93	-	27	27	51	20	15	28
Malaysia	99	100	96	94	95	93	85	99	90	90	90	90	90	90	-	-	-	-	-	-	-
Maldives	83	98	76	59	100	42	100	99	99	98	98	97	98	-	-	22	22	-	-	-	-
Mali	50	78	36	46	59	39	71	82	95	85	84	86	85	3	75	10	36	45	72	8	38
Malta	100	100	100	-	100	-	60	-	94	92	94	86	78	83	-	-	-	-	-	-	-
Marshall Islands	87	82	96	82	93	58	-	93	89	77	88	86	89	69	-	-	-	-	-	-	-
Mauritania	53	59	44	34	49	8	100	87	85	71	71	61	42	-	34	10	41	28	31	2	33
Mauritius	100	100	100	94	95	94	100	99	99	97	97	98	97	-	-	-	-	-	-	-	-
Mexico	97	100	87	79	91	41	100	99	99	98	98	96	98	98	-	-	-	-	-	-	-
Micronesia (Federated States of)	94	95	94	28	61	14	0	70	97	94	94	96	91	74	-	-	-	-	-	-	-
Moldova, Republic of	92	97	88	68	86	52	86	97	98	98	98	97	99	-	-	1	78	52	-	-	-
Monaco	100	100	-	100	100	-	-	90	99	99	99	99	99	99	-	-	-	-	-	-	-
Mongolia	62	87	30	59	75	37	26	99	97	99	99	99	99	28	-	2	78	66	-	-	-
Montenegro[‡]	-	-	-	-	-	-	-	-	-	-	-	-	-	-	-	-	-	-	-	-	-
Morocco	81	99	56	73	88	52	100	95	99	98	98	97	96	-	-	12	38	46	-	-	-
Mozambique	43	72	26	32	53	19	47	87	88	72	70	77	72	-	70	10	54	47	10	-	15
Myanmar	78	80	77	77	88	72	0	76	76	73	73	72	62	-	85	2	66	48	-	-	-
Namibia	87	98	81	25	50	13	100	95	93	86	86	73	-	-	-	18	53	39	7	3	14

TABLE 3. HEALTH

	% of population using improved drinking water sources 2004			% of population using adequate sanitation facilities 2004			% of routine EPI vaccines financed by government 2005	Immunization 2005 — 1-year-old children immunized against (corresponding vaccines):							% new-borns protected against tetanus	% under-fives with suspected pneumonia 1999-2005*	% under-fives with suspected pneumonia taken to health-care provider 1999-2005*	% under-fives with diarrhoea receiving oral rehy-dration and continued feeding 1998-2005*	Malaria 1999-2005*		
	total	urban	rural	total	urban	rural	total	BCG	DPT1	DPT3	polio3	measles	HepB3	Hib3					% under-fives sleeping under a mosquito net	% under-fives sleeping under a treated mosquito net	% under-fives with fever receiving anti-malarial drugs
Nauru	-	-	-	-	-	-	100	90	90	80	80	80	80	-	-	-	-	-	-	-	-
Nepal	90	96	89	35	62	30	32	87	81	75	78	74	41	-	-	23	26	43	-	-	-
Netherlands	100	100	100	100	100	100	-	94	98	98	98	96	-	98	-	-	-	-	-	-	-
New Zealand	-	100	-	-	-	-	100	-	92	89	89	82	87	80	-	-	-	-	-	-	-
Nicaragua	79	90	63	47	56	34	100	-	95	86	87	96	86	86	-	31	57	49	-	-	2
Niger	46	80	36	13	43	4	100	93	97	89	89	83	-	-	54	12	27	43	17	6	48
Nigeria	48	67	31	44	53	36	100	48	43	25	39	35	-	-	51	10	33	28	6	1	34
Niue	100	100	100	100	100	100	100	97	72	85	86	99	86	99	-	-	-	-	-	-	-
Norway	100	100	100	-	-	-	100	-	97	91	91	90	-	93	-	-	-	-	-	-	-
Occupied Palestinian Territory	92	94	88	73	78	61	-	99	99	99	99	99	99	-	-	17	65	-	-	-	-
Oman	-	-	-	-	97	-	100	98	99	99	99	98	99	99	-	-	-	-	-	-	-
Pakistan	91	96	89	59	92	41	61	82	84	72	77	78	73	-	57	16x	66x	33x	-	-	-
Palau	85	79	94	80	96	52	100	-	98	98	98	98	98	98	-	-	-	-	-	-	-
Panama	90	99	79	73	89	51	100	99	95	85	86	99	85	85	-	-	-	-	-	-	-
Papua New Guinea	39	88	32	44	67	41	100	73	80	61	50	60	63	-	10	13x	75x	-	-	-	-
Paraguay	86	99	68	80	94	61	100	78	91	75	74	90	75	75	-	17x	51x	-	-	-	-
Peru	83	89	65	63	74	32	100	93	94	84	80	80	84	84	-	17	68	57	-	-	-
Philippines	85	87	82	72	80	59	100	91	90	79	80	80	44	-	70	10	55	76	-	-	-
Poland	-	-	-	-	-	-	100	94	99	99	99	98	98	22	-	-	-	-	-	-	-
Portugal	-	-	-	-	-	-	-	89	94	93	93	93	94	93	-	-	-	-	-	-	-
Qatar	100	100	100	100	100	100	100	99	99	97	98	99	97	97	-	-	-	-	-	-	-
Romania	57	91	16	-	89	-	100	98	98	97	97	97	98	-	-	-	-	-	-	-	-
Russian Federation	97	100	88	87	93	70	100	97	98	98	98	99	97	-	-	-	-	-	-	-	-
Rwanda	74	92	69	42	56	38	30	91	95	95	95	89	95	95	-	12	20	16	6	5	13
Saint Kitts and Nevis	100	99	99	95	96	96	100	99	99	99	99	99	99	99	-	-	-	-	-	-	-
Saint Lucia	98	98	98	89	89	89	100	99	99	95	95	94	95	95	-	-	-	-	-	-	-
Saint Vincent and the Grenadines	-	-	93	-	-	96	100	95	97	99	93	97	99	99	-	-	-	-	-	-	-
Samoa	88	90	87	100	100	100	100	86	86	64	73	57	60	-	-	-	-	-	-	-	-
San Marino	-	-	-	-	-	-	-	-	94	95	95	94	95	94	-	-	-	-	-	-	-
Sao Tome and Principe	79	89	73	25	32	20	5	98	99	97	97	88	96	-	-	5	47	44	52	-	61
Saudi Arabia	-	97	-	-	100	-	100	96	97	96	96	96	96	96	-	-	-	-	-	-	-
Senegal	76	92	60	57	79	34	70	92	97	84	84	74	84	18	85	7	27	33	14	14	29
Serbia‡	-	-	-	-	-	-	-	-	-	-	-	-	-	-	-	-	-	-	-	-	-
Seychelles	88	100	75	-	-	100	100	99	97	99	99	99	99	-	-	-	-	-	-	-	-
Sierra Leone	57	75	46	39	53	30	0	-	77	64	64	67	-	-	-	9	50	39	15	2	61
Singapore	100	100	-	100	100	-	100	98	96	96	96	96	96	-	-	-	-	-	-	-	-
Slovakia	100	100	99	99	100	98	0	98	99	99	99	98	99	99	-	-	-	-	-	-	-
Slovenia	-	-	-	-	-	-	100	-	92	96	96	94	-	96	-	-	-	-	-	-	-
Solomon Islands	70	94	65	31	98	18	0	84	82	80	75	72	72	-	-	-	-	-	-	-	-
Somalia	29	32	27	26	48	14	0	50	50	35	35	35	-	-	25	-	-	-	-	-	-
South Africa	88	99	73	65	79	46	100	97	98	94	94	82	94	94	-	19x	75x	37	-	-	-
Spain	100	100	100	100	100	100	100	-	98	96	96	97	96	96	-	-	-	-	-	-	-
Sri Lanka	79	98	74	91	98	89	75	99	99	99	99	99	99	-	76	-	-	-	-	-	-
Sudan	70	78	64	34	50	24	0	57	86	59	59	60	52	-	41	5	57	38	23	0	50
Suriname	92	98	73	94	99	76	100	-	99	83	84	91	83	83	-	4	58	43	77	3	-
Swaziland	62	87	54	48	59	44	100	84	77	71	71	60	71	-	-	10	60	24	0	0	26
Sweden	100	100	100	100	100	100	0	16	99	99	99	94	-	98	-	-	-	-	-	-	-
Switzerland	100	100	100	100	100	100	5	-	95	93	95	82	-	91	-	-	-	-	-	-	-
Syrian Arab Republic	93	98	87	90	99	81	100	99	99	99	99	99	99	99	-	18	66	-	-	-	-
Tajikistan	59	92	48	51	70	45	5	98	86	81	84	84	81	-	-	1	51	29	6	2	69
Tanzania, United Republic of	62	85	49	47	53	43	62	91	95	90	91	91	90	-	90	8	59	53	31	16	58
Thailand	99	98	100	99	98	99	100	99	98	98	98	96	96	-	-	-	-	-	-	-	-
The former Yugoslav Republic of Macedonia	-	-	-	-	-	-	100	99	98	97	98	96	53	-	-	-	-	-	-	-	-
Timor-Leste	58	77	56	36	66	33	0	70	64	55	55	48	-	-	45	14	24	-	-	-	19
Togo	52	80	36	35	71	15	100	96	91	82	80	70	-	-	-	9	30	25	56	54	60
Tonga	100	100	100	96	98	96	100	99	99	99	99	99	99	99	-	-	-	-	-	-	-
Trinidad and Tobago	91	92	88	100	100	100	100	98	94	95	97	93	95	95	-	3	74	31	-	-	-
Tunisia	93	99	82	85	96	65	100	-	98	98	98	96	97	80	-	9	43	-	-	-	-
Turkey	96	98	93	88	96	72	100	89	92	90	90	91	85	-	47	29	41	19	-	-	-
Turkmenistan	72	93	54	62	77	50	98	99	99	99	99	99	99	-	-	1	51	-	-	-	-
Tuvalu	100	94	92	90	93	84	100	99	99	93	99	62	79	-	-	-	-	-	-	-	-

	% of population using improved drinking water sources 2004			% of population using adequate sanitation facilities 2004			% of routine EPI vaccines financed by government 2005	Immunization 2005[λ] 1-year-old children immunized against:							% newborns protected against tetanus	% under-fives with suspected pneumonia[±] 1999-2005*	% under-fives with suspected pneumonia taken to health-care provider[±] 1999-2005*	% under-fives with diarrhoea receiving oral rehydration and continued feeding 1998-2005*	Malaria 1999-2005*		
								TB	DPT		Polio	Measles	HepB	Hib					% under-fives sleeping under a mosquito net	% under-fives sleeping under a treated mosquito net	% under-fives with fever receiving anti-malarial drugs
	total	urban	rural	total	urban	rural	total	BCG	DPT1[β]	DPT3[§]	polio3	measles	HepB3	Hib3							
Uganda	60	87	56	43	54	41	9	92	94	84	83	86	84	84	56	22	67	29	7	0	-
Ukraine	96	99	91	96	98	93	100	96	95	96	95	96	97	-	-	-	-	-	-	-	-
United Arab Emirates	100	100	100	98	98	95	100	98	97	94	94	92	92	94	-	-	-	-	-	-	-
United Kingdom	100	100	100	-	-	-	100	-	97	91	91	82	-	91	-	-	-	-	-	-	-
United States	100	100	100	100	100	100	56	-	99	96	92	93	92	94	-	-	-	-	-	-	-
Uruguay	100	100	100	100	100	99	100	99	99	96	96	95	96	96	-	-	-	-	-	-	-
Uzbekistan	82	95	75	67	78	61	64	93	99	99	99	99	99	-	-	0	57	33	-	-	-
Vanuatu	60	86	52	50	78	42	100	65	75	66	56	70	56	-	-	-	-	-	-	-	-
Venezuela (Bolivarian Republic of)	83	85	70	68	71	48	100	95	98	87	81	76	88	87	-	9	72	51	-	-	-
Viet Nam	85	99	80	61	92	50	70	95	94	95	94	95	94	-	-	20	71	39	96	16	7
Yemen	67	71	65	43	86	28	13	66	99	86	87	76	86	57	24	24	47	23x	-	-	-
Zambia	58	90	40	55	59	52	10	94	94	80	80	84	80	80	98	15	69	48	16	7	52
Zimbabwe	81	98	72	53	63	47	1	98	95	-	90	85	90	-	-	16	50	80	3	-	-

MEMORANDUM

	total	urban	rural	total	urban	rural	total	BCG	DPT1	DPT3	polio3	measles	HepB3	Hib3							
Serbia and Montenegro (pre-cession)	93	99	86	87	97	77	100	98	98	98	98	96	65	-	-	3	97	-	-	-	-

SUMMARY INDICATORS

	total	urban	rural	total	urban	rural	total	BCG	DPT1	DPT3	polio3	measles	HepB3	Hib3							
Sub-Saharan Africa	55	81	41	37	53	28	50	76	77	66	68	65	37	-	61	13	39	35	14	4	37
Eastern and Southern Africa	55	76	40	36	49	26	36	81	85	76	75	72	57	-	61	17	43	40	11	5	27
West and Central Africa	56	86	42	38	58	30	64	71	70	57	62	58	19	-	61	10	35	31	17	4	44
Middle East and North Africa	88	95	78	74	90	53	80	89	96	89	90	89	88	-	-	13	66	39	-	-	-
South Asia	85	94	81	37	63	27	81	79	83	65	65	64	23	-	77	19	59	27	-	-	12
East Asia and Pacific	79	92	70	51	73	36	91	87	92	84	84	84	78	-	-	10**	62**	56**	-	-	-
Latin America and Caribbean	91	96	73	77	86	49	96	96	95	91	91	92	85	90	-	-	-	-	-	-	-
CEE/CIS	91	98	79	84	93	70	90	93	96	95	95	96	92	-	-	15	50	25	-	-	-
Industrialized countries[§]	100	100	100	100	100	99	75	-	98	96	94	92	64	90	-	-	-	-	-	-	-
Developing countries[§]	80	92	70	50	73	33	78	83	87	75	76	75	54	-	69	16**	54**	35**	-	-	-
Least developed countries[§]	59	79	51	36	55	29	23	81	86	76	76	72	41	-	64	16	37	40	19	5	36
World	83	95	73	59	80	39	78	83	88	78	78	77	55	-	69	15**	54**	35**	-	-	-

‡ Due to the cession in June 2006 of Montenegro from the State Union of Serbia and Montenegro, and its subsequent admission to the UN on 28 June 2006, disaggregated data for Montenegro and Serbia as separate States are not yet available. Aggregated data presented are for Serbia and Montenegro pre-cession (see Memorandum item).

§ Also includes territories within each country category or regional group. Countries and territories in each country category or regional group are listed on page 136.

DEFINITIONS OF THE INDICATORS

Government funding of vaccines – Percentage of vaccines that are routinely administered in a country to protect children and are financed by the national government (including loans).

EPI – Expanded Programme on Immunization: The immunizations in this programme include those against tuberculosis (TB), diphtheria, pertussis (whooping cough) and tetanus (DPT), polio and measles, as well as vaccination of pregnant women to protect babies against neonatal tetanus. Other vaccines, e.g., against hepatitis B (HepB), *Haemophilus influenzae* type b (Hib) or yellow fever, may be included in the programme in some countries.

BCG – Percentage of infants who received bacille Calmette-Guérin (vaccine against tuberculosis).

DPT1 – Percentage of infants who received their first dose of diphtheria, pertussis (whooping cough) and tetanus vaccine.

DPT3 – Percentage of infants who received three doses of diphtheria, pertussis (whooping cough) and tetanus vaccine.

HepB3 – Percentage of infants who received three doses of hepatitis B vaccine.

Hib3 – Percentage of infants who received three doses of *Haemophilus influenzae* type b vaccine.

% under-fives with suspected pneumonia – Percentage of children (0-4 years) with suspected pneumonia in the past two weeks.

% under-fives with suspected pneumonia taken to health-care provider – Percentage of children (0-4 years) with suspected pneumonia in the past two weeks taken to an appropriate health-care provider.

% under-fives with diarrhoea receiving oral rehydration and continued feeding – Percentage of children (0-4 years) with diarrhoea (in the two weeks preceding the survey) who received either oral rehydration therapy (oral rehydration solutions or recommended home-made fluids) or increased fluids and continued feeding.

Malaria:

% under-fives sleeping under a mosquito net – Percentage of children (0-4 years) who slept under a mosquito net.

% under-fives sleeping under a treated mosquito net – Percentage of children (0-4 years) who slept under an insecticide-treated mosquito net.

% under-fives with fever receiving antimalarial drugs – Percentage of children (0-4 years) who were ill with fever in the past two weeks and received any appropriate (locally defined) antimalarial drugs.

MAIN DATA SOURCES

Use of improved drinking water sources and adequate sanitation facilities – UNICEF, World Health Organization (WHO), Multiple Indicator Cluster Surveys (MICS), and Demographic and Health Surveys (DHS).

Government funding of vaccines – UNICEF and WHO.

Immunization – UNICEF and WHO.

Acute respiratory infection – DHS, MICS and other national household surveys.

Oral rehydration – DHS and MICS.

Malaria – DHS and MICS.

NOTES

-   Data not available.
- x   Data refer to years or periods other than those specified in the column heading, differ from the standard definition, or refer to only part of a country.
- *   Data refer to the most recent year available during the period specified in the column heading.
- **   Excludes China.
- β   Coverage for DPT1 should be at least as high as DPT3. Discrepancies where DPT1 coverage is less than DPT3 reflect deficiencies in the data collection and reporting process. UNICEF and WHO are working with national and territorial systems to eliminate these discrepancies.
- ±   In this year's report, we use the term 'suspected pneumonia' instead of 'acute respiratory infections (ARI)', which was employed in previous editions. However, the data collection methodology has not changed, and estimates presented here are comparable to those in previous reports. For a more detailed discussion regarding this update, please see the 'General note on the data' on page 99.
- λ   In this year's report, immunization coverage estimates, specifically for hepatitis B and *Haemophilus influenzae* type b (Hib), are now also presented for countries where these immunizations have been only partially introduced (such as India). In previous reports, no values were provided for countries with only partial introductions of these vaccines.

TABLE 4. HIV/AIDS

Countries and territories	Estimated adult HIV prevalence rate (15+ years), end-2005	Estimated number of people (all ages) living with HIV, 2005 (thousands) estimate	low estimate - high estimate	Estimated number of women (15+) living with HIV, 2005 (thousands)	HIV prevalence rate in young pregnant women (15-24 years) in capital city — year	median	Estimated number of children (0-14 years) living with HIV, 2005 (thousands)	HIV prevalence among young people (15-24 years), 2005 male	female	% who have comprehensive knowledge of HIV, 1999-2005* male	female	% who used condom at last high-risk sex, 1999-2005* male	female	Orphans — orphaned by AIDS, 2005 estimate (thousands)	orphaned due to all causes, 2005 estimate (thousands)	Orphan school attendance ratio 1999-2005*
Afghanistan	<0.1	<1.0	<2.0	<0.1	-	-	-	-	-	-	-	-	-	-	1600	-
Albania	-	-	<1.0	-	-	-	-	-	-	-	0	-	-	-	-	-
Algeria	0.1	19	9.0 - 59	4.1	-	-	-	-	-	-	-	-	-	-	-	-
Andorra	-	-	-	-	-	-	-	-	-	-	-	-	-	-	-	-
Angola	3.7	320	200 - 450	170	2004	2.8	35	0.9	2.5	-	-	-	-	160	1200	90
Antigua and Barbuda	-	-	-	-	-	-	-	-	-	-	-	-	-	-	-	-
Argentina	0.6	130	80 - 220	36	-	-	-	-	-	-	-	-	-	-	690	-
Armenia	0.1	2.9	1.8 - 5.8	<1.0	-	-	-	-	-	8	7	44	-	-	-	-
Australia	0.1	16	9.7 - 27	<1.0	-	-	-	-	-	-	-	-	-	-	-	-
Austria	0.3	12	7.2 - 20	2.3	-	-	-	-	-	-	-	-	-	-	-	-
Azerbaijan	0.1	5.4	2.6 - 17	<1.0	-	-	-	-	-	-	2	-	-	-	-	-
Bahamas	3.3	6.8	3.3 - 22	3.8	-	-	<0.5	-	-	-	-	-	-	-	8	-
Bahrain	-	<1.0	<2.0	-	-	-	-	-	-	-	-	-	-	-	-	-
Bangladesh	<0.1	11	6.4 - 18	1.4	-	-	-	-	-	-	-	-	-	-	4400	-
Barbados	1.5	2.7	1.5 - 4.2	<1.0	-	-	<0.1	-	-	-	-	-	-	-	3	-
Belarus	0.3	20	11 - 47	5.1	-	-	-	-	-	-	-	-	-	-	-	-
Belgium	0.3	14	8.1 - 22	5.4	-	-	-	-	-	-	-	-	-	-	-	-
Belize	2.5	3.7	2.0 - 5.7	1.0	-	-	<0.1	-	-	-	-	-	-	-	5	-
Benin	1.8	87	57 - 120	45	2003	1.7 - 2.1	9.8	0.4	1.1	14	8	34	19	62	370	-
Bhutan	<0.1	<0.5	<2.0	<0.1	-	-	-	-	-	-	-	-	-	-	78	-
Bolivia	0.1	7.0	3.8 - 17	1.9	-	-	-	-	-	18	-	37	20	-	310	-
Bosnia and Herzegovina	<0.1	<0.5	<1.0	-	-	-	-	-	-	-	-	-	-	-	-	-
Botswana	24.1	270	260 - 350	140	2005	33.5	14	5.7	15.3	33	40	88	75	120	150	99
Brazil	0.5	620	370 - 1000	220	-	-	-	-	-	-	-	-	-	-	3700	-
Brunei Darussalam	<0.1	<0.1	<0.2	<0.1	-	-	-	-	-	-	-	-	-	-	4	-
Bulgaria	<0.1	<0.5	<1.0	-	-	-	-	-	-	-	-	-	-	-	-	-
Burkina Faso	2.0	150	120 - 190	80	2005	1.8	17	0.5	1.4	23	15	67	54	120	710	109
Burundi	3.3	150	130 - 180	79	2004	8.6	20	0.8	2.3	-	24	-	-	120	600	70
Cambodia	1.6	130	74 - 210	59	2002	2.7	-	-	-	-	37	-	-	-	470	71
Cameroon	5.4	510	460 - 560	290	2002	7.0	43	1.4	4.9	34	27	57	46	240	1000	99
Canada	0.3	60	48 - 72	9.6	-	-	-	-	-	-	-	-	-	-	-	-
Cape Verde	-	-	-	-	-	-	-	-	-	-	-	-	-	-	-	-
Central African Republic	10.7	250	110 - 390	130	2002	14.0	24	2.5	7.3	-	5	-	-	140	330	91
Chad	3.5	180	88 - 300	90	2005	3.6	16	0.9	2.2	20	8	25	17	57	600	105
Chile	0.3	28	17 - 56	7.6	-	-	-	-	-	-	-	-	-	-	200	-
China	0.1	650	390 - 1100	180	-	-	-	-	-	-	-	-	-	-	20600	-
Colombia	0.6	160	100 - 320	45	-	-	-	-	-	-	-	-	30	-	870	-
Comoros	<0.1	<0.5	<1.0	<0.1	-	-	<0.1	<0.1	<0.1	-	10	-	-	-	33	59
Congo	5.3	120	75 - 160	61	2002	3.0	15	1.2	3.7	22	10	38	20	110	270	-
Congo, Democratic Republic of the	3.2	1000	560 - 1500	520	2003	3.2	120	0.8	2.2	-	-	-	-	680	4200	72
Cook Islands	-	-	-	-	-	-	-	-	-	-	-	-	-	-	-	-
Costa Rica	0.3	7.4	3.6 - 24	2.0	2002	5.2	-	-	-	-	-	-	-	-	44	-
Côte d'Ivoire	7.1	750	470 - 1000	400	2002	5.2	74	1.7	5.1	-	16	-	-	450	1400	83
Croatia	<0.1	<0.5	<1.0	-	-	-	-	-	-	-	-	-	-	-	-	-
Cuba	0.1	4.8	2.3 - 15	2.6	-	-	-	-	-	-	52	-	-	-	120	-
Cyprus	-	<0.5	<1.0	-	-	-	-	-	-	-	-	-	-	-	-	-
Czech Republic	0.1	1.5	0.9 - 2.5	<1.0	-	-	-	-	-	-	-	-	-	-	-	-
Denmark	0.2	5.6	3.4 - 9.3	1.3	-	-	-	-	-	-	-	-	-	-	-	-
Djibouti	3.1	15	3.9 - 34	8.4	-	-	1.2	0.7	2.1	-	-	-	-	6	48	-
Dominica	-	-	-	-	-	-	-	-	-	-	-	-	-	-	-	-
Dominican Republic	1.1	66	56 - 77	31	-	-	3.6	-	-	-	-	52	29	-	220	96
Ecuador	0.3	23	11 - 74	12	-	-	-	-	-	-	-	-	-	-	230	-
Egypt	<0.1	5.3	2.9 - 13	<1.0	-	-	-	-	-	-	-	-	-	-	-	-
El Salvador	0.9	36	22 - 72	9.9	-	-	-	-	-	-	-	-	-	-	150	-
Equatorial Guinea	3.2	8.9	7.3 - 11	4.7	-	-	<1.0	0.7	2.3	-	4	-	-	5	29	95
Eritrea	2.4	59	33 - 95	31	-	-	6.6	0.6	1.6	-	37	-	-	36	280	83
Estonia	1.3	10	4.8 - 32	2.4	-	-	-	-	-	-	-	-	-	-	-	-
Ethiopia	-	-	420 - 1300	-	2003	11.5	-	-	-	-	-	30	17	-	4800	60
Fiji	0.1	<1.0	0.3 - 2.1	<0.5	-	-	-	-	-	-	-	-	-	-	25	-
Finland	0.1	1.9	1.1 - 3.1	<1.0	-	-	-	-	-	-	-	-	-	-	-	-
France	0.4	130	78 - 210	45	-	-	-	-	-	-	-	-	-	-	-	-
Gabon	7.9	60	40 - 87	33	-	-	3.9	1.8	5.4	22	24	48	33	20	65	98
Gambia	2.4	20	10 - 33	11	-	-	1.2	0.6	1.7	-	15	-	-	4	64	85

	Estimated adult HIV prevalence rate (15+ years), end-2005	Estimated number of people (all ages) living with HIV, 2005 (thousands) estimate	low estimate - high estimate	Estimated number of women (15+) living with HIV, 2005 (thousands)	HIV prevalence rate in young pregnant women (15-24 years) in capital city year	median	Estimated number of children (0-14 years) living with HIV, 2005 (thousands)	HIV prevalence among young people (15-24 years), 2005 male	female	% who have comprehensive knowledge of HIV, 1999-2005* male	female	% who used condom at last high-risk sex, 1999-2005* male	female	Children orphaned by AIDS, 2005 estimate (thousands)	orphaned due to all causes, 2005 estimate (thousands)	Orphan school attendance ratio 1999-2005*
Georgia	0.2	5.6	2.7 - 18	<1.0	-	-	-	-	-	-	-	-	-	-	-	-
Germany	0.1	49	29 - 81	15	-	-	-	-	-	-	-	-	-	-	-	-
Ghana	2.3	320	270 - 380	180	2003	3.9	25	0.2	1.3	44	38	52	33	170	1000	79p
Greece	0.2	9.3	5.6 - 15	2.0	-	-	-	-	-	-	-	-	-	-	-	-
Grenada	-	-	-	-	-	-	-	-	-	-	-	-	-	-	-	-
Guatemala	0.9	61	37 - 100	16	-	-	-	-	-	-	-	-	-	-	370	98
Guinea	1.5	85	69 - 100	53	2004	4.4	7.0	0.5	1.4	-	-	32	17	28	370	113
Guinea-Bissau	3.8	32	18 - 50	17	-	-	3.2	0.9	2.5	-	8	-	-	11	100	103
Guyana	2.4	12	4.7 - 23	6.6	-	-	<1.0	-	-	-	36	-	-	-	26	-
Haiti	3.8	190	120 - 270	96	2000	3.7	17	-	-	28	15	30	19	-	490	87
Holy See	-	-	-	-	-	-	-	-	-	-	-	-	-	-	-	-
Honduras	1.5	63	35 - 99	16	-	-	2.4	-	-	-	-	-	-	-	180	-
Hungary	0.1	3.2	1.9 - 5.3	<1.0	-	-	-	-	-	-	-	-	-	-	-	-
Iceland	0.2	<0.5	<1.0	<0.1	-	-	-	-	-	-	-	-	-	-	-	-
India	0.9	5700	3400 - 9400	1600	-	-	-	-	-	17	21	59	51	-	25700	-
Indonesia	0.1	170	100 - 290	29	-	-	-	-	-	-	7	-	-	-	5300	82
Iran (Islamic Republic of)	0.2	66	36 - 160	11	-	-	-	-	-	-	-	-	-	-	1500	-
Iraq	-	-	-	-	-	-	-	-	-	-	-	-	-	-	-	-
Ireland	0.2	5.0	3.0 - 8.3	1.8	-	-	-	-	-	-	-	-	-	-	-	-
Israel	-	4.0	2.2 - 9.8	-	-	-	-	-	-	-	-	-	-	-	-	-
Italy	0.5	150	90 - 250	50	-	-	-	-	-	-	-	-	-	-	-	-
Jamaica	1.5	25	14 - 39	6.9	-	-	<0.5	-	-	-	-	-	-	-	55	-
Japan	<0.1	17	10 - 29	9.9	-	-	-	-	-	-	-	-	-	-	-	-
Jordan	-	<1.0	<2.0	-	-	-	-	-	-	-	-	-	-	-	-	-
Kazakhstan	0.1	12	11 - 77	6.8	-	-	-	-	-	-	-	65	32	-	-	-
Kenya	6.1	1300	1100 - 1500	740	-	-	150	1.0	5.2	47	34	47	25	1100	2300	95
Kiribati	-	-	-	-	-	-	-	-	-	-	-	-	-	-	-	-
Korea, Democratic People's Republic of	-	-	-	-	-	-	-	-	-	-	-	-	-	-	-	-
Korea, Republic of	<0.1	13	7.9 - 25	7.4	-	-	-	-	-	-	-	-	-	-	450	-
Kuwait	-	<1.0	<2.0	-	-	-	-	-	-	-	-	-	-	-	-	-
Kyrgyzstan	0.1	4.0	1.9 - 13	<1.0	-	-	-	-	-	-	-	-	-	-	-	-
Lao People's Democratic Republic	0.1	3.7	1.8 - 12	<1.0	-	-	-	-	-	-	-	-	-	-	290	-
Latvia	0.8	10	6.1 - 17	2.2	-	-	-	-	-	-	-	-	-	-	-	-
Lebanon	0.1	2.9	1.4 - 9.2	<1.0	-	-	-	-	-	-	-	-	-	-	-	-
Lesotho	23.2	270	250 - 290	150	2004	27.3	18	5.9	14.1	18	26	48	50	97	150	95
Liberia	-	-	-	-	-	-	-	-	-	-	-	-	-	-	250	-
Libyan Arab Jamahiriya	-	-	-	-	-	-	-	-	-	-	-	-	-	-	-	-
Liechtenstein	-	-	-	-	-	-	-	-	-	-	-	-	-	-	-	-
Lithuania	0.2	3.3	1.6 - 10	<1.0	-	-	-	-	-	-	-	-	-	-	-	-
Luxembourg	0.2	<1.0	<1.0	-	-	-	-	-	-	-	-	-	-	-	-	-
Madagascar	0.5	49	16 - 110	13	-	-	1.6	0.6	0.3	16	19	12	5	13	900	76
Malawi	14.1	940	480 - 1400	500	2001	15.0	91	3.4	9.6	36	24	47	35	550	950	93
Malaysia	0.5	69	33 - 220	17	-	-	-	-	-	-	-	-	-	-	480	-
Maldives	-	-	-	-	-	-	-	-	-	-	-	-	-	-	-	-
Mali	1.7	130	96 - 160	66	2002	2.5	16	0.4	1.2	15	9	30	14	94	710	104
Malta	0.1	<0.5	<1.0	-	-	-	-	-	-	-	-	-	-	-	-	-
Marshall Islands	-	-	-	-	-	-	-	-	-	-	-	-	-	-	-	-
Mauritania	0.7	12	7.3 - 23	6.3	-	-	1.1	0.2	0.5	-	-	-	-	7	170	-
Mauritius	0.6	4.1	1.9 - 13	<1.0	-	-	-	-	-	-	-	-	-	-	23	-
Mexico	0.3	180	99 - 440	42	-	-	-	-	-	-	-	-	-	-	1600	-
Micronesia (Federated States of)	-	-	-	-	-	-	-	-	-	-	-	-	-	-	-	-
Moldova, Republic of	1.1	29	15 - 69	16	-	-	-	-	-	-	19	63	44	-	-	-
Monaco	-	-	-	-	-	-	-	-	-	-	-	-	-	-	-	-
Mongolia	<0.1	<0.5	<2.0	<0.1	-	-	-	-	-	-	32	-	-	-	79	-
Montenegro‡	-	-	- - -	-	-	-	-	-	-	-	-	-	-	-	-	-
Morocco	0.1	19	12 - 38	4.0	-	-	-	-	-	-	12	-	-	-	-	-
Mozambique	16.1	1800	1400 - 2200	960	2002	14.7	140	3.6	10.7	33	20	33	29	510	1500	80
Myanmar	1.3	360	200 - 570	110	-	-	-	-	-	-	-	-	-	-	1700	-
Namibia	19.6	230	110 - 360	130	2004	7.5	17	4.4	13.4	41	31	69	48	85	140	92
Nauru	-	-	-	-	-	-	-	-	-	-	-	-	-	-	-	-
Nepal	0.5	75	41 - 180	16	-	-	-	-	-	-	-	-	-	-	970	-

TABLE 4. HIV/AIDS

	Estimated adult HIV prevalence rate (15+ years), end-2005	Estimated number of people (all ages) living with HIV, 2005 (thousands) estimate	low estimate - high estimate	Estimated number of women (15+) living with HIV, 2005 (thousands)	HIV prevalence rate in young pregnant women (15-24 years) in capital city — year	median	Estimated number of children (0-14 years) living with HIV, 2005 (thousands)	HIV prevalence among young people (15-24 years), 2005 male	female	% who have comprehensive knowledge of HIV, 1999-2005* male	female	% who used condom at last high-risk sex, 1999-2005* male	female	orphaned by AIDS, 2005 estimate (thousands)	orphaned due to all causes, 2005 estimate (thousands)	Orphan school attendance ratio 1999-2005*
Netherlands	0.2	18	11 - 29	5.9	-	-	-	-	-	-	-	-	-	-	-	-
New Zealand	0.1	1.4	0.8 - 2.3	-	-	-	-	-	-	-	-	-	-	-	-	-
Nicaragua	0.2	7.3	3.9 - 18	1.7	-	-	-	-	-	-	-	-	17	-	130	-
Niger	1.1	79	39 - 130	42	-	-	8.9	0.2	0.8	-	5	-	-	46	800	-
Nigeria	3.9	2900	1700 - 4200	1600	-	-	240	0.9	2.7	21	18	46	24	930	8600	64p
Niue	-	-	-	-	-	-	-	-	-	-	-	-	-	-	-	-
Norway	0.1	2.5	1.5 - 4.1	<1.0	-	-	-	-	-	-	-	-	-	-	-	-
Occupied Palestinian Territory	-	-	-	-	-	-	-	-	-	-	-	-	-	-	-	-
Oman	-	-	-	-	-	-	-	-	-	-	-	-	-	-	-	-
Pakistan	0.1	85	46 - 210	14	-	-	-	-	-	-	-	-	-	-	4400	-
Palau	-	-	-	-	-	-	-	-	-	-	-	-	-	-	-	-
Panama	0.9	17	11 - 34	4.3	-	-	-	-	-	-	-	-	-	-	53	-
Papua New Guinea	1.8	60	32 - 140	34	-	-	-	-	-	-	-	-	-	-	350	-
Paraguay	0.4	13	6.2 - 41	3.5	-	-	-	-	-	-	-	-	-	-	150	-
Peru	0.6	93	56 - 150	26	-	-	-	-	-	-	-	-	19	-	660	85p
Philippines	<0.1	12	7.3 - 20	3.4	-	-	-	-	-	-	-	-	-	-	2000	-
Poland	0.1	25	15 - 41	7.5	-	-	-	-	-	-	-	-	-	-	-	-
Portugal	0.4	32	19 - 53	1.3	-	-	-	-	-	-	-	-	-	-	-	-
Qatar	-	-	-	-	-	-	-	-	-	-	-	-	-	-	-	-
Romania	<0.1	7.0	3.4 - 22	-	-	-	-	-	-	-	-	-	-	-	-	-
Russian Federation	1.1	940	560 - 1600	210	-	-	-	-	-	-	-	-	-	-	-	-
Rwanda	3.1	190	180 - 210	91	2003	10.3	27	0.4	1.5	54	51	40	26	210	820	82
Saint Kitts and Nevis	-	-	-	-	-	-	-	-	-	-	-	-	-	-	-	-
Saint Lucia	-	-	-	-	-	-	-	-	-	-	-	-	-	-	-	-
Saint Vincent and the Grenadines	-	-	-	-	-	-	-	-	-	-	-	-	-	-	-	-
Samoa	-	-	-	-	-	-	-	-	-	-	-	-	-	-	-	-
San Marino	-	-	-	-	-	-	-	-	-	-	-	-	-	-	-	-
Sao Tome and Principe	-	-	-	-	-	-	-	-	-	-	11	-	-	-	-	-
Saudi Arabia	-	-	-	-	-	-	-	-	-	-	-	-	-	-	-	-
Senegal	0.9	61	29 - 100	33	2005	0.9	5.0	0.2	0.6	-	13	52	36	25	560	74p
Serbia‡	-	-	---	-	-	-	-	-	-	-	-	-	-	-	-	-
Seychelles	-	-	-	-	-	-	-	-	-	-	-	-	-	-	-	-
Sierra Leone	1.6	48	27 - 73	26	2003	3.2	5.2	0.4	1.1	-	16	-	-	31	340	71
Singapore	0.3	5.5	3.1 - 14	1.5	-	-	-	-	-	-	-	-	-	-	26	-
Slovakia	<0.1	<0.5	<1.0	-	-	-	-	-	-	-	-	-	-	-	-	-
Slovenia	<0.1	<0.5	<1.0	-	-	-	-	-	-	-	-	-	-	-	-	-
Solomon Islands	-	-	-	-	-	-	-	-	-	-	-	-	-	-	-	-
Somalia	0.9	44	23 - 81	23	-	-	4.5	0.2	0.6	-	0	-	-	23	630	65
South Africa	18.8	5500	4900 - 6100	3100	2004	25.2	240	4.5	14.8	-	-	-	-	1200	2500	-
Spain	0.6	140	84 - 230	32	-	-	-	-	-	-	-	-	-	-	-	-
Sri Lanka	<0.1	5.0	3.0 - 8.3	<1.0	-	-	-	-	-	-	-	-	-	-	310	-
Sudan	1.6	350	170 - 580	180	-	-	30	-	-	-	-	-	-	-	1700	96
Suriname	1.9	5.2	2.8 - 8.1	1.4	-	-	<0.1	-	-	-	27	-	-	-	10	89
Swaziland	33.4	220	150 - 290	120	2004	37.3	15	7.7	22.7	-	27	-	-	63	95	91
Sweden	0.2	8.0	4.8 - 13	2.5	-	-	-	-	-	-	-	-	-	-	-	-
Switzerland	0.4	17	9.9 - 27	5.9	-	-	-	-	-	-	-	-	-	-	-	-
Syrian Arab Republic	-	-	-	-	-	-	-	-	-	-	-	-	-	-	-	-
Tajikistan	0.1	4.9	2.4 - 16	<0.5	-	-	-	-	-	-	1	-	-	-	-	-
Tanzania, United Republic of	6.5	1400	1300 - 1600	710	2003	8.2	110	2.8	3.8	49	44	47	42	1100	2400	82
Thailand	1.4	580	330 - 920	220	-	-	16	-	-	-	-	-	-	-	1200	-
The former Yugoslav Republic of Macedonia	<0.1	<0.5	<1.0	-	-	-	-	-	-	-	-	-	-	-	-	-
Timor-Leste	-	-	-	-	-	-	-	-	-	-	-	-	-	-	-	-
Togo	3.2	110	65 - 160	61	2004	9.3	9.7	0.8	2.2	-	20	-	-	88	280	96
Tonga	-	-	-	-	-	-	-	-	-	-	-	-	-	-	-	-
Trinidad and Tobago	2.6	27	15 - 42	15	-	-	<1.0	-	-	-	33	-	-	-	28	-
Tunisia	0.1	8.7	4.7 - 21	1.9	-	-	-	-	-	-	-	-	-	-	-	-
Turkey	-	<2.0	<5.0	-	-	-	-	-	-	-	-	-	-	-	-	-
Turkmenistan	<0.1	<0.5	<1.0	-	-	-	-	-	-	-	3	-	-	-	-	-
Tuvalu	-	-	-	-	-	-	-	-	-	-	-	-	-	-	-	-
Uganda	6.7	1000	850 - 1200	520	2005	5.2	110	2.3	5.0	40	28	55	53	1000	2300	95
Ukraine	1.4	410	250 - 680	200	-	-	-	-	-	-	-	-	-	-	-	-

	Estimated adult HIV prevalence rate (15+ years), end-2005	Estimated number of people (all ages) living with HIV, 2005 (thousands) estimate	low estimate - high estimate	Estimated number of women (15+) living with HIV, 2005 (thousands)	HIV prevalence rate in young pregnant women (15-24 years) in capital city year	median	Estimated number of children (0-14 years) living with HIV, 2005 (thousands)	HIV prevalence among young people (15-24 years), 2005 male	female	% who have comprehensive knowledge of HIV, 1999-2005* male	female	% who used condom at last high-risk sex, 1999-2005* male	female	Children (0-17 years) orphaned by AIDS, 2005 estimate (thousands)	orphaned due to all causes, 2005 estimate (thousands)	Orphan school attendance ratio 1999-2005*
United Arab Emirates	-	-	-	-	-	-	-	-	-	-	-	-	-	-	-	-
United Kingdom	0.2	68	41 - 110	21	-	-	-	-	-	-	-	-	-	-	-	-
United States	0.6	1200	720 - 2000	300	-	-	-	-	-	-	-	-	-	-	-	-
Uruguay	0.5	9.6	4.6 - 30	5.3	-	-	-	-	-	-	-	-	-	-	55	-
Uzbekistan	0.2	31	15 - 99	4.1	-	-	-	-	-	7	8	50	-	-	-	-
Vanuatu	-	-	-	-	-	-	-	-	-	-	-	-	-	-	-	-
Venezuela (Bolivarian Republic of)	0.7	110	54 - 350	31	-	-	-	-	-	-	-	-	-	-	480	-
Viet Nam	0.5	260	150 - 430	84	-	-	-	-	-	50	42	68	-	-	1800	-
Yemen	-	-	-	-	-	-	-	-	-	-	-	-	-	-	-	-
Zambia	17.0	1100	1100 - 1200	570	2004	20.7	130	3.8	12.7	33	31	40	35	710	1200	92
Zimbabwe	20.1	1700	1100 - 2200	890	2004	18.6	160	4.4	14.7	-	-	69	42	1100	1400	98

MEMORANDUM

Serbia and Montenegro (pre-cession)	0.2	10	6.0 - 17	2.0	-	-	-	-	-	-	-	-	-	-	-	-

SUMMARY INDICATORS

Sub-Saharan Africa	6.1	24500	21600 - 27400	13200	-	9.7	2000	1.5	4.3	31	23	43	29	12000	46600	79
Eastern and Southern Africa	8.6	17500	15800 - 19200	9400	-	13.5	1400	2.1	6.1	40	31	41	30	8700	24300	80
West and Central Africa	3.5	6900	5300 - 8700	3700	-	4.0	650	0.8	2.5	24	18	46	27	3300	22200	77
Middle East and North Africa	0.2	510	320 - 830	210	-	-	33	-	-	-	-	-	-	-	-	-
South Asia	0.7	5900	3600 - 9700	1600	-	-	130	-	-	17	21	59	51	-	37500	-
East Asia and Pacific	0.2	2300	1800 - 3200	750	-	-	50	-	-	-	-	-	-	-	34800	-
Latin America and Caribbean	0.6	1900	1500 - 2800	640	-	-	54	-	-	-	-	-	-	-	10700	-
CEE/CIS	0.6	1500	1000 - 2300	450	-	-	9	-	-	-	-	-	-	-	-	-
Industrialized countries§	0.4	2000	1400 - 3000	530	-	-	13	-	-	-	-	-	-	-	-	-
Developing countries§	1.1	35100	30300 - 41900	16400	-	-	2300	-	-	-	-	-	-	-	-	-
Least developed countries§	2.7	11700	10100 - 13500	6000	-	7.5	1100	-	-	-	-	-	-	-	-	81
World	1.0	38600	33400 - 46000	17300	-	-	2300	-	-	-	-	-	-	15200	132700	-

‡ Due to the cession in June 2006 of Montenegro from the State Union of Serbia and Montenegro, and its subsequent admission to the UN on 28 June 2006, disaggregated data for Montenegro and Serbia as separate States are not yet available. Aggregated data presented are for Serbia and Montenegro pre-cession (see Memorandum item).

§ Also includes territories within each country category or regional group. Countries and territories in each country category or regional group are listed on page 136.

DEFINITIONS OF THE INDICATORS

Estimated adult HIV prevalence rate – Percentage of adults (15-49 years) living with HIV as of end-2005.

Estimated number of people (all ages) living with HIV – Estimated number of people (all ages) living with HIV as of end-2005.

Estimated number of women (15+ years) living with HIV – Estimated number of women living with HIV as of end-2005.

HIV prevalence rate in young pregnant women in capital city – Percentage of blood samples taken from pregnant women (15-24 years) who test positive for HIV during 'unlinked anonymous' sentinel surveillance at selected antenatal clinics.

Estimated number of children (0-14 years) living with HIV – Estimated number of children 0-14 years living with HIV as of end-2005.

HIV prevalence among young men and women – Percentage of young men and women 15-24 years living with HIV as of end-2005.

Comprehensive knowledge of HIV – Percentage of young men and women (15-24 years) who correctly identify the two major ways of preventing the sexual transmission of HIV (using condoms and limiting sex to one faithful, uninfected partner), who reject the two most common local misconceptions about HIV transmission, and who know that a healthy-looking person can have the AIDS virus.

Condom use at last high-risk sex – Percentage of young men and women (15-24 years) who say they used a condom the last time they had sex with a non-marital, non-cohabiting partner, of those who have had sex with such a partner in the past 12 months.

Children orphaned by AIDS – Estimated number of children (0-17 years) as of end-2005 who have lost one or both parents to AIDS.

Children orphaned due to all causes – Estimated number of children (0-17 years) as of end-2005 who have lost one or both parents due to any cause.

Orphan school attendance ratio – Percentage of children (10-14 years) who lost both biological parents and who are currently attending school as a percentage of non-orphaned children of the same age who live with at least one parent and who are attending school.

MAIN DATA SOURCES

Estimated adult HIV prevalence rate – Joint United Nations Programme on HIV/AIDS (UNAIDS), *Report on the global AIDS epidemic, 2006.*

Estimated number of people living with HIV – UNAIDS, *Report on the global AIDS epidemic, 2006.*

Estimated number of women (15+ years) living with HIV – UNAIDS, *Report on the global AIDS epidemic, 2006.*

HIV prevalence rate in young pregnant women in capital city – UNAIDS, *Report on the global AIDS epidemic, 2006.*

Estimated number of children (0-14 years) living with HIV – UNAIDS, *Report on the global AIDS epidemic, 2006.*

HIV prevalence among young men and women – UNAIDS, *Report on the global AIDS epidemic, 2006.*

Comprehensive knowledge of HIV – Demographic and Health Surveys (DHS), Multiple Indicator Cluster Surveys (MICS), Behavioural Surveillance Surveys (BSS), Reproductive Health Surveys (RHS) (1999-2005) and www.measuredhs.com/hivdata.

Condom use at last high-risk sex – DHS, BSS and RHS (1999-2005), and www.measuredhs.com/hivdata.

Children orphaned by AIDS – UNICEF, UNAIDS and USAID, *Africa's Orphaned and Vulnerable Generations: Children Affected by AIDS, 2006.*

Children orphaned due to all causes – UNICEF, UNAIDS, and USAID, *Africa's Orphaned and Vulnerable Generations: Children Affected by AIDS, 2006.*

Orphan school attendance ratio – MICS, DHS (1999-2005) and www.measuredhs.com/hivdata.

NOTES
- Data not available.
- p Proportion of orphans (10-14 years) attending school is based on 25-49 cases.
- * Data refer to the most recent year available during the period specified in the column heading.

TABLE 5. EDUCATION

Countries and territories	Adult literacy rate 2000-2004* male	female	Number per 100 population 2002-2004* phones	Internet users	Primary school enrolment ratio 2000-2005* gross male	female	net male	female	Primary school attendance ratio (1996-2005*) net male	female	% of primary school entrants reaching grade 5 Admin. data 2000-2004*	Survey data 1997-2005*	Secondary school enrolment ratio 2000-2005* gross male	female	net male	female	Secondary school attendance ratio (1996-2005*) net male	female
Afghanistan	43	13	3	0	127	56	-	-	66	40	-	92	25	5	-	-	18	6
Albania	99	98	44	2	105	104	96	95	54	50	90y	9	79	77	75	73	39	39
Algeria	80	60	22	3	116	107	98	95	94	93	96	95	78	84	65	68	-	-
Andorra	-	-	146	16	102	100	90	87	-	-	-	-	80	83	71	72	-	-
Angola	83	54	3	1	69x	59x	-	-	58	59	-	75	19	15	-	-	22	20
Antigua and Barbuda	-	-	119	26	-	-	-	-	-	-	-	-	-	-	-	-	-	-
Argentina	97	97	58	16	113	112	99	98	-	-	84	78	84	89	76	82	-	-
Armenia	100	99	21	4	99	103	92	95	96	97	-	99	90	93	88	90	91	95
Australia	-	-	141	65	103	103	96	96	-	-	86	-	152	145	85	86	-	-
Austria	-	-	144	48	106	106	-	-	-	-	-	-	104	98	-	-	-	-
Azerbaijan	99	98	30	5	98	96	85	83	91	91	98y	99	84	82	78	76	87	84
Bahamas	-	-	103	29	93	93	83	85	-	-	-	-	76	84	70	78	-	-
Bahrain	89	84	117	21	104	104	96	97	86	87	100	99	96	102	87	93	77	85
Bangladesh	-	-	3	0	107	111	92	95	82	86	65	87y	49	54	45	51	33	41
Barbados	-	-	124	55	108	106	98	97	-	-	97	-	109	111	93	98	-	-
Belarus	100	99	55	25	103	99	91	88	-	-	100y	-	93	94	87	88	-	-
Belgium	-	-	133	40	104	104	99	99	-	-	-	-	111	107	96	97	-	-
Belize	-	-	48	13	126	123	95	96	-	-	91	-	84	87	70	73	-	-
Benin	48	23	6	1	111	86	93	72	60	47	69	92	34	18	23	11	19	12
Bhutan	-	-	6	3	-	-	-	-	73y	67y	91	-	-	-	-	-	-	-
Bolivia	93	81	27	4	114	113	95	96	78	77	86	50	90	87	74	73	57	56
Bosnia and Herzegovina	99	94	58	6	-	-	-	-	93	93	-	99	-	-	-	-	68	71
Botswana	80	82	41	4	105	104	81	83	83	86	91	96y	73	77	58	64	36	44
Brazil	88	89	60	12	145	137	-	-	96	96	84y	84x	97	107	73	78	42	50
Brunei Darussalam	95	90	-	15	109	109	-	-	-	-	93	-	91	96	-	-	-	-
Bulgaria	99	98	96	16	106	104	96	95	-	-	94y	-	104	100	90	87	-	-
Burkina Faso	29	15	4	0	59	47	46	35	35	29	76	93	14	10	11	8	12	10
Burundi	67	52	1	0	87	73	60	54	50	44	63	80	14	10	-	-	6	6
Cambodia	85	64	4	0	142	131	100	96	66	65	60	92	35	24	30	22	17	11
Cameroon	77	60	7	1	126	107	-	-	80	78	64	96	51	36	-	-	34	32
Canada	-	-	111	62	100	100	99	100	-	-	-	-	109	108	94x	94x	-	-
Cape Verde	-	-	29	5	113	108	92	91	-	-	91	-	63	69	52	58	-	-
Central African Republic	65	33	2	0	76	52	-	-	47	39	-	70	-	-	-	-	10	7
Chad	41	13	2	0	86	56	68	46	41	31	46	64y	23	7	16	5	13	7
Chile	96	96	84	28	106	101	-	-	-	-	99	-	89	90	-	-	-	-
China	95	87	50	7	118	117	99	99	-	-	99	-	73	73	-	-	-	-
Colombia	93	93	40	9	112	111	83	84	90	92	77	89	71	78	52	58	64	72
Comoros	-	-	2	1	91	80	60	50	31	31	63	25	40	30	-	-	10	11
Congo	-	-	10	1	92	85	-	-	-	-	66	-	42	35	-	-	-	-
Congo, Democratic Republic of the	81	54	1	0	51x	46x	-	-	55	49	-	54	24	12	-	-	18	15
Cook Islands	-	-	43x	20x	83	81	78	77	-	-	-	-	63	65	55	60	-	-
Costa Rica	95	95	53	24	112	111	-	-	-	-	92	-	67	73	-	-	-	-
Côte d'Ivoire	61	39	9	1	80	63	62	50	62	53	88	94	32	18	26	15	20	16
Croatia	99	97	106	30	95	94	88	87	-	-	100y	-	87	89	84	86	-	-
Cuba	100	100	7	1	103	98	97	95	-	-	98	99	92	93	86	87	-	-
Cyprus	99	95	131	37	98	97	96	96	-	-	99	-	96	99	92	95	-	-
Czech Republic	-	-	139	50	103	101	-	-	-	-	98	-	95	96	-	-	-	-
Denmark	-	-	160	50	101	101	100	100	-	-	100	-	122	127	91	94	-	-
Djibouti	-	-	7	1	44	35	36	29	-	-	88	-	25	18	22	15	-	-
Dominica	-	-	88	29	96	95	87	88	-	-	84	-	107	106	89	92	-	-
Dominican Republic	87	87	39	9	115	109	85	87	84	88	59	91	61	76	45	54	27	39
Ecuador	92	90	39	5	117	117	97	98	-	-	76	-	61	61	52	53	-	-
Egypt	83	59	24	6	103	98	97	94	84	82	99	99	90	84	81	77	73	68
El Salvador	-	-	41	9	116	112	92	92	-	-	73	-	60	61	47	49	-	-
Equatorial Guinea	93	80	9	1	133	121	92	78	61	60	33	72y	38	22	30	18	23	22
Eritrea	-	-	1	1	71	57	50	42	69	64	80	82y	40	23	31	20	23	21
Estonia	100	100	130	51	101	98	94	94	-	-	99	-	97	99	89	91	-	-
Ethiopia	-	-	1	0	101	86	58	55	33	28	73y	65	38	24	34	22	13	10
Fiji	-	-	26	7	107	105	97	96	-	-	99	-	85	91	80	85	-	-
Finland	-	-	141	63	101	100	99	99	-	-	100	-	107	112	94	94	-	-
France	-	-	130	41	105	104	99	99	-	-	98x	-	110	111	95	97	-	-

| | Adult literacy rate 2000-2004* | | Number per 100 population 2002-2004* | | Primary school enrolment ratio 2000-2005* | | | | Primary school attendance ratio (1996-2005*) net | | % of primary school entrants reaching grade 5 | | Secondary school enrolment ratio 2000-2005* | | | | Secondary school attendance ratio (1996-2005*) net | |
| | | | | | gross | | net | | | | Admin. data 2000-2004* | Survey data 1997-2005* | gross | | net | | | |
	male	female	phones	Internet users	male	female	male	female	male	female			male	female	male	female	male	female
Gabon	-	-	39	3	130	129	77	77	94	94	69	91y	49	42	-	-	34	36
Gambia	-	-	10	3	79	84	73	77	55	51	-	96	51	43	49	41	23	19
Georgia	-	-	30	3	95	95	93	92	99y	100y	98y	-	83	82	81	81	-	-
Germany	-	-	153	43	100	100	-	-	-	-	99y	-	101	99	-	-	-	-
Ghana	66	50	9	2	90	87	65	65	62	60	63	98	47	40	39	35	34	35
Greece	98	94	143	18	102	101	100	99	-	-	-	-	96	97	85	88	-	-
Grenada	-	-	74	17	94	90	84	84	-	-	79	-	96	105	75	82	-	-
Guatemala	75	63	34	6	118	108	95	91	80	76	78	73y	51	46	35	32	23	24
Guinea	43	18	2	1	87	71	69	58	60	54	82	94	34	17	28	14	28	19
Guinea-Bissau	-	-	1	2	84	56	53	37	42	36	-	85	23	13	11	6	10	7
Guyana	-	-	27	19	134	125	-	-	96	97	64	97	92	95	-	-	71	75
Haiti	-	-	7	6	-	-	-	-	52	57	-	87	-	-	-	-	17	20
Holy See	-	-	-	-	-	-	-	-	-	-	-	-	-	-	-	-	-	-
Honduras	80	80	16	3	113	113	90	92	-	-	-	-	58	73	-	-	-	-
Hungary	-	-	122	27	99	97	90	88	-	-	97y	-	97	96	91	90	-	-
Iceland	-	-	164	77	102	100	100	98	-	-	100	-	111	118	85	88	-	-
India	73	48	8	3	120	112	92	87	79	72	79	95y	59	47	-	-	54	46
Indonesia	94	87	18	7	118	116	95	93	94	95	92	96y	64	64	57	57	54	56
Iran (Islamic Republic of)	84	70	27	8	98	108	89	88	94y	91y	88	-	84	79	80	76	-	-
Iraq	84	64	6	0	108	89	94	81	84	72	66x	88	54	36	44	31	37	25
Ireland	-	-	143	30	107	106	96	96	-	-	100	-	108	116	84	89	-	-
Israel	98	96	149	47	110	111	97	98	-	-	100	-	93	93	89	89	-	-
Italy	99	98	153	50	102	101	99	99	-	-	96	-	100	98	92	93	-	-
Jamaica	74	86	97	40	95	95	90	91	93y	93y	90	92	87	89	78	81	-	-
Japan	-	-	118	50	100	101	100	100	-	-	-	-	101	102	99	100	-	-
Jordan	95	85	39	11	98	99	90	92	99	99	99	99y	87	88	80	82	85	89
Kazakhstan	100	99	34	3	110	109	93	92	98	99	100y	99	99	97	93	92	73	76
Kenya	78	70	9	5	114	108	76	77	79	79	75	98	50	46	40	40	12	13
Kiribati	-	-	6	2	113	116	96x	98x	-	-	82	-	82	100	65	76	-	-
Korea, Democratic People's Republic of	-	-	4	-	-	-	-	-	-	-	-	-	-	-	-	-	-	-
Korea, Republic of	-	-	131	66	105	104	100	99	-	-	98	-	93	93	90	91	-	-
Kuwait	94	91	98	24	96	97	85	87	-	-	97y	-	87	93	76	80	-	-
Kyrgyzstan	99	98	13	5	98	98	90	90	95	95	96y	100	88	88	-	-	58	60
Lao People's Democratic Republic	77	61	5	0	124	109	87	82	65	60	63	93	52	39	40	34	27	21
Latvia	100	100	96	35	94	91	-	-	-	-	98y	-	97	96	-	-	-	-
Lebanon	-	-	43	17	109	105	94	93	97	97	98	96	85	93	-	-	61	68
Lesotho	74	90	11	2	131	131	83	88	62	69	63	89	32	41	18	28	12	17
Liberia	-	-	0x	0x	115	83	74	58	59x,y	53x,y	-	-	37	27	22	12	-	-
Libyan Arab Jamahiriya	-	-	16	4	113	112	-	-	-	-	-	-	101	107	-	-	-	-
Liechtenstein	-	-	131	64	106	107	87	89	-	-	-	-	67	74	62	69	-	-
Lithuania	100	100	123	28	98	97	90	89	-	-	99y	-	99	98	93	93	-	-
Luxembourg	-	-	199	59	100	99	91	91	-	-	92	-	92	98	77	82	17	21
Madagascar	77	65	2	1	136	131	89	89	74	77	57	93	14x	14x	11x	11x	10	13
Malawi	75	54	3	0	123	126	93	98	80y	84y	44	86	32	26	27	23	-	-
Malaysia	92	85	75	39	94	93	93	93	-	-	98	-	71	81	71	81	-	-
Maldives	96	96	44	6	105	102	89	90	-	-	99y	-	68	78	48	55	15	11
Mali	27	12	4	0	71	56	50	43	45	33	79	93	28	17	-	-	-	-
Malta	86	89	128	75	103	102	94	94	-	-	99	-	109	102	85	90	-	-
Marshall Islands	-	-	9	4	116	109	90	89	-	-	-	-	85	88	72	77	15	9
Mauritania	60	43	19	0	95	93	75	74	46	42	82	69y	22	18	16	13	-	-
Mauritius	88	81	70	15	102	102	94	95	-	-	99	-	89	88	82	83	-	-
Mexico	92	90	54	13	110	108	98	98	-	-	93	-	77	82	63	65	-	-
Micronesia (Federated States of)	-	-	22	11	-	-	-	-	-	-	-	-	-	-	-	-	79	82
Moldova, Republic of	99	98	39	10	95	94	86	86	87	87	90y	99	81	84	76	79	-	-
Monaco	-	-	149x	49x	-	-	-	-	-	-	-	-	-	-	-	-	59	71
Mongolia	98	98	19	8	104	105	84	84	79	80	91y	95	84	95	77	88	39	36
Montenegro‡	-	-	-	-	-	-	-	-	-	-	-	-	-	-	-	-	-	-
Morocco	66	40	36	12	111	100	89	83	91	87	76	86y	52	43	38	32	8	7
Mozambique	-	-	4	1	104	86	75	67	63	57	49	84	13	9	5	4	51	48

TABLE 5. EDUCATION

| | Adult literacy rate 2000-2004* | | Number per 100 population 2002-2004* | | Primary school enrolment ratio 2000-2005* | | | | Primary school attendance ratio (1996-2005*) net | | % of primary school entrants reaching grade 5 | | Secondary school enrolment ratio 2000-2005* | | | | Secondary school attendance ratio (1996-2005*) net | |
| | | | | | gross | | net | | | | Admin. data 2000-2004* | Survey data 1997-2005* | gross | | net | | | |
	male	female	phones	Internet users	male	female	male	female	male	female			male	female	male	female	male	female
Myanmar	94	86	1	0	99	101	89	91	83	84	70	100	41	40	38	37	29	40
Namibia	87	83	21	4	100	102	71	76	78	78	88	95	54	62	32	43	-	-
Nauru	-	-	29x	3x	84	83	-	-	-	-	31	-	46	50	-	-	35	27
Nepal	63	35	2	0	118	108	83	73	80	67	61	92	49	42	-	-	-	-
Netherlands	77	77	140	62	109	106	99	98	-	-	100	-	120	118	89	90	-	-
New Zealand	-	-	124	53	102	102	99	99	-	-	-	-	110	119	93	96	35	47
Nicaragua	-	-	17	2	113	111	89	87	77	84	59	63	59	68	38	43	6	6
Niger	43	15	1	0	52	37	46	32	36	25	74	89	9	6	8	5	38	33
Nigeria	-	-	8	1	107	91	64	57	66	58	36	97	38	31	30	25	-	-
Niue	-	-	84x	48x	80	95	99x	98x	-	-	-	-	100	95	91x	96x	-	-
Norway	-	-	151	39	99	99	99	99	-	-	100	-	114	117	96	97	80	83
Occupied Palestinian Territory	97	88	36	4	93	93	86	86	91y	92y	98y	99	91	96	87	92	-	-
Oman	87	74	43	10	88	87	77	79	-	-	98	-	88	85	74	75	81	80
Pakistan	63	36	6	1	95	69	76	56	62	51	70	90y	31	23	-	-	-	-
Palau	-	-	-	-	111	91	98	94	-	-	-	-	101	115	-	-	-	-
Panama	93	91	39	9	114	111	98	98	-	-	84	-	68	73	61	67	-	-
Papua New Guinea	63	51	1	3	80	70	-	-	-	-	68	-	29	23	-	-	23	18
Paraguay	-	-	35	2	108	104	-	-	95	96	82	90x	62	63	-	-	70	70
Peru	93	82	22	12	114	114	97	97	94	94	90	-	91	92	69	69	55	70
Philippines	93	93	44	5	113	111	93	95	88	89	75	93	82	90	56	67	-	-
Poland	-	-	77	23	99	99	97	98	-	-	100	-	96	97	89	92	-	-
Portugal	-	-	139	28	119	114	99	99	-	-	-	-	92	102	78	87	-	-
Qatar	89	89	92	22	102	101	95	94	-	-	-	-	98	95	88	86	-	-
Romania	98	96	67	21	107	106	92	92	-	-	95y	-	85	86	80	82	-	-
Russian Federation	100	99	79	11	123	123	91	92	-	-	-	-	93	93	-	-	7	7
Rwanda	71	60	2	0	118	120	72	75	75	75	46	78	15	14	-	-	-	-
Saint Kitts and Nevis	-	-	70	21	98	105	91	98	-	-	87	-	111	108	100	97	-	-
Saint Lucia	-	-	41	37	108	103	99	96	-	-	90	-	77	86	68	74	-	-
Saint Vincent and the Grenadines	-	-	75	7	109	103	95	92	-	-	88	-	79	76	62	63	-	-
Samoa	-	-	13	3	100	100	90	91	-	-	94	-	76	85	62	70	-	-
San Marino	-	-	140	56	-	-	-	-	-	-	-	-	-	-	-	-	38	39
Sao Tome and Principe	-	-	8	12	134	132	98	98	83	85	66	69	39	41	25	27	-	-
Saudi Arabia	87	69	52	6	69	66	62	57	-	-	94	-	72	64	54	51	16	10
Senegal	51	29	13	5	78	74	68	64	71	67	78	93	22	16	18	13	-	-
Serbia†	-	-	-	-	-	-	-	-	-	-	-	-	-	-	-	-	-	-
Seychelles	91	92	87	25	109	110	96	97	-	-	99	-	98	106	90	96	14	12
Sierra Leone	47	24	2	0	169	122	-	-	43	39	-	93	14	14	-	-	-	-
Singapore	97	89	133	56	-	-	-	-	-	-	-	-	-	-	-	-	-	-
Slovakia	-	-	103	42	100	98	-	-	-	-	98y	-	94	95	-	-	-	-
Slovenia	-	-	128	48	123	122	98	98	-	-	99y	-	100	100	94	95	-	-
Solomon Islands	-	-	2	1	121	117	80	79	-	-	-	-	33	26	28	24	1	0
Somalia	-	-	6	0	-	-	-	-	13	11	-	68	-	-	-	-	41	48
South Africa	84	81	47	8	107	103	88	89	80	83	84	98y	87	94	58	65	-	-
Spain	-	-	131	33	109	107	100	99	-	-	-	-	116	123	95	99	-	-
Sri Lanka	92	89	16	1	102	101	99	98	-	-	-	-	82	83	-	-	19	20
Sudan	71	52	6	3	64	56	47	39	60	57	92	71	34	32	-	-	40	47
Suriname	92	87	67	7	118	121	90	96	88	91	-	84	63	84	53	74	24	33
Swaziland	81	78	13	3	103	98	76	77	73	72	77	89	42	42	26	32	-	-
Sweden	-	-	180	75	99	99	99	98	-	-	-	-	101	105	97	100	-	-
Switzerland	-	-	156	47	103	102	94	94	-	-	-	-	97	89	86	80	-	-
Syrian Arab Republic	86	74	27	4	126	120	97	92	-	-	92	-	65	61	60	56	88	72
Tajikistan	100	99	4	0	102	97	99	94	89	88	99y	99	89	75	86	73	7	8
Tanzania, United Republic of	78	62	3	1	108	104	92	91	71	75	76	89y	6x	5x	-	-	-	-
Thailand	95	91	55	11	100	95	-	-	-	-	-	-	72	74	-	-	-	-
The former Yugoslav Republic of Macedonia	98	94	62	8	98	98	92	92	-	-	98y	-	85	83	82	80	-	-
Timor-Leste	-	-	-	-	-	-	-	-	76y	74y	-	-	-	-	-	-	27	18
Togo	69	38	6	4	110	92	85	72	75	65	76	88	52	26	30	14	-	-
Tonga	99	99	15	3	118	112	92x	89x	-	-	92	-	94	102	61	75	69	76
Trinidad and Tobago	-	-	74	12	104	101	92	92	96	96	100	98	81	86	70	74	-	-
Tunisia	83	65	48	8	112	108	97	98	95y	93y	97	92	74	80	66	69	49	36
Turkey	95	80	74	14	96	90	92	87	89	88	95	97	90	68	-	-	85	85
Turkmenistan	99	98	8	1	-	-	-	-	77	75	-	100	-	-	-	-	-	-
Tuvalu	-	-	-	30	95	102	-	-	-	-	70	-	87	81	-	-	14	15

| | Adult literacy rate 2000-2004* | | Number per 100 population 2002-2004* | | Primary school enrolment ratio 2000-2005* | | | | Primary school attendance ratio (1996-2005*) net | | % of primary school entrants reaching grade 5 | | Secondary school enrolment ratio 2000-2005* | | | | Secondary school attendance ratio (1996-2005*) net | |
| | | | | | gross | | net | | | | Admin. data 2000-2004* | Survey data 1997-2005* | gross | | net | | | |
	male	female	phones	Internet users	male	female	male	female	male	female			male	female	male	female	male	female
Uganda	77	58	5	1	118	117	-	-	87	87	64	89	18	14	14	12	-	-
Ukraine	100	99	54	8	95	95	82	82	-	-	-	-	94	92	83	84	-	-
United Arab Emirates	-	-	112	32	85	82	72	70	-	-	95	-	65	68	61	64	-	-
United Kingdom	-	-	159	63	107	107	99	99	-	-	-	-	103	106	93	97	-	-
United States	-	-	123	63	100	98	94	90	-	-	-	-	94	95	89	91	-	-
Uruguay	-	-	49	21	110	108	-	-	-	-	88	-	100	116	-	-	86	85
Uzbekistan	-	-	8	3	100	99	-	-	95	94	96y	89	96	93	-	-	-	-
Vanuatu	-	-	8	4	120	116	95	93	-	-	72x	-	44	38	42	36	30	43
Venezuela (Bolivarian Republic of)	93	93	45	9	106	104	92	92	91	93	91	96	67	77	57	66	59	57
Viet Nam	94	87	18	7	101	94	97	91	97	96	87	96y	75	72	-	-	35	13
Yemen	-	-	9	1	102	72	87	63	68	41	73	88y	64	31	46	21	17	19
Zambia	76	60	5	2	101	97	80	80	55	58	98	88	29	23	27	21	44	41
Zimbabwe	-	-	6	7	97	95	81	82	85	87	70	94	38	35	35	33	-	-

MEMORANDUM

	male	female	phones	Internet users	male	female	male	female	male	female	Admin. data	Survey data	male	female	male	female	male	female
Serbia and Montenegro (pre-cession)	99	94	91	19	98	98	96	96	98y	96y	96y	94	88	89	-	-	-	-

SUMMARY INDICATORS

	male	female	phones	Internet users	male	female	male	female	male	female	Admin. data	Survey data	male	female	male	female	male	female
Sub-Saharan Africa	70	53	8	2	103	92	70	66	63	59	63	85	36	28	30	24	21	20
Eastern and Southern Africa	79	67	10	2	109	102	78	76	66	66	71	83	39	33	33	29	16	17
West and Central Africa	60	38	6	1	97	81	63	55	59	52	55	87	33	23	26	20	26	22
Middle East and North Africa	81	62	27	6	98	91	84	78	83	77	91	90	73	66	66	61	50	44
South Asia	72	46	8	3	116	105	90	84	81	75	76	93	54	45	-	-	54	48
East Asia and Pacific	95	87	45	9	115	114	97	97	-	-	94	-	71	71	57**	58**	53**	55**
Latin America and Caribbean	91	90	50	12	119	116	94	94	89	89	85	-	83	90	66	70	44	51
CEE/CIS	99	96	63	11	103	100	91	89	91	89	96	95	92	87	84	83	-	-
Industrialized countries§	-	-	130	52	102	101	97	95	-	-	-	-	101	102	91	93	-	-
Developing countries§	85	72	29	6	112	105	89	85	78	75	82	91	62	57	52**	51**	46**	43**
Least developed countries§	70	50	3	1	103	91	77	72	64	59	69	82	35	29	33	29	22	20
World	86	74	45	13	111	104	90	86	78	75	83	91	67	63	61**	60**	46**	43**

‡ Due to the cession in June 2006 of Montenegro from the State Union of Serbia and Montenegro, and its subsequent admission to the UN on 28 June 2006, disaggregated data for Montenegro and Serbia as separate States are not yet available. Aggregated data presented are for Serbia and Montenegro pre-cession (see Memorandum item).

§ Also includes territories within each country category or regional group. Countries and territories in each country category or regional group are listed on page 136.

DEFINITIONS OF THE INDICATORS

Adult literacy rate – Percentage of persons aged 15 and over who can read and write.

Primary school gross enrolment ratio – The number of children enrolled in primary school, regardless of age, expressed as a percentage of the total number of children of official primary school age.

Secondary school gross enrolment ratio – The number of children enrolled in secondary school, regardless of age, expressed as a percentage of the total number of children of official secondary school age.

Primary school net enrolment ratio – The number of children enrolled in primary school who are of official primary school age, expressed as a percentage of the total number of children of official primary school age.

Secondary school net enrolment ratio – The number of children enrolled in secondary school who are of official secondary school age, expressed as a percentage of the total number of children of official secondary school age.

Primary school net attendance ratio – The number of children attending primary or secondary school who are of official primary school age, expressed as a percentage of the total number of children of official primary school age. These data are from national household surveys.

Secondary school net attendance ratio – The number of children attending secondary or tertiary school who are of official secondary school age, expressed as a percentage of the total number of children of official secondary school age. These data are from national household surveys.

Primary school entrants reaching grade five – Percentage of children entering the first grade of primary school who eventually reach grade five.

MAIN DATA SOURCES

Adult literacy – UNESCO Institute for Statistics (UIS).

Phone and Internet use – International Telecommunications Union (Geneva).

Primary and secondary school enrolment – UIS.

Primary and secondary school attendance – Demographic and Health Surveys (DHS) and Multiple Indicator Cluster Surveys (MICS).

Reaching grade five – Administrative data: UIS. Survey data: DHS and MICS.

NOTES

- Data not available.

x Data refer to years or periods other than those specified in the column heading, differ from the standard definition, or refer to only part of a country, and are not included in the calculation of regional and global averages.

y Data refer to years or periods other than those specified in the column heading, differ from the standard definition, or refer to only part of a country, but are included in the calculation of regional and global averages.

* Data refer to the most recent year available during the period specified in the column heading.

** Excludes China.

TABLE 6. DEMOGRAPHIC INDICATORS

Countries and territories	Population (thousands) 2005 under 18	under 5	Population annual growth rate (%) 1970-1990	1990-2005	Crude death rate 1970	1990	2005	Crude birth rate 1970	1990	2005	Life expectancy 1970	1990	2005	Total fertility rate 2005	% of population urbanized 2005	Average annual growth rate of urban population (%) 1970-1990	1990-2005
Afghanistan	15849	5535	0.7	4.8	26	21	19	51	51	49	39	45	47	7.3	24	3.3	6.7
Albania	1034	253	2.2	-0.3	8	6	7	33	24	17	67	72	74	2.2	45	2.8	1.1
Algeria	11983	3160	3.0	1.7	16	7	5	49	32	21	53	67	72	2.4	60	4.4	2.8
Andorra	12	3	3.8	1.7	-	-	-	-	-	-	-	-	-	-	91	3.8	1.4
Angola	8502	2974	2.7	2.8	28	25	22	52	53	48	37	40	41	6.6	37	5.5	5.1
Antigua and Barbuda	27	8	-0.2	1.7	-	-	-	-	-	-	-	-	-	-	38	0.0	2.2
Argentina	12277	3340	1.5	1.2	9	8	8	23	22	18	66	71	75	2.3	91	2.0	1.4
Armenia	819	162	1.7	-1.1	5	8	9	23	21	11	70	68	72	1.3	64	2.3	-1.4
Australia	4797	1253	1.4	1.2	9	7	7	20	15	12	71	77	81	1.7	93	1.4	1.8
Austria	1552	384	0.2	0.4	13	11	10	15	12	9	70	76	79	1.4	66	0.2	0.4
Azerbaijan	2736	602	1.7	1.0	7	7	7	29	27	16	65	66	67	1.8	50	2.0	0.5
Bahamas	108	30	2.0	1.6	7	7	7	31	24	19	66	68	71	2.2	90	2.8	2.1
Bahrain	232	65	4.0	2.6	9	4	3	40	29	18	62	71	75	2.4	90	4.2	2.7
Bangladesh	59402	17399	2.4	2.1	21	12	8	45	35	26	44	55	64	3.1	25	7.1	3.6
Barbados	63	16	0.4	0.3	9	9	8	22	15	12	69	75	76	1.5	53	0.8	1.4
Belarus	1967	449	0.6	-0.3	7	11	15	16	14	9	71	71	68	1.2	72	2.7	0.2
Belgium	2120	563	0.2	0.3	12	11	10	14	12	11	71	76	79	1.7	97	0.3	0.4
Belize	117	34	2.1	2.5	8	5	5	40	35	26	66	72	72	3.0	49	1.8	2.6
Benin	4300	1441	3.0	3.3	22	15	12	47	47	41	46	53	55	5.6	46	6.7	5.2
Bhutan	983	293	2.2	1.8	23	14	30	43	39	30	41	54	64	4.1	9	5.1	5.3
Bolivia	4090	1239	2.3	2.1	20	11	9	46	36	29	46	59	65	3.7	64	4.0	3.1
Bosnia and Herzegovina	807	186	0.9	-0.7	7	7	9	23	15	9	66	72	74	1.3	45	2.8	0.3
Botswana	800	218	3.2	1.4	13	6	28	48	34	26	55	66	34	3.0	53	11.5	2.8
Brazil	62229	18024	2.2	1.5	11	7	7	35	24	20	59	66	71	2.3	84	3.7	2.3
Brunei Darussalam	130	40	3.4	2.5	7	3	3	36	28	23	67	74	77	2.4	78	3.7	3.6
Bulgaria	1366	335	0.1	-0.8	9	12	14	16	12	9	71	71	73	1.2	70	1.4	-0.4
Burkina Faso	7176	2459	2.4	2.9	23	18	16	50	50	47	43	48	48	6.5	19	6.6	5.0
Burundi	3969	1326	2.4	1.9	20	20	18	44	47	46	44	44	44	6.8	11	7.2	5.4
Cambodia	6242	1835	1.7	2.5	20	13	11	42	44	30	44	55	57	3.9	20	2.1	5.4
Cameroon	7881	2453	2.8	2.2	21	14	17	45	42	35	44	53	46	4.4	53	6.2	4.1
Canada	6970	1698	1.2	1.0	7	7	7	17	14	10	73	78	80	1.5	81	1.3	1.4
Cape Verde	238	72	1.4	2.4	12	8	5	40	39	30	57	65	71	3.6	58	5.5	4.1
Central African Republic	2021	640	2.4	2.0	22	17	22	43	42	37	42	49	39	4.8	44	3.4	3.0
Chad	5257	1867	2.4	3.2	25	19	20	48	48	49	40	46	44	6.7	26	5.3	4.5
Chile	4945	1237	1.6	1.4	10	6	5	29	23	15	62	73	78	2.0	88	2.1	1.8
China	352718	84483	1.6	0.9	8	7	7	33	21	13	62	68	72	1.7	41	3.9	3.5
Colombia	16755	4726	2.2	1.8	9	7	5	38	27	21	61	68	73	2.5	77	3.2	2.6
Comoros	387	127	3.3	2.8	18	11	7	50	41	35	48	56	64	4.6	36	5.1	4.5
Congo	2153	750	3.2	3.2	14	12	13	44	44	44	54	55	53	6.3	54	5.1	4.0
Congo, Democratic Republic of the	31071	11209	3.0	2.8	20	19	20	48	49	50	45	46	44	6.7	33	2.6	3.9
Cook Islands	7	2	-0.8	-0.2	-	-	-	-	-	-	-	-	-	-	73	-0.4	1.4
Costa Rica	1496	393	2.6	2.3	7	4	4	33	27	18	67	75	78	2.2	62	4.2	3.2
Côte d'Ivoire	8908	2773	4.3	2.4	18	14	17	51	45	37	49	52	46	4.8	46	6.2	3.3
Croatia	873	207	0.4	0.1	10	11	12	15	12	9	69	72	75	1.3	60	1.9	0.7
Cuba	2666	682	1.1	0.4	7	7	7	30	17	12	70	74	78	1.6	76	2.1	0.7
Cyprus	205	49	0.5	1.4	10	8	7	19	19	12	71	77	79	1.6	69	2.8	1.8
Czech Republic	1882	453	0.2	-0.1	13	12	11	16	12	9	70	72	76	1.2	75	2.1	-0.1
Denmark	1211	326	0.2	0.4	10	12	11	16	12	11	73	75	78	1.8	86	0.5	0.4
Djibouti	383	120	6.2	2.3	21	15	12	49	43	34	43	51	53	4.8	85	7.6	3.1
Dominica	27	7	0.1	0.6	-	-	-	-	-	-	-	-	-	-	73	1.9	1.1
Dominican Republic	3481	1003	2.4	1.5	11	7	6	42	30	24	58	65	68	2.6	60	3.9	2.1
Ecuador	5100	1445	2.7	1.7	12	6	5	42	29	22	58	68	75	2.7	63	4.4	2.6
Egypt	29691	8933	2.3	1.9	17	9	6	40	32	26	51	63	70	3.1	42	2.4	1.7
El Salvador	2750	805	1.8	2.0	12	7	6	44	30	24	57	65	71	2.8	60	2.9	3.3
Equatorial Guinea	257	88	0.9	2.4	25	20	21	42	44	43	40	46	42	5.9	50	2.2	4.8
Eritrea	2266	759	2.5	2.5	21	16	11	47	42	39	43	48	55	5.3	21	4.0	4.3
Estonia	265	64	0.7	-1.2	11	13	14	15	14	10	71	70	72	1.4	70	1.2	-1.3
Ethiopia	39792	13063	2.7	2.8	21	18	16	49	47	40	43	47	48	5.7	16	4.6	4.4
Fiji	317	92	1.6	1.1	8	6	6	34	29	23	60	67	68	2.8	53	2.5	2.7

	Population (thousands) 2005		Population annual growth rate (%)		Crude death rate			Crude birth rate			Life expectancy			Total fertility rate 2005	% of population urbanized 2005	Average annual growth rate of urban population (%)	
	under 18	under 5	1970-1990	1990-2005	1970	1990	2005	1970	1990	2005	1970	1990	2005			1970-1990	1990-2005
Finland	1100	279	0.4	0.3	10	10	10	14	13	11	70	75	79	1.7	61	1.4	0.3
France	13271	3727	0.6	0.4	11	9	9	17	13	12	72	77	80	1.9	77	0.8	0.7
Gabon	651	193	3.0	2.5	21	11	13	35	39	30	47	60	54	3.8	85	6.9	3.9
Gambia	704	231	3.5	3.2	28	16	11	50	43	34	36	50	57	4.5	26	6.0	3.6
Georgia	1080	242	0.7	-1.3	9	9	11	19	16	11	68	71	71	1.4	51	1.5	-1.8
Germany	14707	3545	0.1	0.3	12	11	10	14	11	8	71	76	79	1.3	88	0.4	0.5
Ghana	10159	3102	2.7	2.4	17	12	11	46	40	31	49	56	57	4.1	46	3.9	4.0
Greece	1944	514	0.7	0.6	8	9	10	17	10	9	72	77	78	1.2	61	1.3	0.9
Grenada	35	10	0.1	0.4	-	-	-	-	-	-	-	-	-	-	42	0.1	2.2
Guatemala	6297	2020	2.5	2.3	15	9	6	44	39	35	52	61	68	4.4	47	3.2	3.2
Guinea	4723	1590	2.2	2.8	27	18	13	50	45	41	38	47	54	5.7	36	5.2	5.2
Guinea-Bissau	856	310	2.8	3.0	29	23	20	49	50	50	36	42	45	7.1	36	5.0	5.7
Guyana	261	75	0.1	0.2	11	10	9	38	25	21	60	60	64	2.2	38	0.7	1.2
Haiti	3846	1147	2.1	1.4	19	16	13	39	38	30	47	49	52	3.8	39	4.1	3.3
Holy See	-	-	-	-	-	-	-	-	-	-	-	-	-	-	100	-	-
Honduras	3317	979	3.2	2.6	15	7	6	48	38	29	52	65	68	3.5	46	4.8	3.6
Hungary	1965	477	0.0	-0.2	11	14	13	15	12	9	69	69	73	1.3	66	1.2	0.2
Iceland	78	21	1.1	1.0	7	7	6	21	18	14	74	78	81	1.9	93	1.4	1.1
India	420678	120011	2.1	1.7	17	11	9	40	31	23	49	58	64	2.9	29	3.4	2.5
Indonesia	75641	21571	2.1	1.4	17	9	7	41	26	20	48	62	68	2.3	48	5.0	4.4
Iran (Islamic Republic of)	25243	6035	3.4	1.4	14	7	5	43	35	19	54	65	71	2.1	68	4.9	2.6
Iraq	13759	4322	3.0	2.9	12	8	9	46	39	34	56	63	60	4.5	67	4.1	2.7
Ireland	1007	303	0.9	1.1	11	9	7	22	15	16	71	75	78	2.0	60	1.3	1.5
Israel	2200	666	2.2	2.7	7	6	6	27	22	20	71	76	80	2.8	92	2.6	2.8
Italy	9837	2662	0.3	0.2	10	10	10	17	10	9	72	77	80	1.3	68	0.4	0.2
Jamaica	992	258	1.2	0.7	8	7	8	35	25	20	68	72	71	2.4	52	2.3	0.8
Japan	21770	5871	0.8	0.2	7	7	8	19	10	9	72	79	82	1.3	66	1.7	0.5
Jordan	2477	732	3.5	3.7	16	6	4	52	37	26	54	67	72	3.3	79	4.7	4.4
Kazakhstan	4394	1075	1.1	-0.7	9	8	11	26	22	16	62	67	64	1.9	56	1.8	-0.8
Kenya	17214	5736	3.7	2.5	15	10	15	51	42	39	52	59	48	5.0	42	8.0	6.0
Kiribati	39	12	2.5	2.2	-	-	-	-	-	-	-	-	-	-	50	4.0	4.6
Korea, Democratic People's Republic of	6756	1723	1.6	0.9	9	8	11	33	21	15	61	65	64	2.0	62	1.9	1.3
Korea, Republic of	10795	2412	1.5	0.7	9	6	6	31	16	10	60	71	78	1.2	81	4.5	1.3
Kuwait	764	241	5.3	1.5	6	2	2	48	24	19	66	75	77	2.3	96	6.3	1.6
Kyrgyzstan	2016	541	2.0	1.2	11	8	7	31	31	22	60	66	67	2.6	34	2.0	0.5
Lao People's Democratic Republic	2830	895	2.1	2.4	23	17	12	44	43	35	40	50	55	4.6	22	4.5	4.7
Latvia	448	101	0.7	-1.1	11	14	13	14	14	9	70	69	72	1.3	66	1.3	-1.5
Lebanon	1225	322	0.7	1.8	8	8	7	33	26	18	65	69	72	2.2	88	2.4	2.2
Lesotho	840	231	2.2	0.8	17	11	26	42	36	28	49	58	34	3.4	18	5.6	1.2
Liberia	1769	631	2.2	2.9	22	21	21	50	50	50	42	43	42	6.8	48	4.6	3.7
Libyan Arab Jamahiriya	2119	636	3.9	2.0	16	5	4	49	28	23	51	68	74	2.9	87	6.7	2.6
Liechtenstein	7	2	1.5	1.2	-	-	-	-	-	-	-	-	-	-	22	1.6	1.5
Lithuania	745	150	0.8	-0.5	9	11	12	17	15	9	71	71	73	1.3	67	2.4	-0.6
Luxembourg	104	29	0.5	1.4	12	10	8	13	13	12	70	75	79	1.7	92	1.7	1.8
Madagascar	9412	3106	2.8	2.9	21	15	12	47	44	38	44	51	56	5.1	27	5.3	3.8
Malawi	6945	2340	3.7	2.1	24	19	21	56	51	43	41	46	40	5.9	17	7.0	4.6
Malaysia	9603	2734	2.5	2.3	10	5	5	37	31	22	61	70	74	2.8	65	4.5	4.1
Maldives	158	46	2.9	2.8	17	10	6	40	41	30	50	60	67	4.0	30	6.1	3.7
Mali	7439	2602	2.5	2.8	28	20	17	55	50	49	37	46	48	6.8	34	5.0	5.1
Malta	88	20	0.9	0.7	9	8	8	17	15	10	70	76	79	1.5	92	1.5	1.1
Marshall Islands	24	7	4.2	1.8	-	-	-	-	-	-	-	-	-	-	67	4.3	2.0
Mauritania	1513	526	2.4	2.8	21	17	14	46	43	41	42	49	53	5.6	64	8.2	5.3
Mauritius	364	98	1.2	1.1	7	6	7	28	20	16	62	69	73	2.0	44	1.0	1.6
Mexico	39654	10857	2.6	1.6	10	5	4	45	29	20	61	71	76	2.3	76	3.6	1.9
Micronesia (Federated States of)	51	16	2.2	0.9	9	7	6	41	34	30	62	66	68	4.3	30	2.7	1.8
Moldova, Republic of	1009	207	1.0	-0.2	10	10	11	18	19	10	65	68	69	1.2	46	2.9	-0.3
Monaco	7	2	1.2	1.0	-	-	-	-	-	-	-	-	-	-	100	1.2	1.0
Mongolia	998	270	2.8	1.2	14	9	7	42	32	22	53	61	65	2.3	57	4.0	1.2
Montenegro‡	-	-	-	-	-	-	-	-	-	-	-	-	-	-	-	-	-

TABLE 6. DEMOGRAPHIC INDICATORS

	Population (thousands) 2005		Population annual growth rate (%)		Crude death rate			Crude birth rate			Life expectancy			Total fertility rate 2005	% of population urbanized 2005	Average annual growth rate of urban population (%)	
	under 18	under 5	1970-1990	1990-2005	1970	1990	2005	1970	1990	2005	1970	1990	2005			1970-1990	1990-2005
Morocco	11743	3378	2.4	1.6	17	8	6	47	29	23	52	64	70	2.7	59	4.1	2.9
Mozambique	10049	3291	1.8	2.6	24	21	20	48	44	39	40	43	42	5.3	38	8.3	6.5
Myanmar	17962	4657	2.1	1.4	18	12	9	41	31	19	48	56	61	2.2	31	2.5	2.8
Namibia	993	268	3.0	2.5	15	9	16	43	42	27	53	62	46	3.7	33	4.8	4.0
Nauru	5	2	1.9	2.4	-	-	-	-	-	-	-	-	-	-	100	1.9	2.4
Nepal	12395	3639	2.3	2.3	21	13	8	42	39	29	43	54	62	3.5	16	6.4	6.1
Netherlands	3559	973	0.7	0.6	8	9	9	17	13	11	74	77	79	1.7	67	1.0	1.3
New Zealand	1048	274	1.0	1.1	9	8	7	22	17	14	71	75	79	2.0	86	1.2	1.2
Nicaragua	2526	731	2.9	2.2	14	7	5	48	38	28	54	64	70	3.1	58	3.5	2.8
Niger	7765	2851	3.1	3.3	28	26	20	58	57	54	38	40	45	7.7	23	6.3	5.8
Nigeria	67371	22257	2.8	2.5	22	18	19	47	47	41	42	47	44	5.6	48	5.5	4.6
Niue	1	0	-	-	-	-	-	-	-	-	-	-	-	-	37	-	-
Norway	1083	283	0.4	0.6	10	11	9	17	14	12	74	77	80	1.8	80	0.9	1.3
Occupied Palestinian Territory	1938	646	3.4	3.6	19	7	4	50	46	37	54	69	73	5.3	72	4.4	4.2
Oman	1054	301	4.5	2.2	17	4	3	50	38	25	50	70	75	3.4	79	13.0	3.8
Pakistan	71800	21115	3.1	2.3	16	11	8	43	41	30	51	60	64	4.0	35	4.2	3.2
Palau	8	2	1.5	1.8	-	-	-	-	-	-	-	-	-	-	68	2.4	1.7
Panama	1163	343	2.4	2.0	8	5	5	38	26	22	65	72	75	2.6	58	3.0	2.4
Papua New Guinea	2751	815	2.4	2.4	19	13	10	42	38	30	44	52	56	3.8	13	3.9	2.4
Paraguay	2722	825	2.9	2.5	9	6	5	37	35	29	65	68	71	3.7	58	4.3	3.7
Peru	10722	2997	2.5	1.7	14	7	6	42	30	22	53	65	71	2.7	75	3.4	2.2
Philippines	34622	9863	2.6	2.0	11	7	5	40	33	24	57	65	71	3.0	63	4.5	3.7
Poland	7984	1811	0.8	0.1	8	10	10	17	15	9	70	71	75	1.2	62	1.5	0.2
Portugal	2007	561	0.7	0.3	11	10	11	21	12	11	67	74	78	1.5	56	3.6	1.5
Qatar	204	67	7.2	3.7	13	3	3	34	23	18	61	69	73	2.9	92	7.5	3.9
Romania	4366	1054	0.7	-0.4	9	11	12	21	14	10	68	69	72	1.3	55	2.1	-0.3
Russian Federation	28830	7225	0.6	-0.2	9	12	16	15	13	11	70	69	65	1.4	73	1.5	-0.2
Rwanda	4658	1500	3.2	1.6	21	33	18	53	48	41	44	32	44	5.5	22	5.7	11.0
Saint Kitts and Nevis	14	4	-0.5	0.3	-	-	-	-	-	-	-	-	-	-	32	-0.4	-0.2
Saint Lucia	56	14	1.4	1.0	8	7	7	41	26	19	64	71	73	2.2	31	2.2	2.1
Saint Vincent and the Grenadines	43	12	0.9	0.6	11	7	7	40	25	20	61	69	71	2.2	60	3.0	3.2
Samoa	88	26	0.6	0.9	10	7	6	39	34	27	55	65	71	4.2	22	0.9	1.2
San Marino	5	1	1.2	1.0	-	-	-	-	-	-	-	-	-	-	89	3.1	0.9
Sao Tome and Principe	73	23	2.3	2.0	13	10	8	47	37	33	56	62	63	3.8	38	4.4	2.2
Saudi Arabia	10690	3200	5.2	2.7	18	5	4	48	36	27	52	68	72	3.8	88	7.6	3.5
Senegal	5804	1845	2.8	2.5	25	14	11	49	44	36	39	53	56	4.8	51	3.7	4.1
Serbia‡	-	-	-	-	-	-	-	-	-	-	-	-	-	-	-	-	-
Seychelles	41	14	1.4	0.8	-	-	-	-	-	-	-	-	-	-	50	4.6	0.8
Sierra Leone	2722	958	2.1	2.0	29	26	23	48	48	46	35	39	41	6.5	40	4.8	4.0
Singapore	1023	216	1.9	2.4	5	5	5	23	18	9	69	75	79	1.3	100	1.9	2.4
Slovakia	1142	255	0.7	0.2	10	10	10	19	15	9	70	72	74	1.2	58	2.3	0.4
Slovenia	345	86	0.7	0.1	10	10	10	17	11	9	69	73	77	1.2	51	2.3	0.2
Solomon Islands	227	72	3.4	2.7	10	9	7	46	38	32	54	61	63	4.1	17	5.5	4.2
Somalia	4152	1482	3.1	1.4	25	22	17	51	46	44	40	42	47	6.2	36	4.4	2.7
South Africa	18417	5223	2.4	1.7	14	8	19	38	29	23	53	62	46	2.7	58	2.5	2.8
Spain	7457	2217	0.8	0.6	9	9	9	20	10	11	72	77	80	1.3	77	1.4	0.7
Sri Lanka	6054	1628	1.7	1.0	9	6	6	31	21	16	62	71	74	1.9	21	1.5	0.9
Sudan	16547	5216	2.9	2.2	21	14	11	47	39	32	44	53	57	4.2	41	5.3	5.0
Suriname	161	45	0.4	0.7	8	7	7	37	24	20	63	68	70	2.5	77	2.1	1.8
Swaziland	514	136	3.2	1.2	18	10	30	50	41	29	48	58	30	3.7	24	7.5	1.5
Sweden	1943	488	0.3	0.4	10	11	10	14	14	11	74	78	80	1.7	83	0.4	0.4
Switzerland	1458	353	0.5	0.4	9	9	9	16	12	9	73	78	81	1.4	68	1.6	0.3
Syrian Arab Republic	8375	2526	3.5	2.6	13	5	3	47	36	28	55	68	74	3.3	50	4.1	2.8
Tajikistan	3055	834	2.9	1.4	10	8	7	40	39	28	60	63	64	3.6	24	2.2	-0.4
Tanzania, United Republic of	19070	6045	3.3	2.5	17	13	17	48	44	37	48	54	46	4.8	38	9.2	6.2
Thailand	18522	5012	2.1	1.1	9	6	7	37	21	16	60	68	71	1.9	32	3.8	1.7
The former Yugoslav Republic of Macedonia	494	117	1.0	0.4	8	8	8	24	17	11	66	71	74	1.5	60	2.0	0.6
Timor-Leste	463	179	1.0	1.6	22	18	12	46	40	51	40	45	56	7.8	8	0.1	1.6
Togo	3095	1014	3.1	2.9	18	12	12	48	44	38	48	58	55	5.1	36	7.0	4.5

	Population (thousands) 2005		Population annual growth rate (%)		Crude death rate			Crude birth rate			Life expectancy			Total fertility rate 2005	% of population urbanized 2005	Average annual growth rate of urban population (%)	
	under 18	under 5	1970-1990	1990-2005	1970	1990	2005	1970	1990	2005	1970	1990	2005			1970-1990	1990-2005
Tonga	43	12	-0.2	0.5	6	6	6	37	30	23	65	70	73	3.3	34	1.6	1.1
Trinidad and Tobago	355	90	1.1	0.5	7	7	8	27	20	14	66	72	70	1.6	76	1.6	1.1
Tunisia	3259	806	2.4	1.4	14	6	5	39	27	16	54	69	74	1.9	64	3.7	2.1
Turkey	25348	7212	2.3	1.6	12	8	7	39	25	20	56	65	69	2.4	67	4.5	2.5
Turkmenistan	1882	488	2.6	1.8	11	8	8	37	35	22	58	63	63	2.6	46	2.3	1.9
Tuvalu	4	1	1.3	0.7	-	-	-	-	-	-	-	-	-	-	57	4.6	2.9
Uganda	16539	5970	3.2	3.2	16	18	15	50	50	51	50	46	49	7.1	12	4.9	3.9
Ukraine	9084	1924	0.5	-0.7	9	13	17	15	13	8	71	69	66	1.1	67	1.5	-0.7
United Arab Emirates	1192	337	10.6	5.9	11	3	1	36	27	16	61	73	79	2.4	85	10.7	6.1
United Kingdom	13117	3367	0.2	0.3	12	11	10	16	14	11	72	76	79	1.7	89	0.9	0.4
United States	74926	20408	1.0	1.0	9	9	8	17	16	14	71	75	78	2.0	81	1.1	1.5
Uruguay	1001	282	0.5	0.7	10	10	9	21	18	16	69	72	76	2.3	93	0.9	1.0
Uzbekistan	10742	2841	2.7	1.7	10	7	7	37	35	23	63	67	67	2.6	36	3.1	1.1
Vanuatu	99	30	2.8	2.3	14	7	5	43	37	30	53	64	69	3.9	24	4.5	3.9
Venezuela (Bolivarian Republic of)	9988	2860	3.1	2.0	7	5	5	37	29	22	65	71	73	2.6	88	3.9	2.3
Viet Nam	30496	7969	2.2	1.6	18	8	6	41	31	20	49	65	71	2.2	27	2.7	3.5
Yemen	11252	3668	3.2	3.7	26	13	8	54	51	40	38	54	62	5.9	26	5.6	5.1
Zambia	6215	2011	3.3	2.2	17	17	22	51	46	40	49	47	38	5.4	37	4.7	1.7
Zimbabwe	6256	1752	3.5	1.4	13	9	23	49	38	29	55	60	37	3.4	36	6.1	2.8

MEMORANDUM

Serbia and Montenegro (pre-cession)	2376	608	0.8	0.2	9	10	11	19	15	12	68	72	74	1.6	52	2.1	0.4

SUMMARY INDICATORS

Sub-Saharan Africa	361301	119555	2.9	2.5	20	16	17	48	45	40	45	50	46	5.4	37	4.8	4.3
Eastern and Southern Africa	177395	57670	2.9	2.4	19	15	17	47	43	38	47	51	46	5.0	31	4.7	4.2
West and Central Africa	183906	61885	2.8	2.6	22	18	18	48	47	42	43	48	46	5.7	42	4.9	4.4
Middle East and North Africa	154130	44711	3.0	2.1	16	8	6	45	35	26	52	63	69	3.1	58	4.4	2.9
South Asia	587319	169666	2.2	1.9	17	11	9	40	33	25	49	58	64	3.1	29	3.7	2.8
East Asia and Pacific	572465	144948	1.8	1.1	10	7	7	35	22	15	59	66	71	1.9	43	3.9	3.4
Latin America and Caribbean	199284	56538	2.2	1.6	11	7	6	37	27	21	60	68	72	2.5	77	3.3	2.2
CEE/CIS	104278	26562	1.0	0.2	9	11	12	21	18	14	67	68	67	1.7	63	2.0	0.2
Industrialized countries[§]	204366	54239	0.7	0.6	10	9	9	17	13	11	71	76	79	1.6	77	1.1	0.9
Developing countries[§]	1928976	550130	2.1	1.6	13	9	9	38	29	23	55	62	65	2.8	43	3.8	3.0
Least developed countries[§]	368348	119352	2.5	2.5	21	16	14	47	43	37	44	50	53	4.9	28	4.9	4.4
World	2183143	616219	1.8	1.4	12	10	9	32	26	21	59	65	68	2.6	49	2.7	2.2

‡ Due to the cession in June 2006 of Montenegro from the State Union of Serbia and Montenegro, and its subsequent admission to the UN on 28 June 2006, disaggregated data for Montenegro and Serbia as separate States are not yet available. Aggregated data presented are for Serbia and Montenegro pre-cession (see Memorandum item).

§ Also includes territories within each country category or regional group. Countries and territories in each country category or regional group are listed on page 136.

DEFINITIONS OF THE INDICATORS

Life expectancy at birth – The number of years newborn children would live if subject to the mortality risks prevailing for the cross section of population at the time of their birth.

Crude death rate – Annual number of deaths per 1,000 population.

Crude birth rate – Annual number of births per 1,000 population.

Total fertility rate – The number of children that would be born per woman if she were to live to the end of her childbearing years and bear children at each age in accordance with prevailing age-specific fertility rates.

Urban population – Percentage of population living in urban areas as defined according to the national definition used in the most recent population census.

MAIN DATA SOURCES

Child population – United Nations Population Division.

Crude death and birth rates – United Nations Population Division.

Life expectancy – United Nations Population Division.

Fertility – United Nations Population Division.

Urban population – United Nations Population Division.

NOTES   -   Data not available.

TABLE 7. ECONOMIC INDICATORS

Countries and territories	GNI per capita (US$) 2005	GDP per capita average annual growth rate (%) 1970-1990	GDP per capita average annual growth rate (%) 1990-2005	Average annual rate of inflation (%) 1990-2005	% of population below $1 a day 1994-2004*	% of central government expenditure (1994-2004*) allocated to: health	education	defence	ODA inflow in millions US$ 2004	ODA inflow as a % of recipient GNI 2004	Debt service as a % of exports of goods and services 1990	Debt service as a % of exports of goods and services 2004
Afghanistan	250x	1.6x	-	-	-	-	-	-	2190	40	-	-
Albania	2580	-0.7x	5.2	22	<2	4	2	4	362	5	4x	2x
Algeria	2730	1.6	1.1	14	<2	4	24	17	313	0	62	19x
Andorra	d	-	-	-	-	-	-	-	-	-	-	-
Angola	1350	0.4x	1.4	407	-	6x	15x	34x	1144	8	7	15
Antigua and Barbuda	10920	6.5x	1.7	2	-	-	-	-	2	0	-	-
Argentina	4470	-0.7	1.1	5	7	5	5	3	91	0	30	14
Armenia	1470	-	4.4	89	<2	-	-	-	254	8	-	5
Australia	32220	1.6	2.5	2	-	14	9	6	-	-	-	-
Austria	36980	2.4	1.8	2	-	14	10	2	-	-	-	-
Azerbaijan	1240	-	0.0	88	<2	1	3	11	176	2	-	4
Bahamas	14920x	1.8	0.4x	3x	-	16	20	3	-	-	-	-
Bahrain	10840x	-1.3x	2.3	2	-	8	15	16	104	1	-	-
Bangladesh	470	0.6	2.9	4	36	7	18	10	1404	2	17	5
Barbados	9270x	1.8	1.5	3x	-	-	-	-	29	-	14	5
Belarus	2760	-	2.2	201	<2	3	4	3	-	-	-	1
Belgium	35700	2.2	1.7	2	-	16	3	3	-	-	-	-
Belize	3500	2.9	2.3	1	-	8	20	5	7	1	5	62
Benin	510	0.0	1.4	6	31	6x	31x	17x	378	10	7	6x
Bhutan	870	6.4x	3.0	8	-	8	13	0	78	12	5x	5x
Bolivia	1010	-1.1	1.3	7	23	10	22	6	767	9	31	18
Bosnia and Herzegovina	2440	-	12.7x	3x	-	-	-	-	671	8	-	3
Botswana	5180	8.3	3.8	8	24x	5	26	8	39	1	4	1x
Brazil	3460	2.3	1.1	90	8	6	6	3	285	0	19	40
Brunei Darussalam	24100x	-	-	-	-	-	-	-	-	-	-	-
Bulgaria	3450	3.4x	1.5	61	<2	12	5	6	-	-	5x	15
Burkina Faso	400	1.4	1.3	4	27	7x	17x	14x	610	14	6	10x
Burundi	100	1.1	-2.8	12	55	2	15	23	351	52	41	63x
Cambodia	380	-	4.7x	3x	34	-	-	-	478	10	-	0
Cameroon	1010	3.4	0.6	5x	17	3	12	10	762	6	18	11x
Canada	32600	2.0	2.3	2	-	9	2	6	-	-	-	-
Cape Verde	1870	-	3.4	4	-	-	-	-	140	16	5	5x
Central African Republic	350	-1.3	-0.6	3	67x	-	-	-	105	9	8	12x
Chad	400	-0.9	1.7	6	-	8x	8x	-	319	14	2	7x
Chile	5870	1.5	3.8	7	<2	14	18	7	49	0	20	24
China	1740	6.6	8.8	5	17	0	2	12	1661	0	10	3
Colombia	2290	2.0	0.6	16	7	9	20	13	509	1	39	32
Comoros	640	0.1x	-0.5	4	-	-	-	-	25	8	2	3x
Congo	950	3.1	-1.0	7	-	4	4	10	116	4	32	3x
Congo, Democratic Republic of the	120	-2.4	-5.2	447	-	0	0	18	1815	28	5x	0x
Cook Islands	-	-	-	-	-	-	-	-	9	-	-	-
Costa Rica	4590	0.7	2.3	14	2	21	22	0	13	0	21	7
Côte d'Ivoire	840	-1.9	-0.5	6	15	4x	21x	4x	154	1	26	5
Croatia	8060	-	2.5	41	<2	13	8	4	121	0	-	27
Cuba	1170x	-	3.5x	4x	-	23x	10x	-	90	-	-	-
Cyprus	17580x	6.1x	2.5x	4x	-	6	12	4	-	-	-	-
Czech Republic	10710	-	1.9	8	<2	17	10	5	-	-	-	10
Denmark	47390	1.5	1.8	2	-	1	12	5	-	-	-	-
Djibouti	1020	-	-2.4	3	-	-	-	-	64	9	-	4x
Dominica	3790	4.7x	1.0	2	-	-	-	-	29	11	4	13x
Dominican Republic	2370	2.0	3.8	11	3	10	13	4	87	0	7	6
Ecuador	2630	1.3	0.7	4	16	11x	18x	13x	160	1	27	33
Egypt	1250	4.3	2.6	7	3	3	15	9	1458	2	18	7
El Salvador	2450	-1.8	1.6	5	19	13	15	3	211	1	14	8
Equatorial Guinea	c	-	16.6x	17x	-	-	-	-	30	-	3	0x
Eritrea	220	-	0.3	11x	-	-	-	-	260	32	-	13x
Estonia	9100	1.5x	4.2	28	<2	16	7	5	-	-	-	15
Ethiopia	160	-	1.5	4	23	6	16	9	1823	24	33	5
Fiji	3280	0.6x	1.3x	3x	-	9	18	6	64	3	12	6x
Finland	37460	2.9	2.6	2	-	3	10	4	-	-	-	-
France	34810	2.2	1.7	1	-	16x	7x	6x	-	-	-	-

	GNI per capita (US$) 2005	GDP per capita average annual growth rate (%)		Average annual rate of inflation (%) 1990-2005	% of population below $1 a day 1994-2004*	% of central government expenditure (1994-2004*) allocated to:			ODA inflow in millions US$ 2004	ODA inflow as a % of recipient GNI 2004	Debt service as a % of exports of goods and services	
		1970-1990	1990-2005			health	education	defence			1990	2004
Gabon	5010	0.0	-0.4	5	-	-	-	-	38	1	4	11x
Gambia	290	0.9	0.1	7	59	7x	12x	4x	63	15	18	3x
Georgia	1350	3.2	0.2	134	7	5	5	5	315	7	-	8
Germany	34580	2.2x	1.4	1	-	19	0	4	-	-	-	-
Ghana	450	-2.1	2.0	26	45	7	22	5x	1358	16	21	5
Greece	19670	1.3	2.4	7	-	7	11	8	-	-	-	-
Grenada	3920	-	2.1	2	-	10	17	-	15	4	2	18x
Guatemala	2400	0.2	1.3	9	14	11	17	11	218	1	11	7
Guinea	370	-	1.2	6	-	3x	11x	29x	279	7	18	17
Guinea-Bissau	180	-0.1	-2.6	18	-	1x	3x	4x	76	30	21	11x
Guyana	1010	-1.5	3.1	9	<2	-	-	-	145	19	-	5
Haiti	450	-0.3	-2.0	19	54	-	-	-	243	-	4	3x
Holy See	-	-	-	-	-	-	-	-	-	-	-	-
Honduras	1190	0.6	0.5	15	21	10x	19x	7x	642	9	30	7
Hungary	10030	2.9	3.1	15	<2	6	5	3	-	-	30	25
Iceland	46320	3.2	2.2	4	-	26	10	0	-	-	-	-
India	720	2.2	4.2	6	35	2	2	13	691	0	25	18x
Indonesia	1280	4.7	2.1	16	8	1	4	7	84	0	31	20
Iran (Islamic Republic of)	2770	-3.5x	2.5	24	<2	7	7	14	189	0	1	4x
Iraq	2170x	-4.3x	-	-	-	-	-	-	4658	-	-	-
Ireland	40150	2.8	6.2	4	-	16	14	3	-	-	-	-
Israel	18620	1.9	1.5	7	-	13	15	18	-	-	-	-
Italy	30010	2.6	1.4	3	-	3	10	3	-	-	-	-
Jamaica	3400	-1.3	0.2	17	<2	7	15	2	75	1	20	14
Japan	38980	3.0	0.9	-1	-	2	6	4x	-	-	-	-
Jordan	2500	2.5x	1.7	2	<2	10	16	19	581	5	18	7
Kazakhstan	2930	-	2.0	92	<2	3	4	5	265	1	-	38
Kenya	530	1.2	-0.2	11x	23	7	26	6	635	4	26	8
Kiribati	1390	-5.3	1.4	3	-	-	-	-	17	18	-	22x
Korea, Democratic People's Republic of	a	-	-	-	-	-	-	-	196			
Korea, Republic of	15830	6.2	4.5	4	<2	0	18	13	-	-	10x	10x
Kuwait	16340x	-6.8x	0.6x	3x	-	6	12	16	-	-	-	-
Kyrgyzstan	440	-	-1.3	57	<2	11	20	10	258	13	-	11
Lao People's Democratic Republic	440	-	3.8	27	27	-	-	-	270	12	8	8x
Latvia	6760	3.4	3.6	25	<2	11	6	4	-	-	-	18
Lebanon	6180	-	2.7	10	-	2	7	11	265	1	1x	63x
Lesotho	960	3.1	2.3	9	36	6	24	6	102	8	4	4
Liberia	130	-4.2	2.3	47	36	5x	11x	9x	210	56	-	0x
Libyan Arab Jamahiriya	5530	-4.8x	-	-	-	-	-	-	-	-	-	-
Liechtenstein	d	-	-	-	-	-	-	-	-	-	-	-
Lithuania	7050	-	1.9	35	<2	15	7	5	-	-	-	13
Luxembourg	65630	2.7	3.6	3	-	13	10	0	-	-	-	-
Madagascar	290	-2.4	-0.7	15	61	8	13	5	1236	24	32	6x
Malawi	160	-0.1	1.0	29	42	7x	12x	5x	476	23	23	6x
Malaysia	4960	4.0	3.3	3	<2	6	23	11	290	0	12	8x
Maldives	2390	-	3.8x	1x	-	11	20	10	28	4	4	5
Mali	380	-0.5	2.2	5	72	2x	9x	8x	567	13	8	5x
Malta	13590	6.5	2.7	3	-	12	13	2	11x	-	0x	3x
Marshall Islands	2930	-	-2.3	5	-	-	-	-	51	36	-	-
Mauritania	560	-0.6	1.9	7	26	4x	23x	-	180	11	24	20x
Mauritius	5260	5.1x	3.7	6	-	9	16	1	38	1	6	6
Mexico	7310	1.6	1.5	15	5	5	25	3	121	0	16	23
Micronesia (Federated States of)	2300	-	-0.1	2	-	-	-	-	86	34	-	-
Moldova, Republic of	880	1.8x	-3.5	63	22	21	8	1	118	5	-	10
Monaco	d	-	-	-	-	-	-	-	-	-	-	-
Mongolia	690	-	0.9	34	27	6	9	9	262	17	-	2
Montenegro‡	-	-	-	-	-	-	-	-	-	-	-	-
Morocco	1730	2.0	1.5	2	<2	3	18	13	706	2	18	14
Mozambique	310	-1.0x	4.6	22	38	5x	10x	35x	1228	23	21	4
Myanmar	220x	1.5	6.6	24	-	5	15	22	121	-	17	3
Namibia	2990	-2.3x	1.4	9	35x	10x	22x	7x	179	4	-	-

TABLE 7. ECONOMIC INDICATORS

	GNI per capita (US$) 2005	GDP per capita average annual growth rate (%)		Average annual rate of inflation (%) 1990-2005	% of population below $1 a day 1994-2004*	% of central government expenditure (1994-2004*) allocated to:			ODA inflow in millions US$ 2004	ODA inflow as a % of recipient GNI 2004	Debt service as a % of exports of goods and services	
		1970-1990	1990-2005			health	education	defence			1990	2004
Nauru	-	-	-	-	-	-	-	-	14	-	-	-
Nepal	270	1.1	1.9	6	24	5	17	10	427	6	12	5
Netherlands	36620	1.5	1.9	2	-	10	11	4	-	-	-	-
New Zealand	25960	0.8	2.1	2	-	17	21	3	-	-	-	-
Nicaragua	910	-3.8	1.5	24	45	13	15	6	1232	27	2	5
Niger	240	-2.2	-0.5	5	61	-	-	-	536	19	12	6x
Nigeria	560	-1.4	0.7	23	71	1x	3x	3x	573	1	22	8
Niue	-	-	-	-	-	-	-	-	14	-	-	-
Norway	59590	3.4	2.6	3	-	16	6	5	-	-	-	-
Occupied Palestinian Territory	1110x	-	-6.0x	9x	-	-	-	-	1136	-	-	-
Oman	7830x	3.3	1.8x	1x	-	7	15	33	55	0	12	7
Pakistan	690	3.0	1.3	10	17	1	2	20	1421	2	16	18
Palau	7630	-	-	3x	-	-	-	-	20	15	-	-
Panama	4630	0.3	2.2	3	7	18	16	0	38	0	3	14
Papua New Guinea	660	-0.7	0.0	8	-	7	22	4	266	8	37	12x
Paraguay	1280	2.8	-0.8	11	16	7	22	11x	0	-	12	13
Peru	2610	-0.6	2.2	15	13	13	7	-	487	1	6	16
Philippines	1300	0.8	1.5	7	16	2	19	5	463	0	23	20
Poland	7110	-	4.3	15	<2	11	12	3	-	-	4	34
Portugal	16170	2.6	1.9	4	<2	16	16	3	-	-	-	-
Qatar	12000x	-	-	-	-	-	-	-	-	-	-	-
Romania	3830	0.9	1.6	67	<2	14	7	5	-	-	0	16
Russian Federation	4460	-	-0.1	85	<2	1	3	12	-	-	-	9
Rwanda	230	1.2	0.0	10	52	5x	26x	-	468	25	10	11
Saint Kitts and Nevis	8210	6.3x	2.9	3	-	-	-	-	0	-	3	34x
Saint Lucia	4800	5.3x	0.4	2	-	-	-	-	-22	-3	2	7x
Saint Vincent and the Grenadines	3590	3.3	1.7	3	-	12	16	-	10	2	3	7x
Samoa	2090	-0.1x	2.5	7	-	-	-	-	31	9	5	5x
San Marino	d	-	-	-	-	18	9	0	-	-	-	-
Sao Tome and Principe	390	-	0.5	34	-	-	-	-	33	55	28	31x
Saudi Arabia	11770	-1.5	-0.3	3	-	6x	14x	36x	32	0	-	-
Senegal	710	-0.3	1.2	4	22	3	14	7	1052	15	14	9x
Serbia‡												
Seychelles	8290	2.9	1.5	2	-	6	10	4	10	1	8	8
Sierra Leone	220	-0.4	-1.4	21	57x	10x	13x	10x	360	32	8	10
Singapore	27490	5.7	3.6	0	-	6	22	29	-	-	-	-
Slovakia	7950	-	2.8	8	<2	20	3	5	-	-	-	13x
Slovenia	17350	-	3.2	18	<2	15	13	3	53x	-	10x	16x
Solomon Islands	590	3.4	-2.6	8	-	-	-	-	122	46	10	7x
Somalia	130x	-0.9	-	-	-	1x	2x	38x	191	-	25x	-
South Africa	4960	0.1	0.7	9	11	-	-	-	617	0	-	6
Spain	25360	1.9	2.3	4	-	15	2	4	-	-	-	-
Sri Lanka	1160	3.0	3.7	9	6	6	10	18	519	3	10	7
Sudan	640	0.1	3.5	40	-	1	8	28	882	5	4	5
Suriname	2540	-2.2x	1.1	59	-	-	-	-	24	2	-	-
Swaziland	2280	2.1	0.2	12	8	8	20	8	117	6	6	2
Sweden	41060	1.8	2.1	2	-	3	6	5	-	-	-	-
Switzerland	54930	1.2	0.6	1	-	0	4	6	-	-	-	-
Syrian Arab Republic	1380	1.9	1.3	7	-	2	9	24	110	0	20	2
Tajikistan	330	-	-4.0	121	7	2	4	9	241	14	-	6
Tanzania, United Republic of	340	-	1.7	16	58	6x	8x	16x	1746	15	25	4
Thailand	2750	4.8	2.7	3	<2	10	21	7	-2	0	14	10
The former Yugoslav Republic of Macedonia	2830	-	-0.1	38	<2	-	-	-	248	5	-	9
Timor-Leste	750	-	-	-	-	-	-	-	153	30	-	-
Togo	350	-0.6	0.0	5	-	5x	20x	11x	61	3	8	0x
Tonga	2190	-	1.9	4	-	7x	13x	-	19	10	2	2x
Trinidad and Tobago	10440	0.5	4.3	5	12x	9	15	2	-1	0	18	4x
Tunisia	2890	2.5	3.3	4	<2	5	20	5	328	1	22	13
Turkey	4710	1.9	1.6	61	3	3	10	8	257	0	27	28
Turkmenistan	1340x	-	-4.7x	329x	12	-	-	-	37	-	-	30x
Tuvalu	-	-	-	-	-	-	-	-	8	-	-	-

	GNI per capita (US$) 2005	GDP per capita average annual growth rate (%) 1970-1990	GDP per capita average annual growth rate (%) 1990-2005	Average annual rate of inflation (%) 1990-2005	% of population below $1 a day 1994-2004*	% of central government expenditure (1994-2004*) allocated to: health	education	defence	ODA inflow in millions US$ 2004	ODA inflow as a % of recipient GNI 2004	Debt service as a % of exports of goods and services 1990	Debt service as a % of exports of goods and services 2004
Uganda	280	-	3.2	8	85	2x	15x	26x	1159	17	47	5
Ukraine	1520	-	-2.4	117	<2	4	6	4	-	-	-	10
United Arab Emirates	18060x	-4.8x	-1.0x	3x	-	7	17	30	-	-	-	-
United Kingdom	37600	2.0	2.4	3	-	15	4	7	-	-	-	-
United States	43740	2.2	2.1	2	-	24	3	20	-	-	-	-
Uruguay	4360	0.9	0.8	21	<2	7	8	4	22	0	31	22
Uzbekistan	510	-	0.3	129	17	-	-	-	246	2	-	21x
Vanuatu	1600	-0.5x	-0.3	3	-	-	-	-	38	13	2	1x
Venezuela (Bolivarian Republic of)	4810	-1.6	-1.0	37	8	8	19	4	49	0	22	16
Viet Nam	620	-	5.9	10	<2	4	14	-	1830	4	7x	3x
Yemen	600	-	2.0	17	16	4	22	19	252	2	4	3
Zambia	490	-2.4	-0.3	37	76	13	14	4	1081	23	13	22x
Zimbabwe	340	-0.4	-2.1	63	56	8	24	7	186	2	19	6x

MEMORANDUM

	GNI per capita (US$) 2005	GDP per capita average annual growth rate (%) 1970-1990	GDP per capita average annual growth rate (%) 1990-2005	Average annual rate of inflation (%) 1990-2005	% of population below $1 a day 1994-2004*	health	education	defence	ODA inflow in millions US$ 2004	ODA inflow as a % of recipient GNI 2004	Debt service 1990	Debt service 2004
Serbia and Montenegro (pre-cession)	3280	-	5.2x	48x	-	-	-	-	1170	5	-	13x

SUMMARY INDICATORS

	GNI per capita (US$) 2005	GDP per capita average annual growth rate (%) 1970-1990	GDP per capita average annual growth rate (%) 1990-2005	Average annual rate of inflation (%) 1990-2005	% of population below $1 a day 1994-2004*	health	education	defence	ODA inflow in millions US$ 2004	ODA inflow as a % of recipient GNI 2004	Debt service 1990	Debt service 2004
Sub-Saharan Africa	764	-	1.1	36	46	-	-	-	22926	6	17	7
Eastern and Southern Africa	1043	-	1.1	36	40	-	-	-	13111	5	14	7
West and Central Africa	491	-	1.0	34	54	-	-	-	9815	7	19	8
Middle East and North Africa	2627	2.4	2.2	11	4	5	14	17	11133	1	21	8
South Asia	691	2.1	3.8	7	32	2	4	14	6758	1	21	-
East Asia and Pacific	2092	5.7	6.6	6	14	1	8	12	6565	0	16	7
Latin America and Caribbean	4078	1.9	1.4	37	9	7	16	4	5627	0	20	24
CEE/CIS	3433	-	-	81	4	4	6	9	-	-	-	15
Industrialized countries§	35410	2.3	1.9	2	-	16	4	12	-	-	-	-
Developing countries§	1801	3.2	4.1	18	22	4	10	10	55058	1	19	13
Least developed countries§	383	-	2.4	59	41	5	15	13	24910	11	12	7
World	7002	2.5	2.3	8	21	13	6	12	57748	0	18	14

‡ Due to the cession in June 2006 of Montenegro from the State Union of Serbia and Montenegro, and its subsequent admission to the UN on 28 June 2006, disaggregated data for Montenegro and Serbia as separate States are not yet available. Aggregated data presented are for Serbia and Montenegro pre-cession (see Memorandum item).

§ Also includes territories within each country category or regional group. Countries and territories in each country category or regional group are listed on page 136.

DEFINITIONS OF THE INDICATORS

GNI per capita – Gross national income (GNI) is the sum of value added by all resident producers plus any product taxes (less subsidies) not included in the valuation of output plus net receipts of primary income (compensation of employees and property income) from abroad. GNI per capita is gross national income divided by midyear population. GNI per capita in US dollars is converted using the World Bank Atlas method.

GDP per capita – Gross domestic product (GDP) is the sum of value added by all resident producers plus any product taxes (less subsidies) not included in the valuation of output. GDP per capita is gross domestic product divided by midyear population. Growth is calculated from constant price GDP data in local currency.

% of population below $1 a day – Percentage of the population living on less than $1.08 a day at 1993 international prices (equivalent to $1 a day in 1985 prices, adjusted for purchasing power parity). As a result of revisions in purchasing power parity exchange rates, poverty rates for individual countries cannot be compared with poverty rates reported in previous editions.

ODA – Net official development assistance.

Debt service – The sum of interest payments and repayments of principal on external public and publicly guaranteed long-term debts.

MAIN DATA SOURCES

GNI per capita – World Bank.

GDP per capita – World Bank.

Rate of inflation – World Bank.

% of population below $1 a day – World Bank.

Expenditure on health, education and defence – International Monetary Fund (IMF).

ODA – Organisation for Economic Co-operation and Development (OECD).

Debt service – World Bank.

NOTES

a: Range: low income ($875 or less).
b: Range: lower-middle income ($876 to $3,465).
c: Range: upper-middle income ($3,466 to $10,725).
d: Range: high income ($10,726 or more).

x Data refer to years or periods other than those specified in the column heading, differ from the standard definition or refer to only part of a country.
* Data refer to the most recent year available during the period specified in the column heading.
- Data not available.

TABLE 8. WOMEN

Countries and territories	Life expectancy: females as a % of males 2005	Adult literacy rate: females as a % of males 2000-2004*	Enrolment ratios: females as a % of males				Contraceptive prevalence (%) 1997-2005*	Antenatal care coverage (%) 1997-2005*	Skilled attendant at delivery (%) 1997-2005*	Maternal mortality ratio[†]		
			primary school 2000-2005*		secondary school 2000-2005*					1990-2005* reported	2000	
			gross	net	gross	net					adjusted	Lifetime risk of maternal death. 1 in:
Afghanistan	101	30	44	-	20	-	10	16	14	1600	1900	6
Albania	108	99	99	99	97	97	75	91	98	17	55	610
Algeria	104	75	92	97	108	105	57	81	96	120	140	190
Andorra	-	-	98	97	104	101	-	-	-	-	-	-
Angola	107	65	86x	-	79	-	6	66	45	-	1700	7
Antigua and Barbuda	-	-	-	-	-	-	53	100	100	65	-	-
Argentina	111	100	99	99	106	108	-	98	99	40	82	410
Armenia	110	99	104	103	103	102	53	93	98	22	55	1200
Australia	106	-	100	100	95	101	-	100x	100	-	8	5800
Austria	107	-	100	-	94	-	51x	100x	100x	-	4	16000
Azerbaijan	112	99	98	98	98	97	55	70	88	19	94	520
Bahamas	109	-	100	102	111	111	-	-	99	-	60	580
Bahrain	104	94	100	101	106	107	62x	97x	98x	46	28	1200
Bangladesh	103	-	104	103	110	113	58	49	13	320	380	59
Barbados	109	-	98	99	102	105	55	100	100	0	95	590
Belarus	118	99	96	97	101	101	50x	100	100	17	35	1800
Belgium	108	-	100	100	96	101	78x	-	-	-	10	5600
Belize	107	-	98	101	104	104	56	96	83	140	140	190
Benin	103	48	77	77	53	48	19	81	66	500	850	17
Bhutan	104	-	-	-	-	-	31	51	37	260	420	37
Bolivia	107	87	99	101	97	99	58	79	67	30	420	47
Bosnia and Herzegovina	108	95	-	-	-	-	48	99	100	8	31	1900
Botswana	97	103	99	102	105	110	48	97	94	330	100	200
Brazil	112	101	94	-	110	107	77x	97	97	72	260	140
Brunei Darussalam	106	95	100	-	105	-	-	100x	99	0	37	830
Bulgaria	110	99	98	99	96	97	42	-	99	6	32	2400
Burkina Faso	103	52	80	76	71	73	14	73	38	480	1000	12
Burundi	104	78	84	90	71	-	16	78	25	-	1000	12
Cambodia	114	75	92	96	69	73	24	38	32	440	450	36
Cameroon	102	78	85	-	71	-	26	83	62	670	730	23
Canada	106	-	100	101	99	100x	75x	-	98	-	6	8700
Cape Verde	109	-	96	99	110	112	53	99	89	76	150	160
Central African Republic	103	51	68	-	-	-	28	62	44	1100	1100	15
Chad	105	32	65	68	30	31	3	39	14	1100	1100	11
Chile	108	100	95	-	101	-	56x	95x	100	17	31	1100
China	105	92	99	100	100	-	87	90	97	51	56	830
Colombia	109	100	99	101	110	112	78	94	96	84	130	240
Comoros	107	-	88	83	75	-	26	74	62	380	480	33
Congo	105	-	92	-	83	-	44	88	86	-	510	26
Congo, Democratic Republic of the	105	67	90x	-	50	-	31	68	61	1300	990	13
Cook Islands	-	-	98	99	103	109	44	-	98	6	-	-
Costa Rica	106	100	99	-	109	-	80	92	99	36	43	690
Côte d'Ivoire	103	64	79	81	56	58	15	88	68	600	690	25
Croatia	110	98	99	99	102	102	-	-	100	8	8	6100
Cuba	105	100	95	98	101	101	73	100	100	37	33	1600
Cyprus	107	96	99	100	103	103	-	-	-	0	47	890
Czech Republic	109	-	98	-	101	-	72	99x	100	4	9	7700
Denmark	106	-	100	100	104	103	-	-	-	10	5	9800
Djibouti	104	-	80	81	72	68	9	67	61	74	730	19
Dominica	-	-	99	101	99	103	50	100	100	67	-	-
Dominican Republic	111	100	95	102	125	120	70	99	99	180	150	200
Ecuador	108	98	100	101	100	102	73	84	75	80	130	210
Egypt	107	71	95	97	93	95	59	70	74	84	84	310
El Salvador	109	-	97	100	102	104	67	86	92	170	150	180
Equatorial Guinea	102	86	91	85	58	60	-	86	65	-	880	16
Eritrea	107	-	80	84	58	65	8	70	28	1000	630	24
Estonia	117	100	97	100	102	102	70x	-	100	8	63	1100
Ethiopia	104	-	85	95	63	65	15	28	6	870	850	14
Fiji	107	-	98	99	107	106	44	-	99	38	75	360
Finland	109	-	99	100	105	100	-	100x	100	6	6	8200
France	109	-	99	100	101	102	75x	99x	99x	10	17	2700

	Life expectancy: females as a % of males 2005	Adult literacy rate: females as a % of males 2000-2004*	Enrolment ratios: females as a % of males				Contraceptive prevalence (%) 1997-2005*	Antenatal care coverage (%) 1997-2005*	Skilled attendant at delivery (%) 1997-2005*	Maternal mortality ratio[†]		
			primary school 2000-2005*		secondary school 2000-2005*					1990-2005* reported	2000	
			gross	net	gross	net					adjusted	Lifetime risk of maternal death. 1 in:
Gabon	102	-	99	100	86	-	33	94	86	520	420	37
Gambia	105	-	106	105	84	84	18	91	55	730	540	31
Georgia	112	-	100	99	99	100	47	95	92	52	32	1700
Germany	108	-	100	-	98	-	75x	-	-	8	8	8000
Ghana	102	76	97	100	85	90	25	92	47	210x	540	35
Greece	107	96	99	99	101	104	-	-	-	1	9	7100
Grenada	-	-	96	100	109	109	54	99	100	1	-	-
Guatemala	111	84	92	96	90	91	43	84	41	150	240	74
Guinea	101	42	82	84	50	50	7	82	56	530	740	18
Guinea-Bissau	106	-	67	70	57	55	8	62	35	910	1100	13
Guyana	110	-	93	-	103	-	37	81	86	120	170	200
Haiti	103	-	-	-	-	-	28	79	24	520	680	29
Holy See	-	-	-	-	-	-	-	-	-	-	-	-
Honduras	106	100	100	102	126	-	62	83	56	110	110	190
Hungary	112	-	98	98	99	99	77x	-	100	7	16	4000
Iceland	105	-	98	98	106	104	-	-	-	-	0	0
India	105	66	93	95	80	-	47	60	43	540	540	48
Indonesia	106	93	98	98	100	100	57	92	72	310	230	150
Iran (Islamic Republic of)	105	83	110	99	94	95	74	77	90	37	76	370
Iraq	105	76	82	86	67	70	44	77	72	290	250	65
Ireland	107	-	99	100	107	106	-	-	100	6	5	8300
Israel	105	98	101	101	100	100	-	-	-	5	17	1800
Italy	108	99	99	100	98	101	60x	-	-	7	5	13900
Jamaica	105	116	100	101	102	104	69	98	97	110	87	380
Japan	109	-	101	100	101	101	56	-	100x	8	10	6000
Jordan	104	89	101	102	101	103	56	99	100	41	41	450
Kazakhstan	119	99	99	99	98	99	66	91	99	42	210	190
Kenya	96	90	95	101	92	100	39	88	42	410	1000	19
Kiribati	-	-	103	102x	122	117	21	88x	85	56	-	-
Korea, Democratic People's Republic of	110	-	-	-	-	-	62x	-	97	110	67	590
Korea, Republic of	110	-	99	99	100	101	81	-	100	20	20	2800
Kuwait	106	97	101	102	107	105	50x	95x	98x	5	5	6000
Kyrgyzstan	113	99	100	100	100	-	60	97	98	49	110	290
Lao People's Democratic Republic	105	79	88	94	75	85	32	27	19	410	650	25
Latvia	116	100	97	-	99	-	48x	-	100	14	42	1800
Lebanon	106	-	96	99	109	-	58	96	89x	100x	150	240
Lesotho	104	122	100	106	128	156	37	90	55	760	550	32
Liberia	104	-	72	78	73	55	10	85	51	580x	760	16
Libyan Arab Jamahiriya	107	-	99	-	106	-	45x	81x	94x	77	97	240
Liechtenstein	-	-	101	102	110	111	-	-	-	-	-	-
Lithuania	117	100	99	99	99	100	47x	-	100	3	13	4900
Luxembourg	108	-	99	100	107	106	-	-	100	0	28	1700
Madagascar	105	84	96	100	100x	100x	27	80	51	470	550	26
Malawi	98	72	102	105	81	85	33	92	56	980	1800	7
Malaysia	106	92	99	100	114	114	55x	74	97	30	41	660
Maldives	99	100	97	101	115	115	39	81	70	140	110	140
Mali	103	44	79	86	61	-	8	57	41	580	1200	10
Malta	106	103	99	100	94	106	-	-	98x	-	0	0
Marshall Islands	-	-	94	99	104	107	34	-	95	-	-	-
Mauritania	106	72	98	99	82	81	8	64	57	750	1000	14
Mauritius	110	92	100	101	99	101	76	-	98	22	24	1700
Mexico	107	98	98	100	106	103	74	86x	83	63	83	370
Micronesia (Federated States of)	102	-	-	-	-	-	45	-	88	120	-	-
Moldova, Republic of	111	99	99	100	104	104	68	98	100	22	36	1500
Monaco	-	-	-	-	-	-	-	-	-	-	-	-
Mongolia	106	100	101	100	113	114	69	94	97	93	110	300
Montenegro[‡]	-	-	-	-	-	-	-	-	-	-	-	-
Morocco	107	61	90	93	83	84	63	68	63	230	220	120
Mozambique	102	-	83	89	69	80	17	85	48	410	1000	14
Myanmar	110	91	102	102	98	97	34	76	57	230	360	75
Namibia	100	95	102	107	115	134	44	91	76	270	300	54

TABLE 8. WOMEN

	Life expectancy: females as a % of males 2005	Adult literacy rate: females as a % of males 2000-2004*	Enrolment ratios: females as a % of males				Contraceptive prevalence (%) 1997-2005*	Antenatal care coverage (%) 1997-2005*	Skilled attendant at delivery (%) 1997-2005*	Maternal mortality ratio[†]		
			primary school 2000-2005*		secondary school 2000-2005*					1990-2005* reported	2000	
			gross	net	gross	net					adjusted	Lifetime risk of maternal death. 1 in:
Nauru	-	-	99	-	109	-	-	-	-	-	-	-
Nepal	101	56	92	88	86	-	38	28	11	540	740	24
Netherlands	107	100	97	99	98	101	79x	-	100	7	16	3500
New Zealand	106	-	100	100	108	103	75x	95x	100x	15	7	6000
Nicaragua	107	-	98	98	115	113	69	86	67	83	230	88
Niger	100	35	71	70	67	63	14	41	16	590	1600	7
Nigeria	101	-	85	89	82	83	13	58	35	-	800	18
Niue	-	-	119	99x	95	105x	-	-	100	-	-	-
Norway	106	-	100	100	103	101	-	-	-	6	16	2900
Occupied Palestinian Territory	104	91	100	100	105	106	51	96	97	-	100	140
Oman	104	85	99	103	97	101	32	100	95	23	87	170
Pakistan	101	57	73	74	74	-	28	36	31	530	500	31
Palau	-	-	82	96	114	-	17	-	100	0x	-	-
Panama	107	98	97	100	107	110	-	72	93	40	160	210
Papua New Guinea	102	81	88	-	79	-	26x	78x	41	370x	300	62
Paraguay	107	-	96	-	102	-	73	94	77	180	170	120
Peru	108	88	100	100	101	100	71	92	73	190	410	73
Philippines	106	100	98	102	110	120	49	88	60	170	200	120
Poland	111	-	100	101	101	103	49x	-	100	4	13	4600
Portugal	109	-	96	100	111	112	-	-	100	8	5	11100
Qatar	107	100	99	99	97	98	43	-	99	10	140	170
Romania	110	98	99	100	101	103	70	94	99	17	49	1300
Russian Federation	122	99	100	101	100	-	-	-	99	32	67	1000
Rwanda	107	85	102	104	93	-	17	94	39	1100	1400	10
Saint Kitts and Nevis	-	-	107	108	97	97	41	100	100	250	-	-
Saint Lucia	104	-	95	97	112	109	47	48	99	35	-	-
Saint Vincent and the Grenadines	108	-	94	97	96	102	58	99	100	93	-	-
Samoa	109	-	100	101	112	113	30x	-	100	-	130	150
San Marino	-	-	-	-	-	-	-	-	-	-	-	-
Sao Tome and Principe	103	-	99	100	105	108	29	91	76	100	-	-
Saudi Arabia	106	79	96	92	89	94	32x	90x	91x	-	23	610
Senegal	105	57	95	94	73	72	12	79	58	430	690	22
Serbia[‡]	-	-	-	-	-	-	-	-	-	-	-	-
Seychelles	-	101	101	101	108	107	-	-	-	57	-	-
Sierra Leone	107	51	72	-	100	-	4	68	42	1800	2000	6
Singapore	105	92	-	-	-	-	62	-	100	6	30	1700
Slovakia	111	-	98	-	101	-	74x	-	99	4	3	19800
Slovenia	110	-	99	100	100	101	74x	98x	100	17	17	4100
Solomon Islands	102	-	97	99	79	86	11x	-	85	550x	130	120
Somalia	105	-	-	-	-	-	-	32	25	-	1100	10
South Africa	103	96	96	101	108	112	60	92	92	150	230	120
Spain	110	-	98	99	106	104	81x	-	-	6	4	17400
Sri Lanka	107	97	99	99	101	-	70	100	96	43	92	430
Sudan	105	73	88	83	94	-	7	60	87	550x	590	30
Suriname	110	95	103	107	133	140	42	91	85	150	110	340
Swaziland	98	96	95	101	100	123	48	90	74	230	370	49
Sweden	106	-	100	99	104	103	-	-	-	5	2	29800
Switzerland	107	-	99	100	92	93	82x	-	-	5	7	7900
Syrian Arab Republic	105	86	95	95	94	93	48	71	77x	65	160	130
Tajikistan	109	99	95	95	84	85	34	71	71	37	100	250
Tanzania, United Republic of	101	79	96	99	83x	-	26	78	43	580	1500	10
Thailand	111	96	95	-	103	-	79	92	99	24	44	900
The former Yugoslav Republic of Macedonia	107	96	100	100	98	98	-	81	99	21	23	2100
Timor-Leste	104	-	-	-	-	-	10	61	18	-	660	30
Togo	107	55	84	85	50	47	26	85	61	480	570	26
Tonga	104	100	95	97x	109	123	33	-	95	-	-	-
Trinidad and Tobago	108	-	97	100	106	106	38	92	96	45	160	330
Tunisia	106	78	96	101	108	105	66	92	90	69	120	320
Turkey	107	84	94	95	76	-	71	81	83	130x	70	480
Turkmenistan	115	99	-	-	-	-	62	98	97	14	31	790
Tuvalu	-	-	107	-	93	-	32	-	100	-	-	-

	Life expectancy: females as a % of males 2005	Adult literacy rate: females as a % of males 2000-2004*	Enrolment ratios: females as a % of males				Contraceptive prevalence (%) 1997-2005*	Antenatal care coverage (%) 1997-2005*	Skilled attendant at delivery (%) 1997-2005*	Maternal mortality ratio†		
			primary school 2000-2005*		secondary school 2000-2005*					1990-2005* reported	2000	
			gross	net	gross	net					adjusted	Lifetime risk of maternal death. 1 in:
Uganda	102	75	99	-	78	86	20	92	39	510	880	13
Ukraine	120	99	100	100	98	101	68	-	100	13	35	2000
United Arab Emirates	106	-	96	97	105	105	28x	97x	99x	3	54	500
United Kingdom	106	-	100	100	103	104	84	-	99	7	13	3800
United States	107	-	98	96	101	102	76x	-	99	8	17	2500
Uruguay	110	-	98	-	116	-	84	94	100	26	27	1300
Uzbekistan	110	-	99	-	97	-	68	97	96	30	24	1300
Vanuatu	106	-	97	98	86	86	28	-	88	68	130	140
Venezuela (Bolivarian Republic of)	108	100	98	100	115	116	77	94	95	58	96	300
Viet Nam	106	93	93	94	96	-	77	86	85	170	130	270
Yemen	105	-	71	72	48	46	23	41	27	370	570	19
Zambia	97	79	96	100	79	78	34	93	43	730	750	19
Zimbabwe	96	-	98	101	92	94	54	93	73	1100	1100	16

MEMORANDUM

Serbia and Montenegro (pre-cession)	107	95	100	100	101	-	58	-	92	7	11	4500

SUMMARY INDICATORS

Sub-Saharan Africa	102	76	89	94	78	80	24	68	43		940	16
Eastern and Southern Africa	102	85	94	97	85	88	30	71	39		980	15
West and Central Africa	102	63	84	87	70	77	18	66	45		900	16
Middle East and North Africa	105	77	93	93	90	92	53	70	76		220	100
South Asia	104	64	91	93	83	-	46	53	37		560	43
East Asia and Pacific	106	92	99	100	100	102**	79	88	87		110	360
Latin America and Caribbean	109	99	97	100	108	106	71	93	87		190	160
CEE/CIS	115	97	97	98	95	99	65	87	93		64	770
Industrialized countries§	108	-	99	98	101	102	-	-	99		13	4000
Developing countries§	106	85	94	96	92	98**	59	71	60		440	61
Least developed countries§	104	71	88	94	83	88	29	59	35		890	17
World	106	86	94	96	94	98**	60	71	63		400	74

‡ Due to the cession in June 2006 of Montenegro from the State Union of Serbia and Montenegro, and its subsequent admission to the UN on 28 June 2006, disaggregated data for Montenegro and Serbia as separate States are not yet available. Aggregated data presented are for Serbia and Montenegro pre-cession (see Memorandum item).

§ Also includes territories within each country category or regional group. Countries and territories in each country category or regional group are listed on page 136.

DEFINITIONS OF THE INDICATORS

Life expectancy at birth – The number of years newborn children would live if subject to the mortality risks prevailing for the cross section of population at the time of their birth.

Adult literacy rate – Percentage of persons aged 15 and over who can read and write.

Enrolment ratios: females as a % of males – Girls' (gross or net) enrolment ratio divided by that of boys', as a percentage.

The gross enrolment ratio – The number of children enrolled in primary or secondary school, regardless of age, expressed as a percentage of the total number of children of official primary or secondary school age.

The net enrolment ratio – The number of children enrolled in primary or secondary school who are of official primary or secondary school age, expressed as a percentage of the total number of children of official primary or secondary school age.

Contraceptive prevalence – Percentage of women in union aged 15-49 currently using contraception.

Antenatal care – Percentage of women aged 15-49 attended at least once during pregnancy by skilled health personnel (doctors, nurses or midwives).

Skilled attendant at delivery – Percentage of births attended by skilled health personnel (doctors, nurses or midwives).

Maternal mortality ratio – Annual number of deaths of women from pregnancy-related causes per 100,000 live births. This 'reported' column shows country-reported figures that are not adjusted for under-reporting and misclassification.

Lifetime risk of maternal death – The lifetime risk of maternal death takes into account both the probability of becoming pregnant and the probability of dying as a result of that pregnancy accumulated across a woman's reproductive years.

MAIN DATA SOURCES

Life expectancy – United Nations Population Division.

Adult literacy – United Nations Educational, Scientific and Cultural Organization (UNESCO).

School enrolment – UIS and UNESCO.

Contraceptive prevalence – Demographic and Health Surveys (DHS), Multiple Indicator Cluster Surveys (MICS), United Nations Population Division and UNICEF.

Antenatal care – DHS, MICS, World Health Organization (WHO) and UNICEF.

Skilled attendant at delivery – DHS, MICS, WHO and UNICEF.

Maternal mortality – WHO and UNICEF.

Lifetime risk – WHO and UNICEF.

---

† The maternal mortality data in the column headed 'reported' are those reported by national authorities. Periodically, UNICEF, WHO and UNFPA evaluate these data and make adjustments to account for the well-documented problems of under-reporting and misclassification of maternal deaths and to develop estimates for countries with no data. The column with 'adjusted' estimates for the year 2000 reflects the most recent of these reviews.

NOTES	-	Data not available.
	x	Data refer to years or periods other than those specified in the column heading, differ from the standard definition or refer to only part of a country.
	*	Data refer to the most recent year available during the period specified in the column heading.
	**	Excludes China.

TABLE 9. CHILD PROTECTION

Countries and territories	Child labour (5-14 years) 1999-2005*			Child marriage 1987-2005*			Birth registration 1999-2005*			Female genital mutilation/cutting 1997-2005* women[a] (15-49 years)			daughters[b]
	total	male	female	total	urban	rural	total	urban	rural	total	urban	rural	total
Afghanistan	31	28	34	43	-	-	6	12	4	-	-	-	-
Albania	23	27	19	-	-	-	99	99	99	-	-	-	-
Angola	24	22	25	-	-	-	29	34	19	-	-	-	-
Argentina	-	-	-	-	-	-	91y	-	-	-	-	-	-
Armenia	-	-	-	19	12	31	97	100	94	-	-	-	-
Azerbaijan	11	11	11	-	-	-	97	98	96	-	-	-	-
Bahrain	5	6	3	-	-	-	-	-	-	-	-	-	-
Bangladesh	7	10	4	69	55	74	7	9	7	-	-	-	-
Benin	26y	23y	29y	37	25	45	70	78	66	17	13	20	6
Bolivia	22	22	22	26	22	37	82	83	79	-	-	-	-
Bosnia and Herzegovina	11	12	10	-	-	-	98	98	99	-	-	-	-
Botswana	-	-	-	10	13	9	58	66	52	-	-	-	-
Brazil	6y	8y	4y	24	22	30	84y	-	-	-	-	-	-
Burkina Faso	57x,y	-	-	52	22	62	-	-	-	77	75	77	32
Burundi	25	26	24	17y	36y	17y	75	71	75	-	-	-	-
Cambodia	-	-	-	25	19	26	22	30	21	-	-	-	-
Cameroon	54	54	54	47	35	64	63	78	51	1	1	2	1
Central African Republic	57	56	59	57	54	59	73	88	63	36	29	41	-
Chad	53	55	52	72	65	73	9	36	3	45	47	44	21
Chile	-	-	-	-	-	-	95y	-	-	-	-	-	-
Colombia	5	6	4	23	19	38	90	97	77	-	-	-	-
Comoros	30	30	31	30	23	33	83	87	83	-	-	-	-
Congo, Democratic Republic of the	32	29	34	-	-	-	34	30	36	-	-	-	-
Costa Rica	50x,y	71x,y	29x,y	-	-	-	-	-	-	-	-	-	-
Côte d'Ivoire	37	35	38	33	24	43	72	88	60	45	39	48	24
Cuba	-	-	-	-	-	-	100y	100y	100y	-	-	-	-
Djibouti	-	-	-	-	-	-	-	-	-	98	98	100	-
Dominican Republic	10	12	7	41	37	51	75	82	66	-	-	-	-
Ecuador	6y	9y	4y	26y	21y	34y	-	-	-	-	-	-	-
Egypt	8y	9y	6y	17	-	-	-	-	-	96	92	98	28y
El Salvador	7y	-	-	27	-	-	-	-	-	-	-	-	-
Equatorial Guinea	30	29	30	-	-	-	32	43	24	-	-	-	-
Eritrea	-	-	-	47	31	60	-	-	-	89	86	91	63
Ethiopia	43y	47y	37y	49	32	53	-	-	-	74	69	76	-
Gabon	-	-	-	34	30	49	89	90	87	-	-	-	-
Gambia	22	23	22	-	-	-	32	37	29	-	-	-	-
Georgia	-	-	-	-	-	-	95	97	92	-	-	-	-
Ghana	57y	57y	58y	28	18	39	67y	-	-	5	4	7	-
Guatemala	24y	-	-	34	25	44	-	-	-	-	-	-	-
Guinea	26	27	25	65	46	75	67	88	56	96	94	96	-
Guinea-Bissau	55	55	55	-	-	-	42	32	47	-	-	-	-
Guyana	19	21	17	-	-	-	97	99	96	-	-	-	-
Haiti	-	-	-	24	18	31	70	78	66	-	-	-	-
Honduras	7y	9y	4y	-	-	-	-	-	-	-	-	-	-
India	14	12	16	46	26	55	35	54	29	-	-	-	-
Indonesia	4y	5y	4y	24	15	33	55	69	43	-	-	-	-
Iraq	13	14	12	-	-	-	98	99	97	-	-	-	-
Jamaica	2	3	1	-	-	-	90y	-	-	-	-	-	-
Jordan	-	-	-	11	11	12	-	-	-	-	-	-	-
Kazakhstan	-	-	-	14	12	17	-	-	-	-	-	-	-
Kenya	27	28	27	25	19	27	48y	64y	44y	32	21	36	21
Korea, Democratic People's Republic of	-	-	-	-	-	-	99	99	99	-	-	-	-
Kyrgyzstan	-	-	-	21	19	22	-	-	-	-	-	-	-
Lao People's Democratic Republic	25	24	26	-	-	-	59	71	56	-	-	-	-
Lebanon	7	8	6	11	-	-	-	-	-	-	-	-	-
Lesotho	23	25	21	23	13	26	26	39	24	-	-	-	-
Liberia	-	-	-	39	-	-	-	-	-	-	-	-	-
Madagascar	32	36	29	39	29	42	75	87	72	-	-	-	-
Malawi	37y	39y	35y	49	-	-	-	-	-	-	-	-	-
Maldives	-	-	-	-	-	-	73	-	-	-	-	-	-
Mali	35	36	34	65	46	74	47y	84y	34y	92	90	93	73
Mauritania	4	5	3	37	32	42	55	72	42	71	65	77	66
Mexico	16y	15y	16y	28y	31y	21y	-	-	-	-	-	-	-
Moldova, Republic of	33	32	33	-	-	-	98	98	98	-	-	-	-
Mongolia	35	35	36	-	-	-	98	98	97	-	-	-	-
Morocco	11	13	9	16	12	21	85	92	80	-	-	-	-
Mozambique	-	-	-	56	41	66	-	-	-	-	-	-	-
Myanmar	-	-	-	-	-	-	65y	66y	64y	-	-	-	-
Namibia	-	-	-	10	9	10	71	82	64	-	-	-	-
Nepal	31	30	33	56	34	60	34	37	34	-	-	-	-
Nicaragua	15	18	11	43	36	55	81	90	73	-	-	-	-
Niger	67	70	65	77	46	86	46	85	40	5	2	5	4
Nigeria	39y	-	-	43	27	52	30	53	20	19	28	14	10
Occupied Palestinian Territory	-	-	-	19	-	-	98	98	97	-	-	-	-
Pakistan	-	-	-	32	21	37	-	-	-	-	-	-	-

| | Child labour (5-14 years) 1999-2005* | | | Child marriage 1987-2005* | | | Birth registration 1999-2005* | | | Female genital mutilation/cutting 1997-2005* | | | |
| | | | | | | | | | | women[a] (15-49 years) | | | daughters[b] |
	total	male	female	total	urban	rural	total	urban	rural	total	urban	rural	total
Paraguay	12y	16y	7y	24	18	32	-	-	-	-	-	-	-
Peru	-	-	-	17	13	30	93	93	92	-	-	-	-
Philippines	12	13	11	14	10	22	83	87	78	-	-	-	-
Romania	1y	-	-	-	-	-	-	-	-	-	-	-	-
Rwanda	35	36	35	20	21	19	65	61	66	-	-	-	-
Sao Tome and Principe	15	16	14	-	-	-	70	73	67	-	-	-	-
Senegal	37	39	36	36	15	53	62	82	51	28	22	35	-
Sierra Leone	59	59	59	-	-	-	46	66	40	-	-	-	-
Somalia	36	31	41	-	-	-	-	-	-	-	-	-	-
South Africa	-	-	-	8	5	12	-	-	-	-	-	-	-
Sri Lanka	-	-	-	12y	-	-	-	-	-	-	-	-	-
Sudan	14	15	13	27y	19y	34y	64	82	46	90	92	88	58
Suriname	-	-	-	-	-	-	95	94	94	-	-	-	-
Swaziland	10	10	10	-	-	-	53	72	50	-	-	-	-
Syrian Arab Republic	8y	10y	6y	-	-	-	-	-	-	-	-	-	-
Tajikistan	10	9	11	13	-	-	88	85	90	-	-	-	-
Tanzania, United Republic of	36	37	34	41	23	49	8	22	4	15	7	18	4
Thailand	-	-	-	21y	13y	23y	-	-	-	-	-	-	-
Timor-Leste	4y	4y	4y	-	-	-	53y	-	-	-	-	-	-
Togo	63	64	62	31	17	41	82	93	78	-	-	-	-
Trinidad and Tobago	2	3	2	34y	37y	32y	95	-	-	-	-	-	-
Tunisia	-	-	-	10y	7y	14y	-	-	-	-	-	-	-
Turkey	-	-	-	23	19	30	-	-	-	-	-	-	-
Turkmenistan	-	-	-	9	12	7	-	-	-	-	-	-	-
Uganda	37	37	36	54	34	59	4	11	3	-	-	-	-
Ukraine	7	8	7	-	-	-	-	-	-	-	-	-	-
Uzbekistan	19	22	17	13	16	11	100	100	100	-	-	-	-
Venezuela (Bolivarian Republic of)	8	9	6	-	-	-	92	-	-	-	-	-	-
Viet Nam	24	24	24	11	5	13	72	92	68	-	-	-	-
Yemen	-	-	-	37	-	-	-	-	-	23	26	22	20
Zambia	11	10	11	42	32	49	10	16	6	1	1	1	-
Zimbabwe	26y	-	-	29	21	36	42	56	35	-	-	-	-

SUMMARY INDICATORS

	total	male	female	total	urban	rural	total	urban	rural	total	urban	rural	total
Sub-Saharan Africa	37	38	37	40	25	48	40	54	32	36	29	40	16
Eastern and Southern Africa	34	36	32	36	21	43	33	44	28	-	-	-	-
West and Central Africa	42	41	42	44	28	56	44	59	34	28	29	29	16
Middle East and North Africa	10	12	9	-	-	-	-	-	-	-	-	-	-
South Asia	14	12	15	48	28	55	32	47	25	-	-	-	-
East Asia and Pacific	11**	11**	10**	20**	12**	25**	65**	77**	56**	-	-	-	-
Latin America and Caribbean	9	10	8	25	24	31	89	92	78	-	-	-	-
CEE/CIS	-	-	-	-	-	-	-	-	-	-	-	-	-
Industrialized countries[§]	-	-	-	-	-	-	-	-	-	-	-	-	-
Developing countries[§]	17**	17**	18**	36**	23**	46**	46**	62**	34**	-	-	-	-
Least developed countries[§]	29	30	28	51	35	57	32	44	28	-	-	-	-
World	-	-	-	-	-	-	-	-	-	-	-	-	-

§ Also includes territories within each country category or regional group. Countries and territories in each country category or regional group are listed on page 136.

DEFINITIONS OF THE INDICATORS

Child labour – Percentage of children aged 5-14 years involved in child labour at the moment of the survey. A child is considered to be involved in child labour under the following conditions: (a) children 5-11 years of age who, during the week preceding the survey, did at least one hour of economic activity or at least 28 hours of domestic work and, (b) children 12-14 years of age who, during the week preceding the survey, did at least 14 hours of economic activity or at least 28 hours of domestic work.

Child labour background variables – Sex of the child; urban or rural place of residence; poorest 20 per cent or richest 20 per cent of the population constructed from household assets (a more detailed description of the household wealth estimation procedure can be found at www.childinfo.org); mother's education reflecting mothers with and without some level of education.

Birth registration – Percentage of children less than five years of age who were registered at the moment of the survey. The numerator of this indicator includes children whose birth certificate was seen by the interviewer or whose mother or caretaker says the birth has been registered. MICS data refer to children alive at the time of the survey.

Child marriage – Percentage of women 20-24 years of age who were married or in union before they were 18 years old.

Female genital mutilation/cutting – (a) Women – the percentage of women aged 15-49 years of age who have been mutilated/cut. (b) Daughters – the percentage of women aged 15-49 with at least one mutilated/cut daughter. Female genital mutilation/cutting (FGM/C) involves the cutting or alteration of the female genitalia for social reasons. Generally, there are three recognized types of FGM/C: clitoridectomy, excision and infibulation. Clitoridectomy is the removal of the prepuce with or without excision of all or part of the clitoris. Excision is the removal of the prepuce and clitoris along with all or part of the labia minora. Infibulation is the most severe form and consists of removal of all or part of the external genitalia, followed by joining together of the two sides of the labia minora using threads, thorns or other materials to narrow the vaginal opening. A more detailed analysis of these data can also be found at www.measuredhs.com and www.prb.org.

MAIN DATA SOURCES

Child labour – Multiple Indicator Cluster Survey (MICS) and Demographic and Health Surveys (DHS).

Child marriage – MICS, DHS and other national surveys.

Birth registration – MICS, DHS, other national surveys and vital registration systems.

Female genital mutilation/cutting – MICS, DHS and other national surveys.

NOTES

- Data not available.
- x Data refer to years or periods other than those specified in the column heading, differ from the standard definition, or refer to only part of a country.
- y Data differ from the standard definition or refer to only part of a country but are included in the calculation of regional and global averages.
- * Data refer to the most recent year available during the period specified in the column heading.
- ** Excludes China.

Summary indicators

Averages given at the end of each table are calculated using data from the countries and territories as grouped below.

Sub-Saharan Africa

Angola; Benin; Botswana; Burkina Faso; Burundi; Cameroon; Cape Verde; Central African Republic; Chad; Comoros; Congo; Congo, Democratic Republic of the; Côte d'Ivoire; Equatorial Guinea; Eritrea; Ethiopia; Gabon; Gambia; Ghana; Guinea; Guinea-Bissau; Kenya; Lesotho; Liberia; Madagascar; Malawi; Mali; Mauritania; Mauritius; Mozambique; Namibia; Niger; Nigeria; Rwanda; Sao Tome and Principe; Senegal; Seychelles; Sierra Leone; Somalia; South Africa; Swaziland; Tanzania, United Republic of; Togo; Uganda; Zambia; Zimbabwe

Middle East and North Africa

Algeria; Bahrain; Djibouti; Egypt; Iran (Islamic Republic of); Iraq; Jordan; Kuwait; Lebanon; Libyan Arab Jamahiriya; Morocco; Occupied Palestinian Territory; Oman; Qatar; Saudi Arabia; Sudan; Syrian Arab Republic; Tunisia; United Arab Emirates; Yemen

South Asia

Afghanistan; Bangladesh; Bhutan; India; Maldives; Nepal; Pakistan; Sri Lanka

East Asia and Pacific

Brunei Darussalam; Cambodia; China; Cook Islands; Fiji; Indonesia; Kiribati; Korea, Democratic People's Republic of; Korea, Republic of; Lao People's Democratic Republic; Malaysia; Marshall Islands; Micronesia (Federated States of); Mongolia; Myanmar; Nauru; Niue; Palau; Papua New Guinea; Philippines; Samoa; Singapore; Solomon Islands; Thailand; Timor-Leste; Tonga; Tuvalu; Vanuatu; Viet Nam

Latin America and Caribbean

Antigua and Barbuda; Argentina; Bahamas; Barbados; Belize; Bolivia; Brazil; Chile; Colombia; Costa Rica; Cuba; Dominica; Dominican Republic; Ecuador; El Salvador; Grenada; Guatemala; Guyana; Haiti; Honduras; Jamaica; Mexico; Nicaragua; Panama; Paraguay; Peru; Saint Kitts and Nevis; Saint Lucia; Saint Vincent and the Grenadines; Suriname; Trinidad and Tobago; Uruguay; Venezuela (Bolivarian Republic of)

CEE/CIS

Albania; Armenia; Azerbaijan; Belarus; Bosnia and Herzegovina; Bulgaria; Croatia; Georgia; Kazakhstan; Kyrgyzstan; Moldova, Republic of; Montenegro; Romania; Russian Federation; Serbia; Tajikistan; the former Yugoslav Republic of Macedonia; Turkey; Turkmenistan; Ukraine; Uzbekistan

Industrialized countries/territories

Andorra; Australia; Austria; Belgium; Canada; Cyprus; Czech Republic; Denmark; Estonia; Finland; France; Germany; Greece; Holy See; Hungary; Iceland; Ireland; Israel; Italy; Japan; Latvia; Liechtenstein; Lithuania; Luxembourg; Malta; Monaco; Netherlands; New Zealand; Norway; Poland; Portugal; San Marino; Slovakia; Slovenia; Spain; Sweden; Switzerland; United Kingdom; United States

Developing countries/territories

Afghanistan; Algeria; Angola; Antigua and Barbuda; Argentina; Armenia; Azerbaijan; Bahamas; Bahrain; Bangladesh; Barbados; Belize; Benin; Bhutan; Bolivia; Botswana; Brazil; Brunei Darussalam; Burkina Faso; Burundi; Cambodia; Cameroon; Cape Verde; Central African Republic; Chad; Chile; China; Colombia; Comoros; Congo; Congo, Democratic Republic of the; Cook Islands; Costa Rica; Côte d'Ivoire; Cuba; Cyprus; Djibouti; Dominica; Dominican Republic; Ecuador; Egypt; El Salvador; Equatorial Guinea; Eritrea; Ethiopia; Fiji; Gabon; Gambia; Georgia; Ghana; Grenada; Guatemala; Guinea; Guinea-Bissau; Guyana; Haiti; Honduras; India; Indonesia; Iran (Islamic Republic of); Iraq; Israel; Jamaica; Jordan; Kazakhstan; Kenya; Kiribati; Korea, Democratic People's Republic of; Korea, Republic of; Kuwait; Kyrgyzstan; Lao People's Democratic Republic; Lebanon; Lesotho; Liberia; Libyan Arab Jamahiriya; Madagascar; Malawi; Malaysia; Maldives; Mali; Marshall Islands; Mauritania; Mauritius; Mexico; Micronesia (Federated States of); Mongolia; Morocco; Mozambique; Myanmar; Namibia; Nauru; Nepal; Nicaragua; Niger; Nigeria; Niue; Occupied Palestinian Territory; Oman; Pakistan; Palau; Panama; Papua New Guinea; Paraguay; Peru; Philippines; Qatar; Rwanda; Saint Kitts and Nevis; Saint Lucia; Saint Vincent/Grenadines; Samoa; Sao Tome and Principe; Saudi Arabia; Senegal; Seychelles; Sierra Leone; Singapore; Solomon Islands; Somalia; South Africa; Sri Lanka; Sudan; Suriname; Swaziland; Syrian Arab Republic; Tajikistan; Tanzania, United Republic of; Thailand; Timor-Leste; Togo; Tonga; Trinidad and Tobago; Tunisia; Turkey; Turkmenistan; Tuvalu; Uganda; United Arab Emirates; Uruguay; Uzbekistan; Vanuatu; Venezuela (Bolivarian Republic of); Viet Nam; Yemen; Zambia; Zimbabwe

Least developed countries/territories

Afghanistan; Angola; Bangladesh; Benin; Bhutan; Burkina Faso; Burundi; Cambodia; Cape Verde; Central African Republic; Chad; Comoros; Congo, Democratic Republic of the; Djibouti; Equatorial Guinea; Eritrea; Ethiopia; Gambia; Guinea; Guinea-Bissau; Haiti; Kiribati; Lao People's Democratic Republic; Lesotho; Liberia; Madagascar; Malawi; Maldives; Mali; Mauritania; Mozambique; Myanmar; Nepal; Niger; Rwanda; Samoa; Sao Tome and Principe; Senegal; Sierra Leone; Solomon Islands; Somalia; Sudan; Tanzania, United Republic of; Timor-Leste; Togo; Tuvalu; Uganda; Vanuatu; Yemen; Zambia

Measuring human development
An introduction to Table 10

If development is to be measured by a comprehensive and inclusive assessment, then the need arises for a method of measuring human as well as economic progress. From UNICEF's point of view, there is a need for an agreed method of measuring the level of child well-being and its rate of change.

The under-five mortality rate (U5MR) is used in Table 10 (next page) as the principal indicator of such progress.

The U5MR has several advantages. First, it measures an end result of the development process rather than an 'input', such as school enrolment level, per capita calorie availability or the number of doctors per thousand population – all of which are means to an end.

Second, the U5MR is known to be the result of a wide variety of inputs: the nutritional health and the health knowledge of mothers; the level of immunization and oral rehydration therapy use; the availability of maternal and child health services (including prenatal care); income and food availability in the family; the availability of safe drinking water and basic sanitation; and the overall safety of the child's environment.

Third, the U5MR is less susceptible to the fallacy of the average than, for example, per capita gross national income (GNI). This is because the natural scale does not allow the children of the rich to be one thousand times as likely to survive, even if the man-made scale does permit them to have one thousand times as much income. In other words, it is much more difficult for a wealthy minority to affect a nation's U5MR, and it therefore presents a more accurate, if far from perfect, picture of the health status of the majority of children (and of society as a whole).

For these reasons, the U5MR is chosen by UNICEF as its single most important indicator of the state of a nation's children.

The speed of progress in reducing the U5MR can be measured by calculating its average annual reduction rate (AARR). Unlike the comparison of absolute changes, the AARR reflects the fact that the lower limits to U5MR are approached only with increasing difficulty. As lower levels of under-five mortality are reached, for example, the same absolute reduction obviously represents a greater percentage of reduction. The AARR therefore shows a higher rate of progress for a 10-point reduction, for example, if that reduction happens at a lower level of under-five mortality. A fall in the U5MR of 10 points from 100 to 90 represents a reduction of 10 per cent, whereas the same 10-point fall from 20 to 10 represents a reduction of 50 per cent. (A negative value for the percentage reduction indicates an increase in the U5MR over the period specified).

When used in conjunction with gross domestic product (GDP) growth rates, the U5MR and its reduction rate can therefore give a picture of the progress being made by any country, territory or region, and over any period of time, towards the satisfaction of some of the most essential of human needs.

As Table 10 shows, there is no fixed relationship between the annual reduction rate of the U5MR and the annual rate of growth in per capita GDP. Such comparisons help to shed light on the relationship between economic advance and human development.

Finally, the table gives the total fertility rate for each country and territory and the corresponding average annual rate of reduction. It is clear that many of the nations that have achieved significant reductions in their U5MR have also achieved significant reductions in fertility.

TABLE 10. THE RATE OF PROGRESS

Countries and territories	Under-5 mortality rank	Under-5 mortality rate			Average annual rate of reduction (%)[e]		Reduction since 1990 (%)[e]	GDP per capita average annual growth rate (%)		Total fertility rate			Average annual rate of reduction (%)	
		1970	1990	2005	1970-1990	1990-2005		1970-1990	1990-2005	1970	1990	2005	1970-1990	1990-2005
Afghanistan	3	320	260	257	1.0	0.1	1	1.6x	-	7.7	8.0	7.3	-0.2	0.6
Albania	121	109	45	18	4.4	6.1	60	-0.7x	5.2	4.9	2.9	2.2	2.6	1.8
Algeria	78	220	69	39	5.8	3.8	43	1.6	1.1	7.4	4.7	2.4	2.3	4.5
Andorra	190	-	-	3	-	-	-	-	-	-	-	-	-	-
Angola	2	300	260	260	0.7	0.0	0	0.4x	1.4	7.3	7.2	6.6	0.1	0.6
Antigua and Barbuda	140	-	-	12	-	-	-	6.5x	1.7	-	-	-	-	-
Argentina	121	71	29	18	4.5	3.2	38	-0.7	1.1	3.1	3.0	2.3	0.2	1.8
Armenia	92	-	54	29	-	4.1	46	-	4.4	3.2	2.5	1.3	1.2	4.4
Australia	161	20	10	6	3.5	3.4	40	1.6	2.5	2.7	1.9	1.7	1.8	0.7
Austria	168	33	10	5	6.0	4.6	50	2.4	1.8	2.3	1.5	1.4	2.1	0.5
Azerbaijan	50	-	105	89	-	1.1	15	-	0.0	4.6	3.0	1.8	2.1	3.4
Bahamas	129	49	29	15	2.6	4.4	48	1.8	0.4x	3.6	2.6	2.2	1.6	1.1
Bahrain	146	82	19	11	7.3	3.6	42	-1.3x	2.3	6.5	3.7	2.4	2.8	2.9
Bangladesh	57	239	149	73	2.4	4.8	51	0.6	2.9	6.4	4.4	3.1	1.9	2.3
Barbados	140	54	17	12	5.8	2.3	29	1.8	1.5	3.1	1.7	1.5	3.0	0.8
Belarus	140	37	19	12	3.3	3.1	37	-	2.2	2.3	1.9	1.2	1.0	3.1
Belgium	168	29	10	5	5.3	4.6	50	2.2	1.7	2.1	1.6	1.7	1.4	-0.4
Belize	125	-	42	17	-	6.0	60	2.9	2.3	6.3	4.5	3.0	1.7	2.7
Benin	21	252	185	150	1.5	1.4	19	0.0	1.4	7.0	6.8	5.6	0.1	1.3
Bhutan	53	267	166	75	2.4	5.3	55	6.4x	3.0	5.9	5.7	4.1	0.2	2.2
Bolivia	64	243	125	65	3.3	4.4	48	-1.1	1.3	6.6	4.9	3.7	1.5	1.9
Bosnia and Herzegovina	129	82	22	15	6.6	2.6	32	-	12.7x	2.9	1.7	1.3	2.7	1.8
Botswana	37	142	58	120	4.5	-4.8	-107	8.3	3.8	6.9	4.5	3.0	2.1	2.7
Brazil	86	135	60	33	4.1	4.0	45	2.3	1.1	5.0	2.8	2.3	2.9	1.3
Brunei Darussalam	151	78	11	9	9.8	1.3	18	-	-	5.7	3.2	2.4	2.9	1.9
Bulgaria	129	32	18	15	2.9	1.2	17	3.4x	1.5	2.2	1.7	1.2	1.3	2.3
Burkina Faso	16	295	210	191	1.7	0.6	9	1.4	1.3	7.6	7.3	6.5	0.2	0.8
Burundi	17	233	190	190	1.0	0.0	0	1.1	-2.8	6.8	6.8	6.8	0.0	0.0
Cambodia	25	-	115	143	-	-1.5	-24	-	4.7x	5.9	5.6	3.9	0.3	2.4
Cameroon	23	215	139	149	2.2	-0.5	-7	3.4	0.6	6.2	5.9	4.4	0.2	2.0
Canada	161	23	8	6	5.3	1.9	25	2.0	2.3	2.2	1.7	1.5	1.3	0.8
Cape Verde	85	-	60	35	-	3.6	42	-	3.4	7.0	5.5	3.6	1.2	2.8
Central African Republic	15	238	168	193	1.7	-0.9	-15	-1.3	-0.6	5.7	5.7	4.8	0.0	1.1
Chad	8	261	201	208	1.3	-0.2	-3	-0.9	1.7	6.6	6.7	6.7	-0.1	0.0
Chile	150	98	21	10	7.7	4.9	52	1.5	3.8	4.0	2.6	2.0	2.2	1.7
China	96	120	49	27	4.5	4.0	45	6.6	8.8	5.6	2.2	1.7	4.7	1.7
Colombia	108	105	35	21	5.5	3.4	40	2.0	0.6	5.6	3.1	2.5	3.0	1.4
Comoros	59	215	120	71	2.9	3.5	41	0.1x	-0.5	7.1	6.1	4.6	0.8	1.9
Congo	43	160	110	108	1.9	0.1	2	3.1	-1.0	6.3	6.3	6.3	0.0	0.0
Congo, Democratic Republic of the	9	245	205	205	0.9	0.0	0	-2.4	-5.2	6.4	6.7	6.7	-0.2	0.0
Cook Islands	113	-	32	20	-	3.1	38	-	-	-	-	-	-	-
Costa Rica	140	83	18	12	7.6	2.7	33	0.7	2.3	5.0	3.2	2.2	2.2	2.5
Côte d'Ivoire	13	239	157	195	2.1	-1.4	-24	-1.9	-0.5	7.4	6.6	4.8	0.6	2.1
Croatia	156	42	12	7	6.3	3.6	42	-	2.5	2.0	1.7	1.3	0.8	1.8
Cuba	156	43	13	7	6.0	4.1	46	-	3.5x	4.0	1.7	1.6	4.3	0.4
Cyprus	168	33	12	5	5.1	5.8	58	6.1x	2.5x	2.6	2.4	1.6	0.4	2.7
Czech Republic	182	24	13	4	3.1	7.9	69	-	1.9	2.0	1.8	1.2	0.5	2.7
Denmark	168	19	9	5	3.7	3.9	44	1.5	1.8	2.1	1.7	1.8	1.1	-0.4
Djibouti	30	-	175	133	-	1.8	24	-	-2.4	7.4	6.3	4.8	0.8	1.8
Dominica	129	-	17	15	-	0.8	12	4.7x	1.0	-	-	-	-	-
Dominican Republic	89	127	65	31	3.3	4.9	52	2.0	3.8	6.2	3.4	2.6	3.0	1.8
Ecuador	102	140	57	25	4.5	5.5	56	1.3	0.7	6.3	3.7	2.7	2.7	2.1
Egypt	86	235	104	33	4.1	7.7	68	4.3	2.6	6.1	4.3	3.1	1.7	2.2
El Salvador	96	162	60	27	5.0	5.3	55	-1.8	1.6	6.4	3.7	2.8	2.7	1.9
Equatorial Guinea	9	-	170	205	-	-1.2	-21	-	16.6x	5.7	5.9	5.9	-0.2	0.0
Eritrea	52	237	147	78	2.4	4.2	47	-	0.3	6.6	6.2	5.3	0.3	1.0
Estonia	156	26	16	7	2.4	5.5	56	1.5x	4.2	2.1	1.9	1.4	0.5	2.0
Ethiopia	19	239	204	164	0.8	1.5	20	-	1.5	6.8	6.8	5.7	0.0	1.2
Fiji	121	65	22	18	5.4	1.3	18	0.6x	1.3x	4.5	3.4	2.8	1.4	1.3
Finland	182	16	7	4	4.1	3.7	43	2.9	2.6	1.9	1.7	1.7	0.6	0.0
France	168	24	9	5	4.9	3.9	44	2.2	1.7	2.5	1.8	1.9	1.6	-0.4

	Under-5 mortality rank	Under-5 mortality rate			Average annual rate of reduction (%)[e]		Reduction since 1990 (%)[e]	GDP per capita average annual growth rate (%)		Total fertility rate			Average annual rate of reduction (%)	
		1970	1990	2005	1970-1990	1990-2005		1970-1990	1990-2005	1970	1990	2005	1970-1990	1990-2005
Gabon	48	-	92	91	-	0.1	1	0.0	-0.4	4.9	5.4	3.8	-0.5	2.3
Gambia	27	311	151	137	3.6	0.6	9	0.9	0.1	6.5	5.9	4.5	0.5	1.8
Georgia	72	-	47	45	-	0.3	4	3.2	0.2	2.6	2.1	1.4	1.1	2.7
Germany	168	26	9	5	5.3	3.9	44	2.2x	1.4	2.0	1.4	1.3	1.8	0.5
Ghana	42	186	122	112	2.1	0.6	8	-2.1	2.0	6.7	5.8	4.1	0.7	2.3
Greece	168	54	11	5	8.0	5.3	55	1.3	2.4	2.4	1.4	1.2	2.7	1.0
Grenada	108	-	37	21	-	3.8	43	-	2.1	-	-	-	-	-
Guatemala	73	168	82	43	3.6	4.3	48	0.2	1.3	6.2	5.6	4.4	0.5	1.6
Guinea	21	345	240	150	1.8	3.1	38	-	1.2	6.8	6.5	5.7	0.2	0.9
Guinea-Bissau	12	-	253	200	-	1.6	21	-0.1	-2.6	6.8	7.1	7.1	-0.2	0.0
Guyana	66	-	88	63	-	2.2	28	-1.5	3.1	5.6	2.6	2.2	3.8	1.1
Haiti	37	221	150	120	1.9	1.5	20	-0.3	-2.0	5.8	5.4	3.8	0.4	2.3
Holy See	-	-	-	-	-	-	-	-	-	-	-	-	-	-
Honduras	76	170	59	40	5.3	2.6	32	0.6	0.5	7.3	5.1	3.5	1.8	2.5
Hungary	154	39	17	8	4.2	5.0	53	2.9	3.1	2.0	1.8	1.3	0.5	2.2
Iceland	190	14	7	3	3.5	5.6	57	3.2	2.2	3.0	2.2	1.9	1.6	1.0
India	54	202	123	74	2.5	3.4	40	2.2	4.2	5.6	4.0	2.9	1.7	2.1
Indonesia	83	172	91	36	3.2	6.2	60	4.7	2.1	5.4	3.1	2.3	2.8	2.0
Iran (Islamic Republic of)	83	191	72	36	4.9	4.6	50	-3.5x	2.5	6.6	5.0	2.1	1.4	5.8
Iraq	33	127	50	125	4.7	-6.1	-150	-4.3x	-	7.2	5.9	4.5	1.0	1.8
Ireland	161	27	10	6	5.0	3.4	40	2.8	6.2	3.9	2.1	2.0	3.1	0.3
Israel	161	27	12	6	4.1	4.6	50	1.9	1.5	3.8	3.0	2.8	1.2	0.5
Italy	182	33	9	4	6.5	5.4	56	2.6	1.4	2.4	1.3	1.3	3.1	0.0
Jamaica	113	64	20	20	5.8	0.0	0	-1.3	0.2	5.5	2.9	2.4	3.2	1.3
Japan	182	21	6	4	6.3	2.7	33	3.0	0.9	2.1	1.6	1.3	1.4	1.4
Jordan	100	107	40	26	4.9	2.9	35	2.5x	1.7	7.9	5.5	3.3	1.8	3.4
Kazakhstan	57	-	63	73	-	-1.0	-16	-	2.0	3.5	2.8	1.9	1.1	2.6
Kenya	37	156	97	120	2.4	-1.4	-24	1.2	-0.2	8.1	5.9	5.0	1.6	1.1
Kiribati	64	-	88	65	-	2.0	26	-5.3	1.4	-	-	-	-	-
Korea, Democratic People's Republic of	70	70	55	55	1.2	0.0	0	-	-	4.3	2.4	2.0	2.9	1.2
Korea, Republic of	168	54	9	5	9.0	3.9	44	6.2	4.5	4.5	1.6	1.2	5.2	1.9
Kuwait	146	59	16	11	6.5	2.5	31	-6.8x	0.6x	7.2	3.5	2.3	3.6	2.8
Kyrgyzstan	63	130	80	67	2.4	1.2	16	-	-1.3	4.9	3.9	2.6	1.1	2.7
Lao People's Democratic Republic	51	218	163	79	1.5	4.8	52	-	3.8	6.1	6.1	4.6	0.0	1.9
Latvia	146	26	18	11	1.8	3.3	39	3.4	3.6	1.9	1.9	1.3	0.0	2.5
Lebanon	90	54	37	30	1.9	1.4	19	-	2.7	5.1	3.1	2.2	2.5	2.3
Lesotho	31	186	101	132	3.1	-1.8	-31	3.1	2.3	5.7	4.9	3.4	0.8	2.4
Liberia	5	263	235	235	0.6	0.0	0	-4.2	2.3	6.9	6.9	6.8	0.0	0.1
Libyan Arab Jamahiriya	117	160	41	19	6.8	5.1	54	-4.8x	-	7.6	4.8	2.9	2.3	3.4
Liechtenstein	182	-	10	4	-	6.1	60	-	-	-	-	-	-	-
Lithuania	151	28	13	9	3.8	2.5	31	-	1.9	2.3	2.0	1.3	0.7	2.9
Luxembourg	168	26	10	5	4.8	4.6	50	2.7	3.6	2.1	1.6	1.7	1.4	-0.4
Madagascar	40	180	168	119	0.3	2.3	29	-2.4	-0.7	6.8	6.2	5.1	0.5	1.3
Malawi	33	341	221	125	2.2	3.8	43	-0.1	1.0	7.3	7.0	5.9	0.2	1.1
Malaysia	140	70	22	12	5.8	4.0	45	4.0	3.3	5.6	3.8	2.8	1.9	2.0
Maldives	74	255	111	42	4.2	6.5	62	-	3.8x	7.0	6.4	4.0	0.4	3.1
Mali	7	400	250	218	2.4	0.9	13	-0.5	2.2	7.5	7.4	6.8	0.1	0.6
Malta	161	32	11	6	5.3	4.0	45	6.5	2.7	2.1	2.0	1.5	0.2	1.9
Marshall Islands	69	-	92	58	-	3.1	37	-	-2.3	-	-	-	-	-
Mauritania	33	250	133	125	3.2	0.4	6	-0.6	1.9	6.5	6.2	5.6	0.2	0.7
Mauritius	129	86	23	15	6.6	2.8	35	5.1x	3.7	3.7	2.2	2.0	2.6	0.6
Mexico	96	110	46	27	4.4	3.6	41	1.6	1.5	6.8	3.4	2.3	3.5	2.6
Micronesia (Federated States of)	74	-	58	42	-	2.2	28	-	-0.1	6.9	5.0	4.3	1.6	1.0
Moldova, Republic of	128	70	35	16	3.5	5.2	54	1.8x	-3.5	2.6	2.4	1.2	0.4	4.6
Monaco	168	-	9	5	-	3.9	44	-	-	-	-	-	-	-
Mongolia	71	-	108	49	-	5.3	55	-	0.9	7.5	4.1	2.3	3.0	3.9
Montenegro[‡]	-	-	-	-	-	-	-	-	-	-	-	-	-	-
Morocco	76	184	89	40	3.6	5.3	55	2.0	1.5	7.1	4.0	2.7	2.9	2.6
Mozambique	24	278	235	145	0.8	3.2	38	-1.0x	4.6	6.6	6.3	5.3	0.2	1.2

TABLE 10. THE RATE OF PROGRESS

	Under-5 mortality rank	Under-5 mortality rate			Average annual rate of reduction (%)[⊖]		Reduction since 1990 (%)[⊖]	GDP per capita average annual growth rate (%)		Total fertility rate			Average annual rate of reduction (%)	
		1970	1990	2005	1970-1990	1990-2005		1970-1990	1990-2005	1970	1990	2005	1970-1990	1990-2005
Myanmar	44	179	130	105	1.6	1.4	19	1.5	6.6	5.9	4.0	2.2	1.9	4.0
Namibia	67	135	86	62	2.3	2.2	28	-2.3x	1.4	6.5	6.0	3.7	0.4	3.2
Nauru	90	-	-	30	-	-	-	-	-	-	-	-	-	-
Nepal	54	250	145	74	2.7	4.5	49	1.1	1.9	5.9	5.2	3.5	0.6	2.6
Netherlands	168	15	9	5	2.6	3.9	44	1.5	1.9	2.4	1.6	1.7	2.0	-0.4
New Zealand	161	20	11	6	3.0	4.0	45	0.8	2.1	3.1	2.1	2.0	1.9	0.3
Nicaragua	82	165	68	37	4.4	4.1	46	-3.8	1.5	7.0	4.9	3.1	1.8	3.1
Niger	4	330	320	256	0.2	1.5	20	-2.2	-0.5	8.1	8.2	7.7	-0.1	0.4
Nigeria	14	265	230	194	0.7	1.1	16	-1.4	0.7	6.9	6.8	5.6	0.1	1.3
Niue	-	-	-	-	-	-	-	-	-	-	-	-	-	-
Norway	182	15	9	4	2.6	5.4	56	3.4	2.6	2.5	1.9	1.8	1.4	0.4
Occupied Palestinian Territory	106	-	40	23	-	3.7	43	-	-6.0x	7.9	6.4	5.3	1.1	1.3
Oman	140	200	32	12	9.2	6.5	63	3.3	1.8x	7.2	6.6	3.4	0.4	4.4
Pakistan	47	181	130	99	1.7	1.8	24	3.0	1.3	6.6	6.1	4.0	0.4	2.8
Palau	146	-	21	11	-	4.3	48	-	-	-	-	-	-	-
Panama	103	68	34	24	3.5	2.3	29	0.3	2.2	5.3	3.0	2.6	2.8	1.0
Papua New Guinea	54	158	94	74	2.6	1.6	21	-0.7	0.0	6.2	5.1	3.8	1.0	2.0
Paraguay	106	78	41	23	3.2	3.9	44	2.8	-0.8	6.0	4.7	3.7	1.2	1.6
Peru	96	174	78	27	4.0	7.1	65	-0.6	2.2	6.3	3.9	2.7	2.4	2.5
Philippines	86	90	62	33	1.9	4.2	47	0.8	1.5	6.3	4.4	3.0	1.8	2.6
Poland	156	36	18	7	3.5	6.3	61	-	4.3	2.2	2.0	1.2	0.5	3.4
Portugal	168	62	14	5	7.4	6.9	64	2.6	1.9	2.8	1.5	1.5	3.1	0.0
Qatar	108	65	26	21	4.6	1.4	19	-	-	6.9	4.4	2.9	2.2	2.8
Romania	117	57	31	19	3.0	3.3	39	0.9	1.6	2.9	1.9	1.3	2.1	2.5
Russian Federation	121	36	27	18	1.4	2.7	33	-	-0.1	2.0	1.9	1.4	0.3	2.0
Rwanda	11	209	173	203	0.9	-1.1	-17	1.2	0.0	8.2	7.6	5.5	0.4	2.2
Saint Kitts and Nevis	113	-	36	20	-	3.9	44	6.3x	2.9	-	-	-	-	-
Saint Lucia	137	-	21	14	-	2.7	33	5.3x	0.4	6.1	3.5	2.2	2.8	3.1
Saint Vincent and the Grenadines	113	-	25	20	-	1.5	20	3.3	1.7	6.0	3.0	2.2	3.5	2.1
Samoa	92	101	50	29	3.5	3.6	42	-0.1x	2.5	6.1	4.8	4.2	1.2	0.9
San Marino	190	-	14	3	-	10.3	79	-	-	-	-	-	-	-
Sao Tome and Principe	41	-	118	118	-	0.0	0	-	0.5	6.5	5.3	3.8	1.0	2.2
Saudi Arabia	100	185	44	26	7.2	3.5	41	-1.5	-0.3	7.3	6.0	3.8	1.0	3.0
Senegal	28	279	148	136	3.2	0.6	8	-0.3	1.2	7.0	6.5	4.8	0.4	2.0
Serbia[‡]	-	-	-	-	-	-	-	-	-	-	-	-	-	-
Seychelles	139	59	19	13	5.7	2.5	32	2.9	1.5	-	-	-	-	-
Sierra Leone	1	363	302	282	0.9	0.5	7	-0.4	-1.4	6.5	6.5	6.5	0.0	0.0
Singapore	190	27	9	3	5.5	7.3	67	5.7	3.6	3.0	1.8	1.3	2.6	2.2
Slovakia	154	29	14	8	3.6	3.7	43	-	2.8	2.5	2.0	1.2	1.1	3.4
Slovenia	182	29	10	4	5.3	6.1	60	-	3.2	2.3	1.5	1.2	2.1	1.5
Solomon Islands	92	97	38	29	4.7	1.8	24	3.4	-2.6	6.9	5.5	4.1	1.1	2.0
Somalia	6	-	225	225	-	0.0	0	-0.9	-	7.3	6.8	6.2	0.4	0.6
South Africa	61	-	60	68	-	-0.8	-13	0.1	0.7	5.6	3.6	2.7	2.2	1.9
Spain	168	34	9	5	6.6	3.9	44	1.9	2.3	2.9	1.3	1.3	4.0	0.0
Sri Lanka	137	100	32	14	5.7	5.5	56	3.0	3.7	4.4	2.5	1.9	2.8	1.8
Sudan	49	172	120	90	1.8	1.9	25	0.1	3.5	6.7	5.6	4.2	0.9	1.9
Suriname	78	-	48	39	-	1.4	19	-2.2x	1.1	5.7	2.7	2.5	3.7	0.5
Swaziland	20	196	110	160	2.9	-2.5	-45	2.1	0.2	6.9	5.7	3.7	1.0	2.9
Sweden	182	15	7	4	3.8	3.7	43	1.8	2.1	2.0	2.0	1.7	0.0	1.1
Switzerland	168	18	9	5	3.5	3.9	44	1.2	0.6	2.0	1.5	1.4	1.4	0.5
Syrian Arab Republic	129	123	39	15	5.7	6.4	62	1.9	1.3	7.6	5.3	3.3	1.8	3.2
Tajikistan	59	140	115	71	1.0	3.2	38	-	-4.0	6.9	5.2	3.6	1.4	2.5
Tanzania, United Republic of	36	218	161	122	1.5	1.8	24	-	1.7	6.8	6.1	4.8	0.5	1.6
Thailand	108	102	37	21	5.1	3.8	43	4.8	2.7	5.5	2.2	1.9	4.6	1.0
The former Yugoslav Republic of Macedonia	125	119	38	17	5.7	5.4	55	-	-0.1	3.2	1.9	1.5	2.6	1.6
Timor-Leste	68	-	177	61	-	7.1	66	-	-	6.3	4.9	7.8	1.3	-3.1
Togo	26	216	152	139	1.8	0.6	9	-0.6	0.0	7.0	6.4	5.1	0.4	1.5
Tonga	103	50	32	24	2.2	1.9	25	-	1.9	5.9	4.6	3.3	1.2	2.2
Trinidad and Tobago	117	57	33	19	2.7	3.7	42	0.5	4.3	3.5	2.5	1.6	1.7	3.0

	Under-5 mortality rank	Under-5 mortality rate			Average annual rate of reduction (%)[Θ]		Reduction since 1990 (%)[Θ]	GDP per capita average annual growth rate (%)		Total fertility rate			Average annual rate of reduction (%)	
		1970	1990	2005	1970-1990	1990-2005		1970-1990	1990-2005	1970	1990	2005	1970-1990	1990-2005
Tunisia	103	201	52	24	6.8	5.2	54	2.5	3.3	6.6	3.6	1.9	3.0	4.3
Turkey	92	201	82	29	4.5	6.9	65	1.9	1.6	5.5	3.0	2.4	3.0	1.5
Turkmenistan	45	-	97	104	-	-0.5	-7	-	-4.7x	6.3	4.3	2.6	1.9	3.4
Tuvalu	80	-	54	38	-	2.3	30	-	-	-	-	-	-	-
Uganda	28	170	160	136	0.3	1.1	15	-	3.2	7.1	7.1	7.1	0.0	0.0
Ukraine	125	27	26	17	0.2	2.8	35	-	-2.4	2.1	1.8	1.1	0.8	3.3
United Arab Emirates	151	84	15	9	8.6	3.4	40	-4.8x	-1.0x	6.6	4.4	2.4	2.0	4.0
United Kingdom	161	23	10	6	4.2	3.4	40	2.0	2.4	2.3	1.8	1.7	1.2	0.4
United States	156	26	12	7	3.9	3.6	42	2.2	2.1	2.2	2.0	2.0	0.5	0.0
Uruguay	129	57	23	15	4.5	2.8	35	0.9	0.8	2.9	2.5	2.3	0.7	0.6
Uzbekistan	61	101	79	68	1.2	1.0	14	-	0.3	6.5	4.2	2.6	2.2	3.2
Vanuatu	80	155	62	38	4.6	3.3	39	-0.5x	-0.3	6.3	4.9	3.9	1.3	1.5
Venezuela (Bolivarian Republic of)	108	62	33	21	3.2	3.0	36	-1.6	-1.0	5.4	3.4	2.6	2.3	1.8
Viet Nam	117	87	53	19	2.5	6.8	64	-	5.9	7.0	3.7	2.2	3.2	3.5
Yemen	46	303	139	102	3.9	2.1	27	-	2.0	8.5	8.0	5.9	0.3	2.0
Zambia	18	181	180	182	0.0	-0.1	-1	-2.4	-0.3	7.7	6.5	5.4	0.8	1.2
Zimbabwe	31	138	80	132	2.7	-3.3	-65	-0.4	-2.1	7.7	5.2	3.4	2.0	2.8

MEMORANDUM

	Under-5 mortality rank	1970	1990	2005	1970-1990	1990-2005	Reduction since 1990	1970-1990	1990-2005	1970	1990	2005	1970-1990	1990-2005
Serbia and Montenegro (pre-cession)	129	71	28	15	4.7	4.2	46	-	5.2x	2.4	2.1	1.6	0.7	1.8

SUMMARY INDICATORS

		1970	1990	2005	1970-1990	1990-2005	Reduction since 1990	1970-1990	1990-2005	1970	1990	2005	1970-1990	1990-2005
Sub-Saharan Africa		244	188	169	1.3	0.7	10	-	1.1	6.8	6.3	5.4	0.4	1.0
Eastern and Southern Africa		219	166	146	1.4	0.9	12	-	1.1	6.8	6.0	5.0	0.6	1.2
West and Central Africa		266	209	190	1.2	0.6	9	-	1.0	6.8	6.7	5.7	0.1	1.1
Middle East and North Africa		195	81	54	4.4	2.7	33	2.4	2.2	6.8	5.0	3.1	1.5	3.2
South Asia		206	129	84	2.3	2.9	35	2.1	3.8	5.8	4.3	3.1	1.5	2.2
East Asia and Pacific		122	58	33	3.7	3.8	43	5.7	6.6	5.6	2.5	1.9	4.0	1.8
Latin America and Caribbean		123	54	31	4.1	3.7	43	1.9	1.4	5.3	3.2	2.5	2.5	1.6
CEE/CIS		88	53	35	2.5	2.8	34	-	-	2.8	2.3	1.7	1.0	2.0
Industrialized countries§		27	10	6	5.0	3.4	40	2.3	1.9	2.3	1.7	1.6	1.5	0.4
Developing countries§		167	105	83	2.3	1.6	21	3.2	4.1	5.8	3.6	2.8	2.4	1.7
Least developed countries§		245	182	153	1.5	1.2	16	-	2.4	6.7	5.9	4.9	0.6	1.2
World		148	95	76	2.2	1.5	20	2.5	2.3	4.7	3.2	2.6	1.9	1.4

‡ Due to the cession in June 2006 of Montenegro from the State Union of Serbia and Montenegro, and its subsequent admission to the UN on 28 June 2006, disaggregated data for Montenegro and Serbia as separate States are not yet available. Aggregated data presented are for Serbia and Montenegro pre-cession (see Memorandum item).

§ Also includes territories within each country category or regional group. Countries and territories in each country category or regional group are listed on page 136.

DEFINITIONS OF THE INDICATORS

Under-five mortality rate – Probability of dying between birth and exactly five years of age expressed per 1,000 live births.

Reduction since 1990 (%) – Percentage reduction in the under-five mortality rate (U5MR) from 1990 to 2005. The United Nations Millennium Declaration in 2000 established a goal of a two-thirds (67 per cent) reduction in U5MR from 1990 to 2015. This indicator provides a current assessment of progress towards this goal.

GDP per capita – Gross domestic product (GDP) is the sum of value added by all resident producers plus any product taxes (less subsidies) not included in the valuation of output. GDP per capita is gross domestic product divided by midyear population. Growth is calculated from constant price GDP data in local currency.

Total fertility rate – The number of children that would be born per women if she were to live to the end of her childbearing years and bear children at each age in accordance with prevailing age-specific fertility rates.

MAIN DATA SOURCES

Under-five mortality – UNICEF, United Nations Population Division and United Nations Statistics Division.

GDP per capita – World Bank.

Fertility – United Nations Population Division.

NOTES
- Data not available.
- x   Data refer to years or periods other than those specified in the column heading, differ from the standard definition or refer to only part of a country.
- Θ   A negative value indicates an increase in the under-five mortality rate since 1990.

INDEX

GLOSSARY

AIDS	acquired immune deficiency syndrome
CAMFED	Campaign for Female Education
CEDAW	Convention on the Elimination of All Forms of Discrimination against Women
CEE/CIS	Central and Eastern Europe/Commonwealth of Independent States
CRC	Convention on the Rights of the Child
DHS	Demographic and Health Surveys
DPKO	Department of Peacekeeping Operations, United Nations
FAWE	Forum for African Women Educationalists
FFE	Food for Education
FGM/C	female genital mutilation/cutting
GCE	Global Campaign for Education
GDP	gross domestic product
GEM	gender empowerment measure
HIV	human immunodeficiency virus

IPU	Inter-Parliamentary Union
MDGs	Millennium Development Goals
MICS	Multiple Indicator Cluster Surveys
OECD	Organisation for Economic Co-operation and Development
SFAI	School Fee Abolition Initiative
UN	United Nations
UNAIDS	Joint United Nations Programme on HIV/AIDS
UNDP	United Nations Development Programme
UNESCO	United Nations Educational, Scientific and Cultural Organization
UNFPA	United Nations Population Fund
UNGEI	United Nations Girls' Education Initiative
UNIFEM	United Nations Development Fund for Women
WHO	World Health Organization

UNICEF Offices

UNICEF Headquarters
UNICEF House
3 United Nations Plaza
New York, NY 10017, USA

UNICEF Regional Office for Europe
Palais des Nations
CH-1211 Geneva 10, Switzerland

UNICEF Central and Eastern Europe, Commonwealth of Independent States Regional Office
Palais des Nations
CH-1211 Geneva 10, Switzerland

UNICEF Eastern and Southern Africa Regional Office
P.O. Box 44145-00100
Nairobi, Kenya

UNICEF West and Central Africa Regional Office
P.O. Box 29720 Yoff
Dakar, Senegal

UNICEF The Americas and Caribbean Regional Office
Avenida Morse
Ciudad del Saber Clayton
Edificio #131
Apartado 0843-03045
Panama City, Panama

UNICEF East Asia and the Pacific Regional Office
P.O. Box 2-154
19 Phra Atit Road
Bangkok 10200, Thailand

UNICEF Middle East and North Africa Regional Office
P.O. Box 1551
Amman 11821, Jordan

UNICEF South Asia Regional Office
P.O. Box 5815
Lekhnath Marg
Kathmandu, Nepal

Further information is available at our website <www.unicef.org>